Lecture Notes in Computer Science   13169

More information about this subseries at https://link.springer.com/bookseries/7408

Raghunath Nambiar · Meikel Poess (Eds.)

Performance Evaluation and Benchmarking

13th TPC Technology Conference, TPCTC 2021
Copenhagen, Denmark, August 20, 2021
Revised Selected Papers

Springer

Editors
Raghunath Nambiar
Advanced Micro Devices Inc.
Santa Clara, CA, USA

Meikel Poess
Oracle Corporation
Redwood Shores, CA, USA

ISSN 0302-9743   ISSN 1611-3349 (electronic)
Lecture Notes in Computer Science
ISBN 978-3-030-94436-0   ISBN 978-3-030-94437-7 (eBook)
https://doi.org/10.1007/978-3-030-94437-7

LNCS Sublibrary: SL2 – Programming and Software Engineering

This Springer imprint is published by the registered company Springer Nature Switzerland AG
The registered company address is: Gewerbestrasse 11, 6330 Cham, Switzerland

Preface

The Transaction Processing Performance Council (TPC) is a non-profit organization established in August 1988. Over the years, the TPC has had a significant impact on the computing industry's use of industry-standard benchmarks. Vendors use the TPC benchmarks to illustrate performance competitiveness for their existing products, and to improve and monitor the performance of their products under development. Many buyers use the TPC benchmark results as points of comparison when purchasing new computing systems.

The information technology landscape is evolving at a rapid pace, challenging industry experts and researchers to develop innovative techniques for evaluation, measurement, and characterization of complex systems. The TPC remains committed to developing new benchmark standards to keep pace with these rapid changes in technology. One vehicle for achieving this objective is the TPC's sponsorship of the Technology Conference Series on Performance Evaluation and Benchmarking (TPCTC) established in 2009. With this conference series, the TPC encourages researchers and industry experts to present and debate novel ideas and methodologies in performance evaluation, measurement, and characterization.

This book contains the proceedings of the 13th the TPC Technology Conference on Performance Evaluation and Benchmarking (TPCTC 2021), held in conjunction with the 44th International Conference on Very Large Data Bases (VLDB 2021) in Copenhagen, Denmark, during August 16–20, 2021.

The hard work and close cooperation of a number of people have contributed to the success of this conference. We would like to thank the members of the TPC and the organizers of VLDB 2021 for their sponsorship; the members of the Program Committee and Publicity Committee for their support; and the authors and the participants who are the primary reason for the success of this conference.

December 2021

Raghunath Nambiar
Meikel Poess

TPCTC 2021 Organization

General Chairs

Raghunath Nambiar   AMD, USA
Meikel Poess   Oracle, USA

Program Committee

Dippy Aggarwal   Intel, USA
Daniel Bowers   Gartner, USA
Michael Brey   Oracle, USA
Ajay Dholakia   Lenovo, USA
Dhabaleswar Panda   Ohio State University, USA
Tilmann Rabl   TU Berlin, Germany
Swapna Raj   Intel, USA
Anil Rajput   AMD, USA
Reza Taheri   VMware, USA

Publicity Committee

Meikel Poess   Oracle, USA
Andrew Bond   Red Hat, USA
Paul Cao   HPE, USA
Gary Little   Nutanix, USA
Raghunath Nambiar   AMD, USA
Reza Taheri   VMware, USA
Michael Majdalany   L&M Management Group, USA
Forrest Carman   Owen Media, USA
Andreas Hotea   Hotea Solutions, USA

About the TPC

Introduction to the TPC

The Transaction Processing Performance Council (TPC) is a non-profit organization focused on developing industry standards for data centric workloads and disseminating vendor-neutral performance data to the industry. Additional information is available at http://www.tpc.org/.

TPC Memberships

Full Members

Full Members of the TPC participate in all aspects of the TPC's work, including development of benchmark standards and setting strategic direction. The Full Member application can be found at http://tpc.org/information/about/join5.asp.

Associate Members

Certain organizations may join the TPC as Associate Members. Associate Members may attend the TPC meetings but are not eligible to vote or hold office. Associate membership is available to non-profit organizations, educational institutions, market researchers, publishers, consultants, governments, and businesses that do not create, market, or sell computer products or services. The Associate Member application can be found at http://tpc.org/information/about/join5.asp.

Academic and Government Institutions

Academic and government institutions are invited join the TPC and a special invitation can be found at http://tpc.org/information/about/join5.asp.

Contact the TPC

TPC
781 Beach Street, Suite 302
San Frnacisco, CA 94109
Voice: 415-561-6272
Fax: 415-561-6120
Email: info@tpc.org

How to Order TPC Materials

All of our materials are now posted free of charge on our web site. If you have any questions, please feel free to contact our office directly or by email at info@tpc.org.

Staying Connected

The TPC offers the option to sign up for E-mail notification when new benchmark results are published or the primary metric of a published benchmark has changed: http://tpc.org/information/about/mailinglist_signup5.asp.

The TPC is also active on LinkedIn
https://www.linkedin.com/company/tpcbenchmarks/

and on Twitter
https://twitter.com/TPCBenchmarks.

TPC 2021 Organization

Full Members

Actian
Alibaba
AMD
Cisco
Dell EMC
Fujitsu
Hewlett Packard Enterprise
Hitachi
Huawei
IBM
Inspur
Intel
Lenovo
Microsoft
Nutanix
Nvidia
Oracle
Red Hat
Transwarp
TTA
VMware

Associate Members

Gartner
University of Coimbra, Portugal
China Academy of Information and Communications Technology
Imec

TPC 2021 Organization

Steering Committee

Michael Brey (Chair), Oracle
Matthew Emmerton, IBM
Jamie Reding, Microsoft
Ken Rule, Intel
Nicholas Wakou, Dell EMC

Public Relations Committee

Paul Cao, HPE
Gary Little, Nutanix
Meikel Poess (Chair), Oracle
Reza Taheri, VMware

Technical Advisory Board

Paul Cao, HPE
Matt Emmerton, IBM
Gary Little, Nutanix
Jamie Reding (Chair), Microsoft
Mike Brey, Oracle
Ken Rul, Intel
Nicholas Wakou, Dell EMC

Technical Subcommittees and Chairs

TPC-C: Jamie Reding, Microsoft
TPC-H: Meikel Poess, Oracle
TPC-E: Matthew Emmerton, IBM
TPC-DS: Meikel Poess, Oracle
TPC-DI: Meikel Poess, Oracle
TPCx-HS: Tariq Magdon-Ismail, VMware
TPCx-IoT: Meikel Poess, Oracle
TPCx-BB: Rodrigo Escobar, Intel
TPCx-V: Reza Taheri, VMware
TPCx-HCI: Reza Taheri, VMware
TPCx-AI: Hamesh Patel, Intel
TPC-Pricing: Jamie Reding, Microsoft
TPC-Energy: Paul Cao, HPE

Working Groups and Chairs

TPC-OSS: Andy Bond, IBM and Reza Taheri, VMware

Contents

A YCSB Workload for Benchmarking Hotspot Object Behaviour in NoSQL Databases

Casper Claesen, Ansar Rafique[✉], Dimitri Van Landuyt, and Wouter Joosen

imec-DistriNet, KU Leuven, Celestijnenlaan 200A, 3001 Leuven, Belgium
{casper.claesen,ansar.rafique,dimitri.vanlanduyt,
wouter.joosen}@cs.kuleuven.be

Abstract. Many contemporary applications have to deal with unexpected spikes or unforeseen peaks in demand for specific data objects – so-called hotspot objects. For example in social networks, specific media items can go viral quickly and unexpectedly and therefore, properly provisioning for such behavior is not trivial.

NoSQL databases are specifically designed for enhanced scalability, high availability, and elasticity to deal with increasing data volumes. Although existing performance benchmarking systems such as the Yahoo! Cloud Serving Benchmark (YCSB) provide support to test the performance properties of different databases under identical workloads, they lack support for testing how well these databases can cope with the above-mentioned unexpected hotspot object behaviour.

To address this shortcoming and fill the research gap, we present the design and implementation of a new YCSB workload that is rooted upon a formal characterization of hotspot-based spikes. The proposed workload implements the Pitman-Yor distribution and is configurable in a number of parameters such as spike probability and data locality. As such, it allows for more extensive experimental validation of database systems.

Our functional validation illustrates how the workload can be used to effectively stress-test different types of databases and we present our comparative results of benchmarking two popular NoSQL databases that are Cassandra and MongoDB in terms of their response to spiked workloads.

Keywords: NoSQL databases · Workload spikes · Hotspot objects · YCSB workload · Performance benchmark · Cassandra · MongoDB

1 Introduction

Context. Many cloud services are running on geographically distributed data centers for offering better reliability and performance guarantees [28]. These cloud services are inherently subject to fluctuations in demand. These fluctuations often are seasonal and thus behave according to predictable patterns

R. Nambiar and M. Poess (Eds.): TPCTC 2021, LNCS 13169, pp. 1–16, 2022.
https://doi.org/10.1007/978-3-030-94437-7_1

(e.g. Christmas shopping patterns are largely similar every year). In such cases, pattern recognition techniques or machine learning algorithms can be employed to determine up front what is the most suited configuration. In the current state of the art, using a wide array of techniques and tactics such as overprovisioning, autoscaling and self-adaptive tuning of servers, fluctuations in service load can be dealt with efficiently, using a combination of reactive and proactive measures.

However, not all fluctuations are equal, and in some cases, the nature of the demand increase can be both explosive and unexpected. One such example is the behaviour of hotspot objects: these are objects in a database that experience a sudden and substantial increase in demand (a.k.a spikes). The canonical example is that of social media items (e.g., a tweet or a video) that have gone viral, but other types of services may also experience similar unexpected peaks or spikes in their respective workload, e.g., emergency service hotlines and information systems during calamities will be faced with similar challenges.

Problem. Existing well-known performance benchmark systems such as the Transaction Processing Performance (TPC) [25] and TPC-C [20] frameworks as well as the Yahoo! Cloud Serving Benchmark (YCSB) [6] are designed to system-atically evaluate different storage technologies in terms of how they cope with a number of pre-defined workloads. Although different workloads exist to evalu-ate how a certain service copes with increasing payloads and fluctuations, there is currently no existing workload in these systems that approximates hotspot behaviour. As such, these existing benchmark systems do not provide us with a clear way to assess the extent to which databases can cope with these types of behavioural patterns and even though a database may be highly scalable and elastic, it may not do so efficiently for the specific case of hotspot workloads.

Contribution. In this paper, we present the design and implementation of a YCSB workload that allow us to systematically benchmark the capabilities of a storage system in dealing with such hotspot-based spikes behaviour. The proposed workload implements the Pitman-Yor distribution [22], which is more effective for stimulating workloads with spikes and allows tuning the parameters of (i) the powerlaw (to set the baseline popularity), (ii) the degree of structuring of the records, (iii) the locality of objects over databases, (iv) the distribution of write, read, update operations, (v) the desired variation in popularity, and (vi) the magnitude and recurrence of spikes.

Validation. We have validated the proposed workload by benchmarking hotspot objects behaviour in NoSQL databases (Cassandra and MongoDB) and compar-ing the results with the core workloads of the YCSB benchmark. The validation results show that the proposed workload generates (unexpected) spikes, which can be used to assess the ability of databases to cope with peaks in demand and hotspot behavior. In addition, we demonstrate the effectiveness of caching strategies in these databases to meet demand considering unpredictable spikes.

Structure. The remainder of this paper is structured as follows: Sect. 2 dis-cusses the relevant background and formulates the problem statement for this paper. In Sect. 3, we present the design and implementation of our proposed workload, which is an extension to the existing workloads supported in YCSB. Then, Sect. 4 reports the results of functional validation and a more extensive evaluation of two popular NoSQL databases (Cassandra and MongoDB) using our proposed workload. Section 5 provides an overview of the related work, and Sect. 6 concludes the paper.

2   Background

This section provides the necessary background to keep the paper self-contained. More specifically, Sect. 2.1 provides a summary of the terminology concerning workload spikes and hotspot objects. In Sect. 2.2, we discuss the overall architecture of the Yahoo! Cloud Serving Benchmark (YCSB) and also describe different data distribution mechanisms and built-in workloads supported in YCSB. Finally, Sect. 2.3 formally describes the problem statement of our paper.

2.1   Spikes

There are two types of workload spikes: (i) volume spikes and (ii) data spikes. A volume spike is an unexpected sustained increase in the total volume of the workload, whereas a data spike is a sudden increase in demand for certain objects or in general a marked change in the distribution of popularity of objects. According to these definitions, a data spike should not be a volume spike and vice versa. In practice, however, volume and data spikes often arise simultaneously. Based on the characterizations of Bodik et al. [4], we define *hotspot objects* and *spikes* as follows:

Hotspot Objects. An increasing fluctuation of spikes in workloads create hotspot objects. For example, an object is denoted as a *hotspot object* if the change of the workload of this specific object compared to before represents a significant spike. More formally, an object is a *hotspot object* as $\triangle_{i,Ts} > D$ with D a given threshold and $\triangle_{i,Ts}$ the change of the workload of the object i at the starting point of the spike [4].

Workload Spikes. Four factors determine the spikes of a workload: (i) steepness, (ii) magnitude, (iii) duration, and (iv) spatial locality. The steepness expresses how fast the volume of the workload goes up. The magnitude is the difference in popularity between the hotspot objects in the spikes and the normal workload. The duration determines how long the spike lasts. Finally, the spatial locality of a spike defines where the hotspot objects are located. The objects that correspond to spike and more specifically consider all these four factors are called the hotspot objects.

A spike can be represented by a couple of parameters. The symbol s represents a spike. A spike in symbols is then equal to $s = (t0, t1, t2, t3, M, L, N, V)$.

A spike is determined by N the number of hotspot objects and V the variation of the hotspot popularity. M defines the magnitude of the spike. The duration is expressed by $t0$, $t1$, $t2$ and $t3$. The combination of M with $t0$, $t1$, $t2$ and $t3$ determines the steepness. Finally, the L parameter determines the spatial locality of the hotspot objects [4].

2.2   Yahoo Cloud Serving Benchmark (YCSB)

The Yahoo Cloud Serving Benchmark (YCSB) [6] is one of the most popular and frequently-used benchmark systems to evaluate the performance of NoSQL databases. It supports a wide range of NoSQL databases out of the box and is also extensible in this regard. Section 2.2.1 describes the overall architecture of YCSB, while Sect. 2.2.2 describes different types of workloads currently supported in YCSB.

2.2.1   YSCB Architecture

As shown in Fig. 1, the architecture of YCSB [6] consists of four core compo-nents: (i) the `Workload Executor`, (ii) different `Client` threads, (iii) the `DB interface` layer, and (iv) the `Stats` component. The `Workload Executor` com-ponent is responsible for executing specific runs of the benchmark, which involves creating and coordinating a specified number of `Client` threads. These threads execute insert, read, update, delete (CRUD) operations on the target database through the `DB Interface` layer. This layer in turn makes an abstraction of the underlying database in order to support easy switching to different database technologies. The `Stats` component collects all the results (measured latencies) of the experiment.

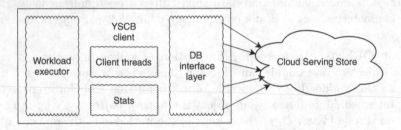

Fig. 1. Architecture of the YCSB benchmark system [6].

2.2.2   YCSB Workloads and Distribution

Out of the box, YCSB supports three distributions: (i) *Uniform*, (ii) *Zipfian*, and (iii) the *Latest*. In the case of Uniform distribution, all records have an equal chance to occur in the next operation. On the other hand, when Zip-fian distribution is chosen, some records are very popular (the head), whereas others are unpopular (the tail). The Latest distribution is the same as Zipfian only the latest added results are set to be the most popular ones. Next to these three distributions, YCSB also supports Multinomial distribution, in which the probability can be configured on a per-item basis. In addition, YCSB currently supports five distinct workloads: *A*, *B*, *C*, *D* and *E*, each with their own charac-teristics. Table 1 summarizes these workloads, indicating the type of distribution being used and the different types of applications these workloads mimic.

Table 1. An overview of core workloads supported in YCSB [6].

Workload	Operations	Record selection	Type of application
A: Update heavy	Read: 50% Update: 50%	Zipfian	Session store recording recent actions in a user session
B: Read heavy	Read: 95% Update: 5%	Zipfian	Photo tagging; add a tag is an update, but most operations are to read tags
C: Read only	Read: 100%	Zipfian	User profile cache, where profiles are constructed elsewhere (e.g., Hadoop)
D: Read latest	Read: 95% Insert: 5%	Latest	User status updates; people want to read the latest statuses
E: Short ranges	Scan: 95% Insert: 5%	Zipfian/Uniform[a]	Threaded conversations, where each scan is for the posts in a given thread (assumed to be clustered by thread id)

[a]The Zipfian distribution chooses the first key in the range and the Uniform distribution determines the number of records to scan.

2.3 Problem Statement

Existing benchmark systems[1] mainly focus on generating flat workloads and as such lack support to simulate workloads with spikes. These systems do not take into account the sudden change in the popularity of the objects. As an example, some cold (unpopular) objects suddenly can become hot (popular) objects. However, testing how a database deals with sudden and unpredictable spikes is essential to evaluate the resilience and scaling capabilities of the systems. In addition, the current implementations (e.g., YCSB framework) rely extensively on the *Zipfian* (or the derived *Latest*) distribution to determine the popularities of the objects. *These power-law distributions are insufficiently realistic. The popularity of the most popular objects is not high enough or the tail of the distribution falls too slow [4] and as such these distributions can not be used to benchmark hotspot behaviour.* In summary, there is a strong need for: (i) a new workload that supports unpredictable spikes and (ii) a more realistic distribution.

3 YCSB Workload for Benchmarking Hotspot Object

In this section, we present our extension of YCSB by introducing a new workload that enables us to benchmark hotspot objects behaviour in different NoSQL databases. As such, a new YCSB workload is introduced that is capable of generating spikes and thus imitating data and volume spikes. The proposed workload uses a new generator that is based on the Pitman-Yor distribution [22]. In addition, extra functionality is added to support a more precise way of configuring the objects in terms of locality and structure.

---

[1] In this paper, we mainly focus on YCSB. However, a more extensive discussion of other benchmark systems is covered in Sect. 5.

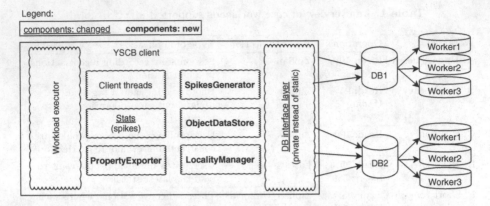

Fig. 2. Architecture of our proposed system, which extends YCSB [6] by introducing a new workload for benchmarking hotspot behaviour in NoSQL databases.

Figure 2 provides a graphical overview of our proposed architecture. As shown (in bold), we have introduced a number of new components, which include (i) the `SpikesGenerator` component, (ii) the `ObjectDataStore` component, (iii) the `LocalityManager` component, and (iv) the `PropertyExporter` component. In addition, we have also modified the existing components of the YCSB benchmark. The rest of this section provides a high-level overview of the key features of these new components, which are added in YCSB, while each component is further discussed in detail in the following subsections.

The `SpikesGenerator` component is the key part of our system and is responsible for generating the spikes based on parameters such as the baseline popularity. The `ObjectDataStore` component is an index that keeps information about the intended role and the functionality of each generated object. Examples are the baseline popularity, locality, etc. The `LocalityManager` component provides support for experiments over multiple databases. The `PropertyExporter` component allows exporting these generated properties in order to support performing an experiment with the same overall configuration, and thus increases reproducibility. It also ensures that the information about the records and the generated parameters are the same during the load and the run phase. All parameters have also a forced alternative. For example, the parameters *powerlaw* (1.2) and *maxPop* (0.3) generate the baseline popularity, but the alternative parameter *objForcedPopularity* (0.1, 0.0, 0.2, . . .) sets a fixed baseline popularity.

The YCSB components that were changed to accommodate for this new workload type are (i) the `Stats` component and (ii) the `DB interface` layer. The `Stats` component has been expanded so that more information about the latencies of the hotspot objects can be reported, whereas the `DB interface` layer needed minor changes to allow connections to different databases simultaneously.

The extension maximally adheres to the design principles of the YCSB, extending base classes and leveraging existing configuration facilities where possible. We discuss the introduced components (except for the `PropertyExporter`) in further detail below.

3.1   SpikesGenerator

The `SpikesGenerator` component consists of two classes: (i) *Pitman Yor-SpikesGenerator* and (ii) *SpikesWorkload.*

PitmanYorSpikesGenerator uses the Pitman-Yor distribution, as explained in the paper of Bodik et al. [4], to determine the baseline popularity (B) of the objects. These popularities are used to decide on which objects the operations execute when no spikes occur. The implementation adds an extra parameter *maxPop* that determines the mapping range from $[0.0, maxPop]$ instead of $[0.0, 1.0]$. At the end, a random permutation is taken from these popularities. The process is called as $PY(1/a, 0.5))$ with a the configurable power-law parameter.

The *PitmanYorSpikesGenerator* is a YCSB generator that extends the existing abstract class *NumberGenerator*. However, a major difference between the new generator and the existing generators is that it records the relevant properties of each object in the *ObjectDataStore*, which is explained in Sect. 3.2.

To support spikes, a hotspot popularity (H) is calculated with the Dirichlet distribution [4]. The object popularities are set between 0.0 and 1.0, with their sum equal to 1.0. With N the number of hotspot objects and V the variation of the popularity of the hotspot objects (which ranges from 0.0 (equal) to $\frac{N-1}{N^2}$ (heavy tailed)), the parameters for the Dirichlet distribution are calculated as follows [4]:

$$\alpha_i = \frac{N - 1 - V * N^2}{V * N^3}$$

Then after N hotspot popularities are calculated, N objects are chosen with the global locality parameter L to become the hotspot objects. The value of L ranges from 0.0 to 1.0 meaning uniform and heavy-tailed selected over the possible locations. Finally, the popularity P at time t with magnitude factor c_t (0 if normal, $(M-1)/M$ at peak of the spike) is equal to:

$$P_t = (1 - c_t)B + c_t H$$

SpikesWorkload implements a workload class that is capable of simulating spikes[2]. The *SpikesWorkload* class is an extension of the *CoreWorkload* which is responsible for setting the parameters of this class. At pre-determined times, the popularities of an object are switched from the baseline to the spike popularities and the scheduling of the operations is influenced correspondingly. In this way, data and volume spikes can be generated. For this purpose, it uses *PitmanY-orSpikesGenerator*. The classes *SpikeObject* and *LocalityObject* are responsible to maintain the information about the spike and the locality on a per-object basis. The *SpikesWorkload* generates the events of the spike in the function *doSpikeEvents*. Possible events are (i) the start ($t0$), (ii) rising ($t0 - t1$), (iii) flat ($t1 - t2$), (iv) declining ($t2 - t3$), and (v) the end ($t3$) of the spike.

---

[2] In the YCSB config, it will be used when the parameter *workload* is set to *site.ycsb.workloads.SpikesWorkload.*

3.2   ObjectDataStore

The `ObjectDataStore` component represents an index that keeps track of the different properties of each generated object in the *DataObject* record. This record consists of (i) an identifier, (ii) a boolean that indicates if the object is a hotspot, (iii) the baseline popularity, (iv) the hotspot popularity, (v) the locality, and (vi) a boolean to determine if the object is structured or not.

As YCSB supports structured data and not unstructured data, a new parameter *objStructProportion* is introduced. It determines the proportion of the structured items. The value ranges from 0.0 (all unstructured) to 1.0 (all structured). The extra information is stored in the *DataObject* class. When a new record is constructed and the object is unstructured, all fields are concatenated and stored in the first field. In this way, it is possible to simulate blobs.

3.3   LocalityManager

YCSB has been developed under the main assumption that an experiment only involves a single database technology. A setup with multiple databases can be tested through multiple independent experiments on each database. In this way, there is no support to take the data locality aspect of hotspot objects into account. This is necessary to know in detail what happens when spikes occur.

DBContainer solves the problem of supporting multiple databases by retaining the different databases. If the parameter *hosts* is an array of IP-addresses, a container with the corresponding databases is created. For each database operation (insert, read, update, scan, and delete), new functions are implemented with the *DBContainer* as a parameter instead of the *DB*. The database-specific calls are determined at run-time through method overloading, where a specific target database is chosen in the *SpikesWorkload* class by the information of the *DataObject* class of the *ObjectDataStore* component.

As discussed in Sect. 3.1, the global locality parameter L is used to determine objects that have become the hotspot objects based on their location. The global locality parameter *objLocality* defines if the objects must be grouped on one database (1.0) or spread over different multiple databases (0.0). As such, it determines the locality value where the first IP-address of hosts is mapped to 1, the second to 2, etc.

4   Functional Validation

As a functional validation, we illustrate the importance of our proposed workload in terms of benchmarking hotspot objects behavior in NoSQL databases. More precisely, the goal of this functional validation is to show the differences between the core workloads of the YCSB benchmark (cf. Table 1 for more information about different workloads supported in YCSB) and our proposed workload, which is specifically designed to simulate hotspot behaviour in NoSQL databases (cf. Sect. 3 for more details about our proposed workload). Section 4.1

gives an overview of the experimental setup and also provides details on software and hardware used for the experiments. The subsequent section (Sect. 4.2) presents the main results with a critical discussion.

4.1   Experiment Setup

In order to validate our approach, we implemented two application prototypes that use different workloads. The first prototype (Prototype YCSB) is based on the core workload of type A (workload_A) of the YCSB benchmark (cf. Table 1), which consists of 50% read operations and 50% update operations, generates no spikes, and relies on the Zipfian distribution. The second prototype (Prototype YCSB^{Hotspot}) is based on our proposed workload, which also consists of 50% read and 50% update operations, but instead generates spikes and relies on Pitman-Yor distribution. Moreover, in the current implementation, the proposed workload contains one hotspot object (cf. Table 2 (a)) for more details about different hotspot object properties).

Table 2(a) describes the popularity and object parameters of our proposed workload, while the spike and experiment parameters are listed in Table 2(b). For both application prototypes, we have used 10 000 records and performed 100 000 operations with the same number of threads (10 threads) where the proportion of read and update operations is 0.5 (50%). The warm-up phase (first 10 000 operations in our case) is excluded from the presented results, as it involves higher latencies and eventually leads to inconsistency in results.

The experiments are conducted in a client-server environment where the client process runs application prototypes and the server process runs different databases. In our case, both client and server processes run on a single-node setup[3], which consists of Intel(R) Core(TM) i5-2400 CPU @ 3.10 GHz × 4 processor and 3.7 GB RAM with Ubuntu Bionic (18.04.4) installed. For all the experiments, we have used both Cassandra and MongoDB with their default configurations: cache is disabled in Cassandra by default, whereas enabled in MongoDB. In addition, we have cleaned both databases at the start of every new experiment.

4.2   Results

This section presents the results of our experiments for both Cassandra and MongoDB databases. Section 4.2.1 presents and discusses the results of the Cassandra database, while Sect. 4.2.2 outlines the results of the MongoDB database followed by the discussion in Sect. 4.2.3.

4.2.1   Results of the Cassandra Database

The results of all the experiments where application prototypes use the Cassandra database are presented in Fig. 3. The left-hand side of the Fig. 3 (Figs. 3a

---

[3] The experiments for a multi-node setup will be considered in the future work.

Table 2. Different parameters of our proposed workload, which generates spikes and contains one hotspot object.

baseline popularity	
powerlaw	1.2
maxPop	0.3
hotspot popularity	
objForced-	[1.0, 0.0,
PopularitySpike	0.0, ...]
all objects	
objLocality	1.0
hotspot objects	
L	1.0
all objects	
recordcount	10000
fieldcount	10
fieldlength-	uniform
distribution	
fieldlength	35
minfieldlength	25
objStructProportion	1.0

one spike	
t0	20000
t1	26666
t2	33333
t3	40000
all spikes	
t	50000
M	3
waitingTime-	100
OperationNoSpike	
characteristics	
experiment	
operationcount	100000
read-	0.5
proportion	
update-	0.5
proportion	
threads	10

(a) Popularity and object parameters. (b) Spike and experiment parameters

and 3b) represents the results of prototype YCSB, which is based on the core workload of type A (workload_A) of the YCSB benchmark (cf. Table 1), whereas the right-hand side of the Fig. 3 (Figs. 3c and 3d) shows the results of prototype YCSB^{Hotspot}, which is based on our proposed spike workload.

Figures 3a and 3c display the operation latencies, while Figs. 3b and 3d present the number of processed operations per discrete time bucket in terms of throughput. The rainbow visualization of these graphs ensures a better visualization of the bars and does not have any functional meaning. The black dots in Fig. 3c and Fig. 4c present respectively $t0$, $t1$, $t2$ and $t3$ of the spike as explained in Sect. 2.1. As visible in the results, Cassandra is optimized for the write-heavy workloads. The maximum latencies of prototype YCSB^{Hotspot} are much higher when the spikes occur [(91830 μs, 92037 μs) vs (37066 μs, 37293 μs)]. The average latencies of prototype YCSB^{Hotspot} are much lower than prototype YCSB [(711 μs, 694 μs) vs (782 μs, 764 μs)]. This goes against intuition, but the small waiting time before each operation to simulate spikes and the relatively small time period of spikes explains it. The comparison of the x-axis of Fig. 3a with Fig. 3c makes it clear that prototype YCSB requires less time [±7000 μs vs. ±15000 μs] to execute all operations.

4.2.2 Results of the MongoDB Database

The results of all the experiments where application prototypes use the MongoDB database are presented in Fig. 4. The left-hand side of the Fig. 4 (Figs. 4a and 4b) presents the results of Prototype YCSB, which is based on the core work-

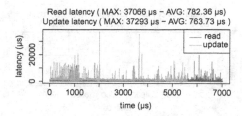

(a) Operation latencies in μs for Prototype YCSB, which is based on the core workload of type A (workload_A) of the YCSB benchmark.

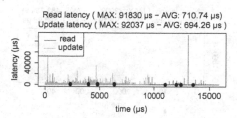

(c) Operation latencies in μs for Prototype YCSB^{Hotspot}, which is based on the proposed spike workload.

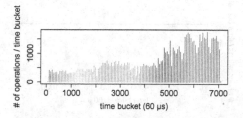

(b) Number of processed operations per discrete time bucket of 60 μs (throughput) for Prototype YCSB.

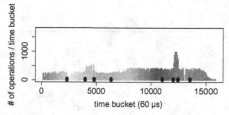

(d) Number of processed operations per discrete time bucket of 60 μs (throughput) for Prototype YCSB^{Hotspot}.

Fig. 3. Results of both application prototypes (prototype YCSB and prototype YCSB^{Hotspot}) which include (i) operation latencies in μs and (ii) number of processed operations per discrete time bucket of 60 μs (throughput) for the Cassandra database.

load of type A (workload_A) of YCSB (cf. Table 1), while the right-hand side of the Fig. 4 (Figs. 4c and 4d) displays the results of Prototype YCSB^{Hotspot}, which is based on our proposed workload. As clearly visible in the results, MongoDB is optimized for the read-heavy workloads. As shown, prototype YCSB^{Hotspot} again performs better than prototype YCSB [avg:(228 μs, 257 μs) vs. (483 μs, 498 μs) and max: (13144 μs, 13427 μs) vs. (33009 μs, 30891 μs)]. The reason that prototype YCSB^{Hotspot} performs better than prototype YCSB is that the new Pitman-Yor distribution (baseline popularity) is, in this case, generating a small amount of very popular items, so that less swap caching occurs. The peaks of the latencies when a spike occurs are clearly visible between the black dots indicating the spikes in Fig. 4c.

4.2.3 Discussion

Due to space constraints, this section only focuses on the functional validation of the generation of spikes. Hence, the proof of the functional correctness of the generated popularity, locality and the structure/size of the objects by the corresponding parameters are left out. Figures 3d and 4d clearly show that the workload generates spikes in the throughput that are visible between the black dots indicating the spikes. The corresponding latencies when the spikes occur

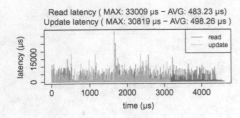

(a) Operation latencies in µs for Prototype YCSB, which is based on the core workload of type A (workload_A) of the YCSB benchmark.

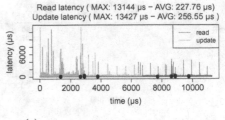

(c) Operation latencies in µs for Prototype YCSB^{Hotspot}, which is based on the proposed spike workload.

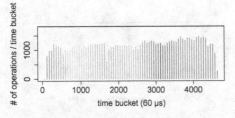

(b) Number of processed operations per discrete time bucket of 60 µs (throughput) for Prototype YCSB.

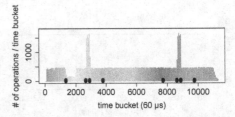

(d) Number of processed operations per discrete time bucket of 60 µs (throughput) for Prototype YCSB^{Hotspot}.

Fig. 4. Results of both application prototypes (prototype YCSB and prototype YCSB^{Hotspot}) which include (i) operation latencies in µs and (ii) number of processed operations per discrete time bucket of 60 µs (throughput) for the MongoDB database.

are also visible in Figs. 3c and 4c (indicated with the black dots), and these illustrate the resulting increase in read and write latencies.

The different results of Cassandra and MongoDB can entirely be attributed to caching: in this case, the results confirm that object caching is a suited tactic when spikes occur. As such, we show that the proposed benchmark is an enabler for experimenting with and optimizing different tactics (e.g. caching or adaptive provisioning such as autoscaling) for specific spike-based workload profiles.

5   Related Work

Existing benchmarks such as TPC-C [16,20] and TPC-E [26] focus on emulating database applications to compare different relational database management systems (RDBMS). These benchmarks use predefined queries, which are executed within the context of transactions to measure the performance (e.g., throughput) of different RDBMS. Similarly, Difallah et al. [10] proposed an extensible and easy-to-use testbed, which contains fifteen workloads that all differ in complexity and system demands for benchmarking relational databases. Cloud service benchmark such as YCSB [6], on the other hand, is designed to evaluate the performance of distributed databases. Although YCSB is the de-facto standard for evaluating the performance properties of distributed database systems (e.g., NoSQL databases), it fails to adequately mimic the hotspot behaviour in these databases. More specifically, the *Zipfian* (or the derived *Latest*) distributions of YCSB mainly focus on generating flat workloads and as such lack support to simulate workloads with spikes. In addition, these distributions do not take into account the locality of objects and also lack in supporting sudden and unexpected change of popularity in objects.

In recent years, significant research efforts focus on extending YCSB in a number of different ways to support and evaluate other properties of distributed databases. For example, YCSB++ [19] is designed to evaluate non-transactional access to distributed key-value stores. It extends the API to achieve bulk loading of data into databases such as HBase and Accumulo. YCSB+T [9], an extension of YCSB is designed with the ability to wrap multiple database operations into transactions and to improve performance understanding and debugging of advanced features such as ingest speed-up techniques and function shipping filters. Dayarathna et al. [8] conducted an in-depth study focusing on existing benchmarks for graph processing systems, graph database benchmarks, and bigdata benchmarks with graph processing workloads. One such example is XGDBench [7], a benchmarking platform, which is designed to operate in both current cloud service infrastructures and future exascale clouds. XGDBench extends YCSB and mainly tends to focus on benchmarking graph databases (such as AllegroGraph, Fuseki, Neo4j, OrientDB), which are beyond the scope of this work. Kumar et al. [15] proposed a system that extends YCSB in order to enable users to select the right storage system for a given application by evaluating the performance and other tradeoffs such as consistency, latency, and availability.

Barahmand et al. [3] proposed BG, a benchmark system that rates different databases for processing social networking actions using pre-defined SLAs. BG is also inspired by prior benchmark systems such as YCSB and YCSB++ and can be used for multiple purposes such as comparing different databases and quantifying the performance characteristics in the presence of failures. Sidhanta et al. [24] introduced Dyn-YCSB, a system that is built upon YCSB and eliminates the need for users to manually change the workload configurations whenever the workload parameters are changed. According to user-specified functions, Dyn-YCSB automatically varies the parameters in YCSB workloads. BSMA [29] is mainly designed for benchmarking the performance of analytical queries over social media data. In comparison to existing benchmark systems (e.g., YCSB) that only provide a synthetic data generator, BSMA is different in the sense that it also provides a real-life dataset with a built-in synthetic data generator. The real-life dataset contains tweets of 1.6 million users and also allows to generate both social networks and synthetic timelines.

Smartbench [14] evaluates the suitability level of RDBMS in supporting both real-time and analysis queries in Internet of Things (IoT) settings. BigBench [13] is an end-to-end benchmark that contains data model and synthetic data generator to address different aspects (volume, velocity, and variety) of big data. In comparison to previous research efforts that mainly focus on structured data,

BigBench also takes into account semi-structured and unstructured data. To accomplish this, the BigBench data model is adopted from the TPC-DS benchmark [18,23], which is enriched with semi-structured and unstructured data components. BigBench V2 [12] is a major rework of BigBench where a new data model and the generator is proposed that rather reflects simple data models and late binding requirements. In contrast to the previous work, BigBench V2 is completely independent of TPC-DS with a new data model and an overhauled workload. BigFUN [21] is a micro-benchmark that is based on a synthetic social network scenario with a semi-structured data model to evaluate the performance of four representative Big Data management systems (BDMSs): MongoDB, Hive, AsterixDB, and a commercial parallel shared-nothing relational database system. BigDataBench [11] compares the performance of systems for analyzing semi-structured data, including their ability to efficiently process machine learning algorithms in a map/reduce setting. These frameworks focus specifically on evaluating the performance and scalability factors of databases. To cope with the challenge of testing ACID properties, Waudby et al. [27] presented a set of data model-agnostic ACID compliance tests for graph databases.

There also exist other recent works that deal with spikes and variation in workload. Arasu et al. [1] proposed Linear Road, a benchmark to compare the performance of Stream Data Management Systems (SDMS) with relational databases. As such, it simulates a toll system for motor vehicles in a large metropolitan area. This benchmark can mimic a form of spike behaviour that is very use-case specific. Hereby, the solution is not applicable to other use cases. However, our proposed solution can easily be extended and applied to a wide range of use cases. Similarly, other benchmark systems use traces from the past that are reused to simulate the expected behaviour. An example of such a system is Linkbench [2], which provides a realistic and challenging test for persistent storage of social and web service data. The solution ensures testing of the reused spikes, but completely new and unexpected sudden spikes are out of the scope. In comparison, our work focuses on the imitations of different traces on the hand of the new parameters. In this way, new kinds of spikes that never occurred before and are difficult to anticipate in advance can also be simulated. Lu et al. [17] presented AutoFlow, a hotspot-aware system that supports dynamic load balance in distributed stream processing. AutoFlow contains a centralized scheduler, which monitors the load in the dataflow dynamically and implements state migrations accordingly. HotRing [5] is a hotspot-aware system that leverages a hash index, which provides fast access to hot objects by moving head pointers closer to them. These systems generate a flat workload and do not take into account the locality of objects.

In summary, benchmark frameworks described in this section are mostly designed to address different aspects (performance, scalability, availability, etc.) of big data management systems as well as big data processing frameworks. As such, these systems mainly focus on generating flat workloads. Other recent works focus on dealing with spikes and variations in workloads. However, they fail to predict (unexpected) sudden spikes that have not occurred previously. In essence, none of these existing systems are designed to approximate hotspot behaviour in databases, particularly distributed NoSQL databases. This highlights and confirms the need for a configurable benchmark to mimic the hotspot behaviour in distributed databases, such as the workload proposed in this paper.

6   Conclusion

The current state of NoSQL benchmark systems does not appear to be sufficient to mimic spikes. To bridge this gap, we extended YCSB [6] by introducing a new workload that supports the generation of spikes with hotspot behaviour and uses a similar approach described by Bodik et al. [4]. Besides, a number of new parameters have been introduced in the workload, which makes it easy to generate the requested volume and/or data spikes. The workload has been validated, in comparison to the core workloads of YCSB on the default configuration of Cassandra and MongoDB databases. The results show that our proposed workload can be used to test the resilience of NoSQL databases caused by hotspot objects behaviour, which is currently lacking in the existing workloads of the YCSB benchmark system.

Acknowledgements. This research is partially funded by the Research Fund KU Leuven and the Cybersecurity Initiative Flanders (CIF) project.

References

1. Arasu, A., et al.: Linear Road: A Stream Data Management Benchmark (2004). https://doi.org/10.1016/B978-012088469-8/50044-9
2. Armstrong, T., Ponnekanti, V., Borthakur, D., Callaghan, M.: LinkBench: a database benchmark based on the Facebook social graph, pp. 1185–1196 (2013)
3. Barahmand, S., Ghandeharizadeh, S.: BG: a benchmark to evaluate interactive social networking actions. Citeseer (2013)
4. Bodik, P., Fox, A., Franklin, M., Jordan, M., Patterson, D.: Characterizing, modeling, and generating workload spikes for stateful services, pp. 241–252 (2010). https://doi.org/10.1145/1807128.1807166
5. Chen, J., et al.: HotRing: a hotspot-aware in-memory key-value store. In: 18th USENIX Conference on File and Storage Technologies (FAST 20), Santa Clara, CA, pp. 239–252. USENIX Association, February 2020. https://www.usenix.org/conference/fast20/presentation/chen-jiqiang
6. Cooper, B.F., Silberstein, A., Tam, E., Ramakrishnan, R., Sears, R.: Benchmarking cloud serving systems with YCSB. In: Proceedings of the 1st ACM Symposium on Cloud Computing, pp. 143–154 (2010)
7. Dayarathna, M., Suzumura, T.: XGDBench: a benchmarking platform for graph stores in exascale clouds, pp. 363–370 (2012)
8. Dayarathna, M., Suzumura, T.: Benchmarking Graph Data Management and Processing Systems: A Survey. arXiv preprint arXiv:2005.12873 (2020)
9. Dey, A., Fekete, A., Nambiar, R., Rohm, U.: YCSB+T: benchmarking web-scale transactional databases, pp. 223–230 (2014)
10. Difallah, D.E., Pavlo, A., Curino, C., Cudre-Mauroux, P.: Oltp-bench: an extensible testbed for benchmarking relational databases. Proc. VLDB Endow. **7**(4), 277–288 (2013)

11. Gao, W., et al.: Bigdatabench: a scalable and unified big data and AI benchmark suite. arXiv preprint arXiv:1802.08254 (2018)
12. Ghazal, A., et al.: BigBench V2: the new and improved BigBench. In: 2017 IEEE 33rd International Conference on Data Engineering (ICDE), pp. 1225–1236. IEEE (2017)
13. Ghazal, A., et al.: BigBench: towards an industry standard benchmark for big data analytics. In: Proceedings of the 2013 ACM SIGMOD International Conference on Management of Data, pp. 1197–1208 (2013)
14. Gupta, P., Carey, M.J., Mehrotra, S., Yus, O.: SmartBench: a benchmark for data management in smart spaces. Proc. VLDB Endow. **13**(12), 1807–1820 (2020)
15. Kumar, S.P., Lefebvre, S., Chiky, R., Soudan, E.G.: Evaluating consistency on the fly using YCSB. In: 2014 International Workshop on Computational Intelligence for Multimedia Understanding (IWCIM), pp. 1–6, November 2014. https://doi.org/10.1109/IWCIM.2014.7008801
16. Leutenegger, S.T., Dias, D.: A modeling study of the TPC-C benchmark. ACM SIGMOD Rec. **22**(2), 22–31 (1993)
17. Lu, P., Yuan, L., Zhang, Y., Cao, H., Li, K.: AutoFlow: Hotspot-Aware, Dynamic Load Balancing for Distributed Stream Processing. arXiv preprint arXiv:2103.08888 (2021)
18. Nambiar, R.O., Poess, M.: The making of TPC-DS. In: VLDB, vol. 6, pp. 1049–1058 (2006)
19. Patil, S., et al.: YCSB++: benchmarking and performance debugging advanced features in scalable table stores, pp. 1–14 (2011)
20. PilHo, K.: Transaction processing performance council (TPC). Guide d'installation (2014)
21. Pirzadeh, P., Carey, M.J., Westmann, T.: BigFUN: a performance study of big data management system functionality. In: 2015 IEEE International Conference on Big Data (Big Data), pp. 507–514. IEEE (2015)
22. Pitman, J., Yor, M.: The two-parameter Poisson-Dirichlet distribution derived from a stable subordinator. Ann. Probab. 855–900 (1997)
23. Poess, M., Smith, B., Kollar, L., Larson, P.: TPC-DS, taking decision support benchmarking to the next level (2002)
24. Sidhanta, S., Mukhopadhyay, S., Golab, W.: DYN-YCSB: benchmarking adaptive frameworks. In: 2019 IEEE World Congress on Services (SERVICES), vol. 2642–939X, pp. 392–393, July 2019. https://doi.org/10.1109/SERVICES.2019.00119
25. TPC: Transaction Processing Performance Council. `tpcorg` http://www.tpc.org/. Accessed 14 Feb 2020
26. TPC-E: TPC-E is an On-Line Transaction Processing Benchmark. http://www.tpc.org/tpce/ (2020). Accessed 20 Feb 2021
27. Waudby, J., Steer, B.A., Karimov, K., Marton, J., Boncz, P., Szárnyas, G.: Towards testing ACID compliance in the LDBC social network benchmark. In: Nambiar, R., Poess, M. (eds.) TPCTC 2020. LNCS, vol. 12752, pp. 1–17. Springer, Cham (2021). https://doi.org/10.1007/978-3-030-84924-5_1
28. Wu, Z., Butkiewicz, M., Perkins, D., Katz-Bassett, E., Madhyastha, H.V.: SPANStore: cost-effective geo-replicated storage spanning multiple cloud services. In: Proceedings of the Twenty-Fourth ACM Symposium on Operating Systems Principles, pp. 292–308 (2013)
29. Xia, F., Li, Y., Yu, C., Ma, H., Qian, W.: BSMA: a benchmark for analytical queries over social media data. Proc. VLDB Endow. **7**(13), 1573–1576 (2014)

IoTDataBench: Extending TPCx-IoT for Compression and Scalability

Yuqing Zhu[1,2]($\boxtimes$) (iD), Yanzhe An[2,3], Yuan Zi[2,3], Yu Feng[2,3],
and Jianmin Wang[1,2,3]

[1] BNRIST, Tsinghua University, Beijing 100084, China
{zhuyuqing,jimwang}@tsinghua.edu.cn
[2] NELBDS, Tsinghua University, Beijing 100084, China
{ayz19,ziy20,y-feng19}@mails.tsinghua.edu.cn
[3] School of Software, Tsinghua University, Beijing 100084, China

Abstract. We present a record-breaking result and lessons learned in practicing TPCx-IoT benchmarking for a real-world use case. We find that more system characteristics need to be benchmarked for its application to real-world use cases. We introduce an extension to the TPCx-IoT benchmark, covering fundamental requirements of time-series data management for IoT infrastructure. We characterize them as data compression and system scalability. To evaluate these two important features of IoT databases, we propose IoTDataBench and update four aspects of TPCx-IoT, i.e., data generation, workloads, metrics and test procedures. Preliminary evaluation results show systems that fail to effectively compress data or flexibly scale can negatively affect the redesigned metrics, while systems with high compression ratios and linear scalability are rewarded in the final metrics. Such systems have the ability to scale up computing resources on demand and can thus save dollar costs.

Keywords: Benchmarking · IoT data management · Time-series database · Internet of Things · TPC

1 Introduction

The Internet of Things (IoT) are increasingly attracting attentions from both industry and academia. The increasing number of IoT devices and sensors has driven IoT data management system, i.e., time-series database, to be the most popular among all types of databases [7]. Hence, there are increasing demands to benchmark and compare various design and implementations of time-series databases.

TPCx-IoT [22] is an industrial standard for benchmarking IoT data management systems. It targets at the databases deployed for the Internet-of-Things architecture. It addresses the important aspects in IoT data management such as intensive data ingestion and time-range based queries. In comparison to alternative benchmarks for IoT data management like TSBS [8], TPCx-IoT can increase

© Springer Nature Switzerland AG 2022
R. Nambiar and M. Poess (Eds.): TPCTC 2021, LNCS 13169, pp. 17–32, 2022.
https://doi.org/10.1007/978-3-030-94437-7_2

the generated workload by horizontal scale-out. This is important for IoT data management, as IoT data workload features intensive writes that are not common in other workloads such as key-value or relational data. The intensive write demands can be as high as many tens of millions of points per second.

Despite the benefits of TPCx-IoT, we find that it has not addressed some key aspects of IoT data management scenarios. On running TPCx-IoT benchmark over our open-sourced distributed IoT database, IginX[1] over Apache IoTDB[2], we achieved a record-breaking result, **4,116,821 IoTps**. When communicating the result to our users for a use case, we find that the result is not as useful as expected, because data compression and system scalability are not tested.

Data compression is very important for IoT data management, as the data volume is unprecedentedly huge. The target deployment environment of IoT database might not install computing resources to hold such a large volume of data in its original size. Data compression is the fundamental measure to reduce storage requirement. Moreover, the limited computing resource of the target deployment environment requires processing before synchronization with the cloud environment. Such processing does not include the time-range based queries, but also aggregation queries [8,15], which are extremely common for detailed data from IoTs. These aggregation-based workloads are considered in some common tests for IoT data management [8,15], but not in TPCx-IoT.

Furthermore, IoT devices can increase as time passes, leading to so-called cardinality problem that is difficult to handle [9]. Due to the inherently limited computing resources of a single server, system scalability is the inevitable measure to handle this requirement of applications. It is in fact a pressing requirement when considering the highly increasing velocity and volume of IoT data, due to the potentially fast increase of IoT devices and sensors.

Existent benchmarks commonly used [8] have not covered or even considered data compression and database system scalability. Neither have academic benchmarks [15]. While each of these benchmarks has its own advantage respectively, we amalgamate their features and add two new features, i.e., data compression and system scalability tests. As TPCx-IoT is currently the industrial standard for IoT database benchmarking, we extend TPCx-IoT and propose the new benchmark for IoT data management, IoTDataBench.

IoTDataBench features data compression test and database scalability test. Data compression is largely related to data type and data distribution. To benchmark data compression capability properly, IoTDataBench integrates a data modeling framework such that various real-world time-series data can be plugged into the framework to train models for later data generation. We extend the TPCx-IoT benchmark procedure to include the new data generation component. We also adapt the workload execution run to include the system scalability test procedure. Finally, we update the benchmark metrics to incorporate the results of data compression test and system scalability test. In sum, we make the following contributions:

---

[1] https://github.com/thulab/IginX.
[2] https://github.com/apache/IoTDB.

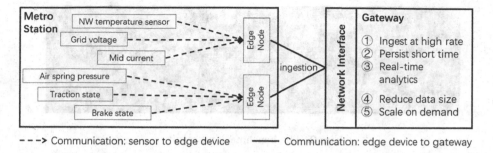

- - -> Communication: sensor to edge device   —— Communication: edge device to gateway

Fig. 1. Overview of a gateway architecture serving metro trains.

- We present a record-breaking result and the lessons learned in practicing TPCx-IoT benchmarking for a real-world use case.
- We make an apple-to-apple comparison between common benchmarks for IoT and time-series data management, summarizing their features and shortcomings.
- We propose IoTDataBench by extending the TPCx-IoT benchmark to include data compression test and system scalability test.
- We implement IoTDataBench based on TPCx-IoT, updating metric computation, data generation, workload generation and test procedure.
- Our preliminary evaluation results validate the design of IoTDataBench and indicate the future directions for improving IoT database systems.

2   Use Case: Benchmarking for Train Monitoring

In this section, we present a use case when we try to exercise TPCx-IoT for selecting the database for an IoT data management scenario. We have analyzed the benchmarking requirements and studied the in-depth analysis of the TPCx-IoT benchmark [22]. In the following, we present our results in practicing TPCx-IoT. In the process, we learned a few lessons that make us to extend TPCx-IoT and develop IoTDataBench.

One of our user, Shanghai Metro, has a monitoring system for its subway trains. The monitoring system must support dashboard-like functionality. It must keep all the monitoring data received from all sensors on all trains by MQTT protocol. As shown in Fig. 1, it is facing a scenario resembling the gateways in a typical IoT infrastructure [22]. As a result, we try benchmarking our database by TPCx-IoT, an industrial benchmark for IoT databases. We aim to see how well our database can go and whether it satisfies the user's requirements.

2.1   Benchmarking Result and Settings

In our benchmarking test, the final measured run lasts for 1821.794 s, leading to the record-breaking result of **4,116,821 IoTps**, as shown in Fig. 2.

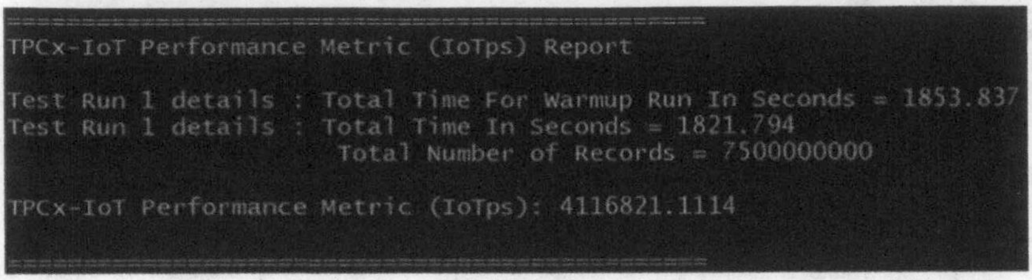

```
===========================================================
TPCx-IoT Performance Metric (IoTps) Report

Test Run 1 details : Total Time For Warmup Run In Seconds = 1853.837
Test Run 1 details : Total Time In Seconds = 1821.794
                     Total Number of Records = 7500000000

TPCx-IoT Performance Metric (IoTps): 4116821.1114
===========================================================
```

Fig. 2. The benchmarking result.

We run TPCx-IoT benchmark tests on IginX over Apache IoTDB. While IoTDB is a standalone database for IoT time-series data management, IginX is the middleware that can manage multiple instances of standalone IoT time-series databases to form an elastic cluster. As long as a standalone IoT time-series database implements the database interface, it can be integrated into and managed by IginX. Currently, IginX supports IoTDB and InfluxDB. Both IginX and IoTDB are open-sourced. The tests are run on a cluster of five servers, each with the following configuration:

- 4 Intel(R) Xeon(R) CPU Platinum 8260 clocked at 2.40 GHz, each with 24 cores and 48 threads.
- 768 GB RAM
- Mellanox HDR (200 Gbps per server node)
- 1.6 TB Nvme Disk

We used the following tuning parameters for IginX and IoTDB:

- IginX, sessionPoolSize = 130
- IginX, asyncExecuteThreadPool = 100
- IginX, syncExecuteThreadPool = 120
- IoTDB, mlog_buffer_size = 16777216
- IoTDB, enable_mem_control = false
- IoTDB, max_deduplicated_path_num = 10000
- IoTDB, compaction_strategy=NO_COMPACTION
- IoTDB, enable_unseq_compaction = false
- IoTDB, enable_last_cache = false

For TPCx-IoT, we set the number of clients to be five, each of which co-locates with one IginX instance and one IoTDB instance on a server node. Each client is set with 12 threads. The database records count is 7.5 billion. Except for environmental-setting related parameters, no modifications are made to the original TPCx-IoT distribution files.

2.2 Learned Lessons

While our benchmarking results are promising, our users find that the results are not as helpful as expected for their application scenarios. In fact, after fully analyzing the requirements in the use case and the TPCx-IoT specification, we find that TPCx-IoT falls short in the following aspects.

First, TPCx-IoT is not considering data compression. Sensors on the trains are generating more than 10TB data every month. While the company would like to preserve all the data for future analysis, the storage cost is causing a burden for this non-Internet company. As time-series database is suited for managing IoT data and performs well in data compression, the company would like to compare which database performs best in data compression and thus reduces storage costs most. Besides, data compression is also important to reduce bandwidth consumption when transferring data from gateways back to the cloud systems.

Second, TPCx-IoT does not take the database scalability into account, although it has well considered the scalability of workload generation so as to simulate the fast-ingestion workload pattern of IoT scenarios. Shanghai Metro has to scale out the whole database system every month for more storage space, since sensors are generating more than 10TB data per month [27]. Unfortunately, the company finds that the database system in use takes longer and longer time for the scale-out process, during which the database performance degrades severely. Besides, when new lines are opened or new sensors are added to trains, the database system will also need to scale out accordingly. But TPCx-IoT lacks scalability tests on database system.

Third, TPCx-IoT has not used real-world data in the benchmarking tests. The distribution of data in the workload is key to measuring the performance of IoT databases. On the one hand, data compression is highly correlated with data distribution. For example, sensor data without white noise can be compressed much better than one with. Besides, data types also matter, because numerics can be encoded but strings normally cannot. On the other hand, while TPCx-IoT uses values of exactly 1KB and considers only evenly-spacing time-series data, real-world data are commonly sent back in the original size without padding to the same size, and unevenly-spacing data are also common in IoT scenarios. These factors have also impacts on the results of data compression. Furthermore, while some time-series databases have devised specific accelerating mechanisms for data queries, data type and distribution also play an important role in affecting the performance of queries.

From the above analyses about the use case, we learn that 1) the system's capability in scaling-out must be measured to meet the increased workloads that are highly possible in future; 2) users need to be informed about the system performance on data compression to estimate their future cost of their storage space; and, 3) real-world data are needed for a valid evaluation result of the IoT data management system.

The use case of Shanghai Metro is among the common scenarios for IoT data management, e.g., aeroplane flight test monitoring and truck monitoring. As a result, we believe that TPCx-IoT need be extended to include data compression and system scalability. Besides, data types and distribution must be taken into account instead of using padding bytes.

Table 1. Comparing benchmarks for IoT data management.

Benchmarks	Queries	Mixed R/Ws	Scalability		Compression
			Benchmark	Database	
TSBS	Time-range and aggregation	NO	NO	NO	NO
SmartBench	Time-range and aggregation	NO	NO	NO	NO
TPCx-IoT	Time-range-only	YES	YES	NO	NO
IoTDataBench	Time-range and aggregation	YES	YES	YES	YES

3   Related Works

As for benchmarking IoT databases, three representative benchmarks exist for common usage. The first is TPCx-IoT [22], which is proposed by the TPC organization as a standard. The second is TSBS, which is first setup by the InfluxDB project and then improved by the TimescaleDB project. While InfluxDB is ranked as the most popular project and TimescaleDB the tenth popular, TSBS has become a defacto standard benchmark for open-source time-series database. As IoT data are typically time-series data, TSBS [8] can also be used for IoT database benchmarking. The third is SmartBench, which is an academic work. SmartBench [15] mainly considers comprehensive analytical requirements of IoT data. Therefore, it has a more inclusive query workloads.

TPCx-IoT mainly addresses three key aspects of IoT data management. The first is whether intensive writes can be generated. Intensive writes are typical of IoT data management scenarios. This features differ greatly from KV or relational data management. To settle this, TPCx-IoT designs a highly scalable architecture that can distribute the workload generator across multiple nodes. The second is whether typical queries can be simulated. Time-range queries are common in IoT data processing. TPCx-IoT mainly simulate such query workloads. The third is whether data reliability is guaranteed. TPCx-IoT checks the number of replicas in the benchmarking procedure. Besides, it also sends writes and queries on the same data to different clients for verification.

We compare the three benchmarks in Table 1, along with our proposal of IoT data benchmark, i.e., IoTDataBench. As for query workloads, while TPCx-IoT is expected to cover aggregation queries, we find its official implementation only supports time-range queries. But TSBS and SmartBench cannot support mixed read-write workloads. In comparison, TPCx-IoT adopts the YCSB framework and can flexibly generate any mixture of read-write workloads. As for scalability, TSBS and SmartBench lacks both benchmark scalability and tests on database scalability. TPCx-IoT has great benchmark scalability, but cannot test the scalability of database. None of the three benchmarks have considered benchmarking the database' capability on data compression. Extending from TPCx-IoT, IoTDataBench inherits its features and advantages. Besides, IoTDataBench has all the desired features of scalability test on database and data compression test.

4   IoTDataBench: A TPCx-IoT Evolution

IoTDataBench extends the use cases supported by TPCx-IoT to more general scenarios, where new IoT devices can be added in an ad-hoc way. In such sce-

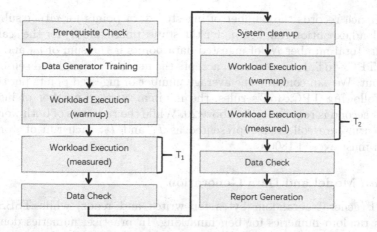

Fig. 3. IoTDataBench benchmarking procedure.

narios, workloads will increase accordingly, requiring the database to have the capability to scale-out in an on-demand manner. The use case that motivates our design of IoTDataBench also represents the use case when system scalability is demanded for storage expansion.

4.1   Benchmarking Procedure

IoTDataBench has a benchmarking procedure resembling TPCx-IoT's execution rules. IoTDataBench modifies the execution rules to include a data generator modeling phase such that real-world data can be incorporated in the benchmarking tests. Although execution rules might require long lasting discussions to reach an agreement, the benchmarking procedure of IoTDataBench updates the execution rules only for real-world data inclusion. This data generator modeling phase is not in the measured steps. Hence, the addition of this phase does not change the main thread of TPCx-IoT's execution rules.

As illustrated in Fig. 3, a typical benchmark run of IoTDataBench consists of two benchmark iterations. In each benchmark iteration, the warmup phase of workload execution runs stable workloads with mixed ingestion (write) and query (read) as in TPCx-IoT; and, the measured run of workload execution differs from the warmup phase by including database scale-out test procedures. Besides, data check is carried out in each iteration for data validation. The first iteration has an extra phase for data generator modeling, which trains a model for data generation used in both iterations. After the first iteration, the system is cleaned up for the second iteration. Before the benchmark run, a set of prerequisite checks are carried out for specification-conformity tests. After the benchmark run, results are summarized with a report generated.

During benchmark tests, IoTDataBench records the total volume S_i of ingested data and collects the final on-disk storage size S_d of the database system under test. These metrics are collected for data compression test. Besides,

IoTDataBench records the number of ingested data points for either subphase of a workload execution run, i.e., n_0 for the stable phase and n_s for the scale-out phase. The total number N_p of ingested data points is the sum of n_0 and n_s.

As in TPCx-IoT, IoTDataBench accepts the number of simulated sensors m_s as the input. We can compute the average number of ingested points per second by $\frac{N_p}{m_s}$. Following TPCx-IoT's rules, the minimal average number of ingested points per second is required to be above 20. While the runtimes of both workload execution runs are collected, represented as T_1 and T_2, each run of workload execution must exceed 1800 s.

4.2   Data Model and Data Generation

TPCx-IoT generates random bytes for writes and reads, while TSBS pre-generates random numerics for benchmarking. In practice, numerics dominate the data types of time-series values. For DevOps scenarios, strings are also common for logging purposes. IoTDataBench considers both literals and numerics.

IoTDataBench provides three methods for data generation. The first is generating numerics by stochastic distributions. Currently, TPCx-IoT supports constant, uniform, Zipfian, and histogram random number generation. These generators are mainly for integers. Besides, they do not follow the real-world distributions of IoT data. Therefore, we provide data generator for floating point numbers. We integrate multiple generators for common distributions, e.g., Poisson, Pareto, and exponential distributions. These generators can be used for both timestamps and values.

The second method is to let users input a sample of their target dataset and to generate more data by copying the sample periodically. Data generated in this way naturally follow the distribution of real-world data. Besides, the common periodicity of time-series data is instantiated in the generated data.

The third method also allows users to input a sample of their target dataset. Instead of just copying the original data, this method trains a data generation model by the data sample. Then the model is used for data generation. While this method can take longer time for data generation than other methods, the time taken by data generation phase is not counted in the running time of benchmark tests.

Currently, IoTDataBench exploits Poisson, Pareto and exponential distributions to generate floating point numbers for tests [10]. However, the other two methods are also provided with configurable parameters for users such that it can be applied to broader range of applications. Furthermore, to enable the generation of periodical patterns, IoTDataBench keeps 10 sets of 6710886 points, leading to approximately 1GB data. Each set is recursively passed to some client threads as input to form periodical patterns.

4.3   Workload Generation: Ingestion and Query

Ingestion Workloads. We integrate the workload generator with the ingestion procedure. Different from TPCx-IoT having exactly 1KB values for each write, IoTDataBench generates variable-type values by the trained data generator. Such values includes integers, floating numbers, and strings. The different data types of values are to examine the data compression capability of system under tests. Besides evenly-spaced time-series data, IoTDataBench also considers unevenly-spaced time-series data with stochastically distributed timestamps.

Query Workloads. We integrate IoTDataBench with query types considered in counterparts, i.e., TSBS and SmartBench. These queries are specific to IoT data. Besides, data compression can also influence the query performance. The system scalability test is also possible to influence the overall system performance. Queries are generated from the following four query templates, which represent typical dash-board-like queries [8,15]:

1. Time-range based observations ($S \subseteq Sensors, t_s, t_e$): selects observations from sensors in the list of sensors S in a time range of $[t_s, t_e]$.
2. Aggregation based statistics ($S \subseteq Sensors, F, t_s, t_e$): retrieves statistics (e.g., average, max, min, first, last), based on functions specified in F during the time range $[t_s, t_e]$.
3. Down-sampled observations ($S \subseteq Sensors, t_u, t_s, t_e$): selects downsampled observations by the time unit t_u from sensors in the list of sensors S in a time range of $[t_s, t_e]$.
4. Filtered observations ($S \subseteq Sensors, cond, t_s, t_e$): selects observations that satisfied the condition *cond* from sensors in the list of sensors S in a time range of $[t_s, t_e]$. *cond* is in the form of $< s_v > \theta < value >$, where s_v is the sensor name, *value* is in its range, and *theta* is a comparison operator, e.g., equality.

IoTDataBench groups the queries of TPCx-IoT, TSBS and SmartBench to form four representative query types. As compared to TPCx-IoT, the latter two types of query workloads are new. While it is possible to implement the latter three types of queries based on the first type of queries, it is much costly than the implementation of directly supporting these queries. Directly support of the latter three query types are typical of databases designed for IoT data management.

4.4   Database Scalability Test

IoTDataBench features database scalability test. This test is run within the workload execution process. Each measured run of workload execution is divided into a stable phase and a scale-out phase. The stable phase lasts for half of the warmup runtime. Then, the system is scaled out to *one* node by the supplied database command. Afterwards, one more TPCx-IoT client is added for generating more workloads. Here, IoTDataBench requires the scale-out process to be node-by-node, because this fits better with real-world application scenarios. In case that a system cannot support the scale-out process, the system can be specified with `non-scalable`. It is required that each round of workload execution must run for at least 30 min.

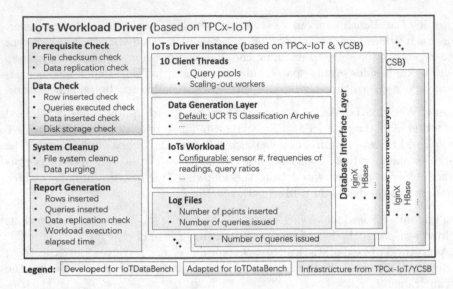

Fig. 4. IoTDataBench architecture.

On generating workloads for database scalability test, there exists the key problem of deciding the number of records for each client. With k clients configured for workload generation, one client is used for scalability test. For the N_p database records, each of the k clients is assigned with $2N_p/(2k-1)$ records, while the remaining client is assigned with $N_p/(2k-1)$ records. As the stable phase lasts for only half of the warmup runtime, the $k-1$ clients should finish generating half of their workloads before the scalability test. Hence, all clients are generating approximately the same workloads, again following the original uniform pattern of client workload generation in TPCx-IoT.

We simulate the scale-out scenario for situations when new IoT devices are installed and connected to the system as planned. We require the system to automatically scale out because automatic scalability of system can save maintenance cost. Besides, research on edge resiliency has attracted attentions. We believe benchmarks for IoT data management should consider aspects for the future. The increase ingestion workload exerts pressures on the system's capability in handling high cardinality, as well as in handling intra-system workloads during scale-out process.

4.5   Benchmark Driver Architecture

IoTDataBench inherits the same benchmarking architecture as TPCx-IoT [22], with a few noticeable differences. Figure 4 illustrates the overall architecture of IoTDataBench. The workload driver is responsible for running the entire workload. Before initiating the main benchmarking process, some prerequisite checks are carried out. Then, IoTDataBench workload driver also accepts three arguments for initiating its driver instances, i.e., *the number n_i of driver instances* and *the total number N_p vof points*. The workload driver spawn n_i driver instances accordingly. After the measured workload execution phase finishes, the workload driver initiates data check, system cleanup and report generation as needed.

In Fig. 4, white components are developed for IoTDataBench, and components with gradually changing color are adapted for IoTDataBench. The shaded components are directly inherited from TPCx-IoT and YCSB. IoTDataBench implements two new components. The first is a data generation component for a data modeling phase such that data can be generated in an ad-hoc manner. The second is a new workload generator for IoTDataBench to suit the different application scenarios for IoT data management.

IoTDataBench adapts three components from TPCx-IoT, i.e., data check, thread pool and database interface layer. Two more checks are added to data check phase. They are *data inserted check* for checking the ingested data volume S_i in bytes, and *disk storage check* for checking the total storage size S_d consumed by the database for the test. Results from these two checks are used to compute the data compression metric. IoTDataBench adds the function of scaling out workers to the three management component. This addition is for the scalability test of the benchmark. As for database interface layer, IoTDataBench extends the original database interface to accept more IoT data-specific processing operations such as aggregation queries.

4.6 Metrics

IoTDataBench extends TPCx-IoT to measure two more aspects, i.e., data compression ratio and scalability. To follow TPC benchmarks' virtue of publishing only one performance metric and one price/performance metric, we incorporate these two aspects into the original two metrics of TPCx-IoT respectively, i.e., performance metrics (IoTps) and price-performance metrics ($/IoTps).

IoTps: The performance metric reflects the effective ingestion rate in seconds that the SUT can support during a 30-min measurement interval, while executing real-time analytic queries and scaling out once. The total number N_p of points ingested into the database is used to calculate the performance metric. For the two measured runs, the performance run is defined as the one with the longer running time $T_i = max(T_1, T_2)$. IoTps is calculated as follows:

$$IoTps = \frac{N_p}{T_i} \tag{1}$$

As N_p is summarized from two parts, i.e., n_0 and n_s, it naturally reflects the system's capability to scale out. As data compression must be exerted in the process of workload execution, the compression performance is also considered in a comprehensive way.

$/IoTps: The price-performance metric reflects the total cost of ownership per unit IoTps performance. To incorporate the consideration of data compression and scalability, IoTDataBench makes the following adaptation. First, the cost of the storage component is not considered in a whole. Rather, given the cost C_0 of the storage component and its storage space S_0, the final cost of the storage component is computed as $C_0 \frac{S_d}{S_i}$, where S_0 must be larger than or equal to S_i. Hence, a higher compression ratio, i.e., $r = \frac{S_i}{S_d}$ leads to a lower storage cost.

The unit cost of storage can be computed as $\frac{C_0 S_d}{N_p S_i}$. To support $IoTps$ workload, the storage cost should be compute as $IoTps \frac{C_0 S_d}{N_p S_i}$. Given that storage cost takes up more and more portion of the total system cost as time passes, we further augment the storage cost by a weight $w_i = 2 * 24 * 365 = 17520$. This augmentation weight is given by assuming that the system will keep data for one-year long and that the system will run for 24 h in the whole year.

Second, we further take into account scalability in the price-performance metric. As the system can be consisted of different number of nodes at different stage of the workload execution run, we compute the system cost by a weighted sum. Assume the system before scale-out costs c_0 and that after scale-out costs c_s. The total cost C_S of the system is computed as $\frac{1}{2} c_0 + \frac{1}{2} c_s$.

5   Evaluation

Metric is paramount in the design of a benchmark. We present our preliminary evaluation of the extended metrics, along with a description of our IoT-DataBench implementation. Preliminary evaluation results show systems that fail to effectively compress data or flexibly scale can negatively affect the redesigned metrics, while systems with high compression ratios and linear scalability are rewarded in the final metrics. Such systems have the ability to scale up computing resources on demand and can thus save dollar costs.

5.1   Implementation

For the evaluation of IoTDataBench, we implemented data generation and workload generation extensions within the YCSB [13] codes extended by TPCx-IoT. As for data generation, we added two data generation classes for Poisson and Pareto distributions. Following TPCx-IoT's implementation, we modified the source codes of the `CoreWorkload`, `DB`, and `DBWrapper` class. While time-range query was already implemented, we implemented the other three types of queries by adding two methods, with the aggregation and the down-sample queries supported in one method.

The scalability test and the metric computation were implemented by adapting the shell scripts, including `TPC-IoT-master.sh` and `TPC-IoT-client.sh`. The disk storage check was implemented as a new shell script to be executed at each of the database server nodes.

5.2   Performance Metric Evaluation

We first evaluate whether the performance metric can reflect the scalability feature of the system under test. Let n_0 and n_s be the total number of points

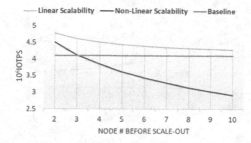

Fig. 5. Performances computed based on Eq. (5) for systems with linear and non-linear scalability. The baseline performance in the stable phase is plotted for reference.

ingested during the stable phase and the scale-out phase of the workload execution procedure respectively. Besides, let t_0 and t_s be the time taken by the two phases respectively. Assume the system under test is scaled from m nodes to $m+1$ nodes. If the system is linearly scalable, according to the new performance definition, we have:

$$n_s = \frac{n_0}{t_0} \frac{m+1}{m} w_s, w_s = 1 \tag{2}$$

$$N_p = n_0 + n_s \tag{3}$$

$$T_i = t_0 + t_s \tag{4}$$

$$IoTps = \frac{1}{t_0 + t_s}(t_s \frac{n_0}{t_0} \frac{m+1}{m} w_s + n_0) = \frac{N_p}{T_i} \tag{5}$$

According Eq. (5), w_s reflects the scalability property of the system under test, while m rewards systems consisting of powerful nodes in smaller numbers. This complies with the design assumption of TPCx-IoT. Assume the system under test can achieve 4100 *KIoTps* in TPCx-IoT with different numbers of nodes. We plot the corresponding performances for systems with different numbers of nodes, assuming linear scalability, i.e., $w_s = 1$, and non-linear scalability, i.e., $w_s = 0.9$. For non-linear systems, the linearity decreases as the system size increases, modeled as w_s^m.

Figure 5 presents the results. Assume that a system can achieve 4100 *KIoTps* before scaling out to one more node. If the system is linear scalable, it can always achieve a performance higher than the baseline. The performance gain from scaling out decreases as the number of system nodes increases. In comparison, systems that are not linearly scalable will have a performance even lower than before scaling out. This is especially true when the system has to migrate data during scale-out process [27]. Hence, systems that fail to effectively scale can negatively affect the redesigned metrics, while systems with linear scalability are rewarded in the final metrics.

5.3 Price/Performance Metric Evaluation

We evaluate the new prices/performance metric along with the added data compression test. We observe how it can change with different compression ratios.

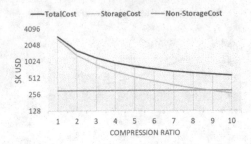

Fig. 6. The storage cost and the total cost of the system, under varied compression ratios.

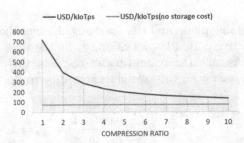

Fig. 7. Price/performance metric, $USD/kIoTps$, under varied compression ratios.

Assuming a system with 4100 $KIoTps$ performance. Using the currently top result of TPCx-IoT as the baseline, we consider a system costing about $300K$, with each 16-byte record making a storage cost of $2.039E - 08$. Following the new price/performance definition of IoTDataBench, we compute the storage cost and the total cost of a system running at 4100 $KIoTps$, under varied compression ratios. Figure 6 plots the result, with the corresponding price/performance results presented in Fig. 7.

From Fig. 6, we can see that the storage cost dominates the total cost when the compression ratio is small. On when the compression ratio reaches 10 can the storage cost be smaller than the non-storage component cost. IoTDataBench assumes one-year preservation of data when designing the price/performance metric. If the data preservation time is longer, the storage cost can be intolerable. This is exactly the reason why users of IoT databases are highly concerned with data compression. The corresponding effects of compression ratio are clearly demonstrated by the price/ performance metric, as shown in Fig. 7.

6   Discussion

System scalability has key impacts on the performance metric of the system under test. According to DB-Engines, the most popular time-series databases include InfluxDB [17], OpenTSDB [5], KairosDB [4], TimescaleDB [24], and Druid [26]. While the details of InfluxDB's distributed version are unknown for its closed source, OpenTSDB, KairosDB, TimescaleDB and Druid are exploiting existent distributed systems for scalability, i.e., HBase [2], Cassandra [1], distributed PostgreSQL database [6] and HDFS [3]. These distributed systems are designed for file, key-value, or relational data. IoT time-series data have features and workload characteristics different from these types of data. In fact, the data distribution design of existent scalable systems cannot meet the workload characteristics of time-series data [27]. We believe a new data distribution architecture for IoT time-series data is demanded.

As for data compression, existent time-series databases have employed both lossless compression [11,14,18,21,23] and lossy compression [12,16,20]. They have also commonly adopted the data retention policy to control storage consumption by discarding data passing a given time [17]. But discarding historical data is causing a loss [25]. For example, historical data are crucial for long-term observations and enabling new scientific knowledge creation in the future [19]. Considering the cost of storage, we believe it is desirable to have time-series database that can store as much data as possible within a given storage space.

7   Conclusions

IoT data management is becoming prevalent due to the increase of IoT devices and sensors. As an industrial standard for benchmarking IoT databases, TPCx-IoT is gaining attention gradually. In this paper, we present our practicing experience of TPCx-IoT in achieving a record-breaking result, as well as lessons learned when applying TPCx-IoT to our real-world use case. Driven by users' needs to evaluate data compression and system scalability, we extend TPCx-IoT and propose IoTDataBench, which updates four aspects of TPCx-IoT, i.e., data generation, workloads, metrics and test procedures. Preliminary implementation and evaluation results of IoTDataBench are provided. Based on our design process of IoTDataBench, we summarize two demanding aspects to be addressed by IoT time-series database designers, i.e., how to distribute IoT time-series data that suits its workload characteristics, and how to store as much data as possible within a given storage space.

Acknowledgements. This work was supported by NSFC Grant (No. 62021002).

References

1. Apache cassandra (2020). https://cassandra.apache.org/
2. Apache hbase (2020). https://hbase.apache.org/
3. Apache hdfs (2020). https://hadoop.apache.org/docs/r1.2.1/hdfs_design.html
4. Kairosdb (2020). https://kairosdb.github.io/
5. Opentsdb (2020). http://opentsdb.net/
6. Postgresql (2020). https://www.postgresql.org/
7. Db-engines ranking of time series dbms (2021). https://db-engines.com/en/ranking/time+series+dbms

8. Time series benchmark suite (tsbs) (2021). https://github.com/timescale/tsbs
9. What is high cardinality, and how do time-series databases like influxdb and timescaledb compare? (2021). https://blog.timescale.com/blog/what-is-high-cardinality-how-do-time-series-databases-influxdb-timescaledb-compare/
10. Agrawal, N., Vulimiri, A.: Low-latency analytics on colossal data streams with summarystore. In: Proceedings of the 26th Symposium on Operating Systems Principles, pp. 647–664 (2017)
11. Blalock, D., Madden, S., Guttag, J.: Sprintz: time series compression for the internet of things. In: Proceedings of the ACM on Interactive, Mobile, Wearable and Ubiquitous Technologies, vol. 2, no. 3, pp. 1–23 (2018)
12. Chandak, S., Tatwawadi, K., Wen, C., Wang, L., Ojea, J.A., Weissman, T.: LFZip: lossy compression of multivariate floating-point time series data via improved prediction. In: 2020 Data Compression Conference (DCC), pp. 342–351. IEEE (2020)
13. Cooper, B.F., Silberstein, A., Tam, E., Ramakrishnan, R., Sears, R.: Benchmarking cloud serving systems with YCSB. In: Proceedings of the 1st ACM Symposium on Cloud Computing, pp. 143–154 (2010)
14. Group, N.W.: RFC 3229: Delta encoding in http (2002). https://tools.ietf.org/html/rfc3229
15. Gupta, P., Carey, M.J., Mehrotra, S., Yus, O.: SmartBench: a benchmark for data management in smart spaces. Proc. VLDB Endow. **13**(12), 1807–1820 (2020)
16. Hübbe, N., Wegener, A., Kunkel, J.M., Ling, Y., Ludwig, T.: Evaluating lossy compression on climate data. In: Kunkel, J.M., Ludwig, T., Meuer, H.W. (eds.) ISC 2013. LNCS, vol. 7905, pp. 343–356. Springer, Heidelberg (2013). https://doi.org/10.1007/978-3-642-38750-0_26
17. InfluxDB: Influxdb home page (2020). https://www.influxdata.com/
18. Lindstrom, P., Isenburg, M.: Fast and efficient compression of floating-point data. IEEE Trans. Visual Comput. Graph. **12**(5), 1245–1250 (2006)
19. Murillo, A.P.: Data at risk initiative: examining and facilitating the scientific process in relation to endangered data. Data Sci. J. 12–048 (2014)
20. Nuijten, R.J., Gerrits, T., Shamoun-Baranes, J., Nolet, B.A.: Less is more: onboard lossy compression of accelerometer data increases biologging capacity. J. Anim. Ecol. **89**(1), 237–247 (2020)
21. Pelkonen, T., et al.: Gorilla: a fast, scalable, in-memory time series database. Proc. VLDB Endow. **8**(12), 1816–1827 (2015)
22. Poess, M., Nambiar, R., Kulkarni, K., Narasimhadevara, C., Rabl, T., Jacobsen, H.A.: Analysis of TPCx-IoT: the first industry standard benchmark for IoT gateway systems. In: 2018 IEEE 34th International Conference on Data Engineering (ICDE), pp. 1519–1530. IEEE (2018)
23. Robinson, A., Cherry, C.: Results of a prototype television bandwidth compression scheme. Proc. IEEE **55**(3), 356–364 (1967)
24. TimescaleDB: Timescaledb home page (2020). https://www.timescale.com/
25. Visheratin, A., et al.: Peregreen-modular database for efficient storage of historical time series in cloud environments. In: 2020 USENIX Annual Technical Conference (USENIX ATC'20), pp. 589–601 (2020)
26. Yang, F., Tschetter, E., Léauté, X., Ray, N., Merlino, G., Ganguli, D.: Druid: a real-time analytical data store. In: Proceedings of the 2014 ACM SIGMOD International Conference on Management of Data, pp. 157–168 (2014)
27. Zhu, Y.: When load rebalancing does not work for distributed hash table. CoRR abs/2012.15027 (2020). https://arxiv.org/abs/2012.15027

EvoBench: Benchmarking Schema Evolution in NoSQL

André Conrad[1]([✉]), Mark Lukas Möller[2], Tobias Kreiter[3],
Jan-Christopher Mair[3], Meike Klettke[2], and Uta Störl[1]

[1] University of Hagen, Hagen, Germany
{andre.conrad,uta.stoerl}@fernuni-hagen.de
[2] University of Rostock, Rostock, Germany
{mark.moeller2,meike.klettke}@uni-rostock.de
[3] Darmstadt University of Applied Sciences, Darmstadt, Germany
bdcc.fbi@h-da.de

Abstract. Since NoSQL database schema evolution is an important cost and time factor in the development of software applications, a standardized benchmark is essential for the comparison and evaluation of different schema evolution management systems. This benchmark should be simple to be set up, its design and usage ergonomic, its results straightforward for interpretation and reproduction – even after decades. Therefore, we present the implementation of a benchmark using Docker containers. By using containers with databases that already contain the test data, containers with the schema evolution system to be measured and the possibility to use the benchmark system itself in a container, it is very convenient to get the benchmark up and running. We also provide a data generator that creates individual data sets and/or reproduces real data once the schema is known. We demonstrate the flexibility and easy application of our approach by means of several experiments and discuss their results.

Keywords: Database evolution benchmark · Schema evolution · Containerized benchmark · Reproducibility

1 Introduction

Software applications are dynamic systems and subject to regular maintenance and development processes. Such processes may involve changes to the schema of the database systems used. Especially with the use of agile development methods where data models are subject to frequent changes, schema-flexible NoSQL data stores have become very popular. For example, a study of the schema evolution of 10 different real world applications using NoSQL databases showed regular changes to the schema during the entire lifespan of the applications [13].

This work has been funded by Deutsche Forschungsgemeinschaft (DFG, German Research Foundation) – 385808805.

A common approach to dealing with software updates or version releases and resulting changes to the database schema is to provide "update scripts" that migrate existing data for a given version jump.

With the commonly used "update scripts", all existing data are usually transferred to the changed schema (eager migration). Using *database-as-service* products such as Amazon AWS or Google Cloud Datastores may also increase costs since not all existing data are accessed regularly and thus not all data need to be migrated eagerly.

However, schema changes or evolution in the life cycle of an application can result in an error-prone and time-consuming effort. To address the complexity that schema evolution in NoSQL involves, methods and tools for the management and automation of such processes are an ongoing topic in database research [7,11,12]. For the development and/or comparison of such systems, a uniform benchmark is required. Even if such a benchmark exists for relational databases, none does yet exist for NoSQL database systems.

Contributions

- We present the implementation of the first benchmark for *Schema Evolution Systems* (SES) for NoSQL databases.
- The implementation of the benchmark uses Docker containers to provide an easy workflow to setup, run and reproduce the benchmark.
- We provide several Docker containers to the public to run and reproduce the benchmark. First, we provide generic containers with the benchmark and the data generator. Containers for MongoDB and Cassandra pre-filled with test data are also provided.
- Using five example experiments with different data sets, databases and versions of a SES, we show the ease of use and flexibility of the benchmark as a proof of concept.

This paper is organized as follows: Sect. 2 presents related work regarding the benchmark for schema evolution. Section 3 describes the implementation and functionality of our benchmark. Section 4 explains the data generator provided, as well as various data sets generated by this generator. In Sect. 5, the capabilities and flexibility of the benchmark are demonstrated using 5 different example experiments. Section 6 explains our conclusions and future work.

2   Related Work

So far, schema evolution benchmarks exist only for relational systems, but not for NoSQL databases: In [3] a schema evolution benchmark based on an indepth analysis of MediaWiki's schema evolutions history called *Pantha Rei* is presented. *Twente* [16] is an extension of the TPC-C benchmark to measure the blocking behaviour of schema transformations in relational database systems. *UniBench* [18] is a benchmark for multi-model databases and provides the data model for a social commerce application. In [10], we present a detailed comparison and analysis of these and further benchmark systems as well as the requirements for a benchmark in the context of schema evolution in NoSQL databases.

To fill the gap of a schema evolution benchmark for NoSQL, we present a concept for a NoSQL schema evolution benchmark called *EvoBench* in [9]. This includes a detailed description of the data model used, based on the social commerce scenario of *UniBench* and the concept of chaining *Schema Evolution Operations* (SMOs) with respect to the initial scheme. In this paper, we present the implementation of the *EvoBench* benchmark and demonstrate its usability. A strong focus was put on the scalability and reproducibility of the benchmark. Moreover, *EvoBench* has been designed and implemented for the use of different databases supported by various Schema Evolution Systems.

In [15] a middleware for managing schema evolution in NoSQL databases called *Darwin* is introduced. Besides other features, a database independent schema evolution language with different SMOs like *add, rename, delete, copy* and *move* which was introduced in [12] is provided. For the migration of data into the newest schema version, different strategies are available. For example, all existing data can be migrated eagerly to the latest schema version. Another strategy is to migrate the entities lazily once accessed. Various hybrid strategies are also available between these two strategies. We use *Darwin* in this paper as Schema Evolution System for proof of concept of the benchmark.

MigCast, proposed in [5] and [6], is an advisor that calculates the monetary migration costs and the latency of queries in the context of schema evolution when using *Darwin*. It applies both an internal cost model and the generation of required test data and workload. However, it is not a generic benchmark for different Schema Evolution Systems as is the case with *EvoBench*.

In [13] an in-depth analysis of the design and evolution of the implicit schema of 10 different applications with NoSQL databases is presented. Apart from the evolution history, other metrics such as the size or the denormalization of the schema are considered.

In [4], the performance of a native installation of a MySQL database system is compared with the use of a Docker container and KVM hypervisor. Similarly, in [14] a performance comparison is made between non-virtualization and multiple instances of VMware VMs and Docker Containers running with Apache Cassandra as workload. The results show that the Docker container solutions require very low overhead and system resource consumption. For example, the performance in terms of the maximum number of transactions per second was at least as high for the Docker solution as for the non-virtualized case.

3 Benchmark Implementation

This section presents the implementation of a benchmark for Schema Evolution Systems, based on the *EvoBench* concept presented in [9]. We first describe primary design criteria for the implementation. Afterwards, the description of the design will address the implementation of the criteria.

3.1 Design Criteria

In the following, basic design criteria for the implementation of the benchmark are presented [1, 10]:

Reproducibility: The repeatability of experiments and the reproducibility of results has come more and more into the focus of database system research [2]. For example, it can be time-consuming and difficult to set up certain environments from which results were obtained in a particular constellation for the reproduction of results. This commences with the operating system used and also affects complex software stacks of certain versions and corresponding setting parameters. In addition, there is the problem of the availability of used data sets and software. For example, web links may no longer work indefinitely and/or the data sets or software used may no longer be findable or runnable. This problem concerns not only the reproduction of results by others, but also the repetition of own experiments possibly carried out "long" ago.

Simplicity: The benchmark must be easy to install, configure and use. This also applies to the required database systems, the import of data sets, creation of indexes and further settings of the software stack. It should also be possible to use it on different systems and architectures without any difficulties.

Extensibility: With regard to the benchmark presented here, this means that it should be easily extensible by other database systems and SES to be used.

Clear Results: Results or, more precisely, recorded metrics need to be easily interpreted and compared. This also refers to a corresponding representation. In addition to the collected "raw data", for example, an easy-to-interpret graphical representation should be generated automatically.

3.2 Design Overview

To address the problem of the continuous *reproducibilty* of benchmarks and/or on different systems and to keep it simple to set up the necessary software stack (*simplicity*), containerization with Docker[1] is used. On the one hand to provide images with pre-filled and configured databases and on the other hand for providing the SES as a ready to run Docker image. This also has the advantage to easily use Docker images automatically built and delivered to a container registry by using CI/CD concepts such as GitLab.

The benchmark can either be run directly on the host or within a Docker container. Running directly on the host requires, that all dependencies of the benchmark are additionally installed to Docker. Figure 1 shows an overview of the design described.

A REST interface is used for the communication with the SES of choice, e.g. for executing SMOs or performing data migration. This allows to easily extend the benchmark to support additional SESs which provide a REST API (*extensibility*).

---

[1] https://www.docker.com.

To keep the configuration of the benchmark as simple as possible one central configuration file in the JSON format is provided. This means that the entire configuration necessary for the execution of the benchmark can be made within this file. To be able to define different benchmark scenarios it is possible to specify several of these files.

The results of each benchmark execution are stored in a folder structure. This concerns the raw data of the measurements in JSON format as well as the visualization of the results in arbitrary formats like PDF or SVG. Additionally, the mean values and standard deviations are calculated automatically in the case of the multiple execution of the measurements. This presents the results in a clear and easy-to-interpret manner (*clear results*). Figure 6 shows such an automatically generated plot as an example.

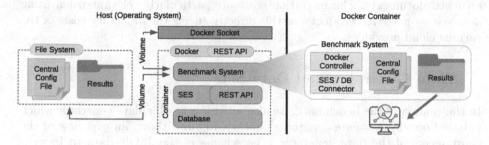

Fig. 1. Overview of the benchmark's implementation design using Docker containers.

3.3 Configuration

Within the central configuration file (see Fig. 1), the workload of the benchmark is defined in the form of one or more sequences (so-called workload chains) of different commands. The concept of these workload chains was introduced in [9] and is illustrated in Fig. 2. For each of the chains, different parameters that affect the entire chain are first defined. These are:

– The *repository* and *tag* of the database and SES Docker images, that will be used. This also includes the necessary environment parameter for the SES container to set up the database connection for instance.
– The number of times the workload chain is executed.

Each workload chain inside the configuration file consists of a sequence of different commands. In the case of an eager migration these consist of one or more SMOs and data migration calls that include various parameters provided by the SES used. The commands and parameters are sent to the SES via the REST interface. Figure 2 illustrates the configuration of the workload chains.

3.4 Metrics

Two metrics are currently recorded during the execution of the benchmark. First, the *Performance* of each command inside a workload chain is captured.

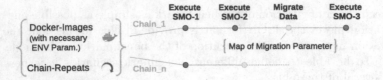

Fig. 2. Representation of the workload chains and their configuration parameters.

More specifically, the time of execution of the various REST API calls. Then, the *Migration Costs* consist of the number of entities written and read, captured for each command inside a chain. For example, when using MongoDB, the *serverStatus*[2] is used to receive the number of all inserted, updated, deleted and returned documents. The migration costs are particularly relevant when using *database-as-a-service* products, as this directly affects the monetary costs of the various cloud providers.

4   Data Generator and Data Sets

In the context of the benchmark, we also provide a flexible data generator which is based on the *json-data-generator*[3] library. Figure 3 shows an overview of the components of the data generator. The schema of the JSON data to be generated will be described by using a "pseudo" JSON file per entity type. Over 50 combinable functions are available to generate attribute values, so that most realistic data can be received.

Since an incorrect use of the functions provided in the schema definition can lead to malformed JSON data, a *JSON Syntax Validator* component was integrated into the data generator. Furthermore, a *JSON Schema Builder* component was added that generates a JSON schema[4] in addition to the data received (see Fig. 3).

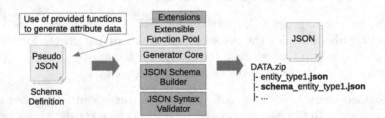

Fig. 3. Components of the data generator. Components provided by the library used are shown in light grey. Newly added components and extensions are dark grey.

---

[2] https://docs.mongodb.com/manual/reference/command/serverStatus/.
[3] https://github.com/vincentrussell/json-data-generator (v1.12).
[4] https://json-schema.org.

Relations: Since the used *json-data-generator* library cannot define relations between different entity types, additional functions were implemented (*Extensions* in Fig. 3). These serve to define 1:1, 1:n (or n:1) and m:n relationships. When generating the entities, a foreign key is randomly selected from all existing entities of the related entity type. In the case of a m:n relationship, foreign keys are stored in arrays. Also, a minimum and maximum length of the array can be specified.

Social Commerce Data: To be able to generate data for social commerce scenarios like product names, feedbacks or posts as realistic as possible, open data sources were added to the data generator to obtain such information. For this the *jHound* data scraping and analysing tool [8] was used to download such information from open data repositories.

4.1 Data Sets

At this point, four data sets based on two different models are presented which are then used in the example experiments. These data sets were generated using our data generator and deployed as ready-to-use Docker images for Cassandra and MongoDB. MongoDB and Cassandra were used as they are the most popular[5] document and wide column stores. Indexes for all primary and foreign key attributes were already included.

UniBench: This model was initially introduced as part of the *UniBench* multi-model benchmark in [17], describing a social commerce scenario and was also used in the *EvoBench* benchmark concept [9]. Since the schema was originally developed as a multi-model scenario, we adapted this model and reduced it to 8 entity types (see Fig. 4).

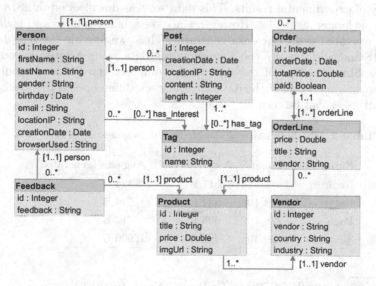

Fig. 4. UML model of the adapted *UniBench* social commerce scenario [17].

We provide two data sets of this scheme with a scaling of 0.1 (see Table 1). The scaling refers to the size of the data sets[6] provided for the multi-model benchmark *UniBench*. The data sets only differ in the average size of the *Post* and *Feedback* entities by a factor of about 10. This was achieved by having the "smaller" data set for the *Feedback.feedback* and *Post.content* attributes contained between 2 and 8 paragraphs while the "big" data set contained between 32 and 64 paragraphs. The attribute *Person.gender* is present in both data sets with a probability of 50% to mimic the structural variability in NoSQL databases.

Table 1. Characteristics of the "big" and "small" data sets of the *UniBench* scheme. The *OrderLine* is included in *Order*.

Entity type	Count	Avg size (small)	Avg size (big)
Person	995	513 B	-
Post	123,200	2,800 B	25,900 B
Tag	910	171 B	-
Product	969	327 B	-
Vendor	64	230 B	-
Feedback	15,000	2,600 B	25,700 B
Order	14,225	825 B	-

MediaWiki: The MediaWiki *pages-articles* data set from 2018-06-20 (see Fig. 5) illustrates the problem of availability of test data with respect to the reproducibility of experimental results. This data set was downloaded in 2018 and is currently no longer available[7]. However, since the schema is known, this data set was also recreated using our data generator. Thus, we provide the real data set from 2018 and additionally the corresponding data set generated by our data generator. Since the size of the data of the different attributes was only estimated for the generation of the data set, there are differences in the average size of the entities as can be seen in Table 2.

Table 2. Characteristics of the MediaWiki *pages-articles* data sets.

Entity type	Count	Avg size (real)	Avg size (generated)
Redirect	1,724	511 B	424 B
Revision	228,108	534 B	536 B
Page	228,108	695 B	717 B
Text	228,108	1,400 B	1,000 B

[6] https://github.com/HY-UDBMS/UniBench/releases/tag/0.2.
[7] https://dumps.wikimedia.org/.

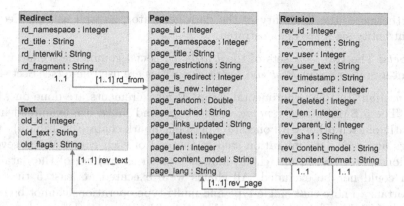

Fig. 5. UML model of the MediaWiki *pages-articles* data set from 2018-06-20.

5   Proof of Concept

In this section we demonstrate the flexibility and ease of use of the benchmark. In the following an overview of the 5 experimental setups is given which will later be analysed in detail. All measurements were done on a machine with 2 x Intel Xeon CPU E5-2695v3 @ 2.30 GHz (14 cores each), 128G RAM (DDR4, 2133 MHz), 200 GB SSD and the following software: Ubuntu 20.04.2, Docker 20.10.3, MongoDB 4.0 and Cassandra 3.0.15. In all experiments the prototype of the *Darwin Schema Evolution Management System* [15] was used as SES. *Darwin* is treated as a "black box", since the focus is not on how it works, but on demonstrating the applicability of our Benchmark.

1. The first experiment examines the differences between an SES-side and a DB-side migration. The impact of "big" and "small" entities will then also be looked at. Both measurements are done on the same database system.
2. A comparison between two different database systems will be presented next.
3. We then test the effects of a revised version of the Schema Evolution System in comparison to the default one.
4. The differences between stepwise and composite migration are then examined.
5. Finally, a real data set and a synthetic data set of the same schema will be compared.

5.1   Effects of SES-Side, DB-Side and Different Entity Sizes

At the start, the effects of a SES-side and a DB-side migration are considered. A data migration can be performed in different ways with regard to the "place of execution". In a SES-side migration, the entities are loaded into the application context, necessary changes are made and then written back to the database. In a DB-side migration, necessary changes to the data are performed by appropriate queries in the database [7]. Depending on the SMO and the capabilities of the NoSQL database system, a DB-side migration is not always possible.

Furthermore, the flexibility of the data generator, as well as the effect of different entity sizes are demonstrated.

Data Sets: The two data sets of the *UniBench* social commerce scenario with different average sizes of *Post* and *Feedback* entities are used here (see Sect. 4.1).

Configuration: In this experimental setup all measurements are done on MongoDB. The 5 SMOs: *add, rename, delete, copy* and *move* are examined independently of each other with one SMO per benchmark chain (see Table 3). This includes an eager data migration step at the end of each chain. When several operations were used in one chain, influences such as caching of the database system could not be excluded. All chains were executed at least 5 times. It is important to note that single-type and multi-type operations cannot be compared on the basis of the metrics recorded. A multi-type operation involves more than one entity type compared to a single-type operation. Therefore, it is possible to compare *add, rename* and *delete*. The same applies to *copy* and *move*. The following experiments were then based on the configuration described here.

Table 3. The 5 SMOs, each in one benchmark chain.

chain-1:	`add integer Post.rating = 0`
chain-2:	`rename Post.content to postContent`
chain-3:	`delete Post.content`
chain-4:	`copy Person.email to Post.email where Person.id = Post.person_id`
chain-5:	`move Person.email to Post.email where Person.id = Post.person_id`

Results: Initially, the effects of an SES-side migration in comparison to a DB-side migration are analysed. For such comparison the "big" data set (see Sect. 4.1) is used in each case. With regard to a DB-side migration an average performance improvement by 51.6% was recorded (see Fig. 6). It can also be observed that *delete* achieves a better performance despite the same migration cost, compared to *add* and *rename*. Then there is a striking behaviour between *copy* and *move*. As with all other operations, a DB-side migration would be expected to have better performance than a SES-side migration, but in the case of *move* it is the other way around. It is also interesting that *copy* causes higher migration costs than *move* in the case of a SES-side migration which has no impact on the performance.

Next, two data sets of the same schema with the same number of entities, but different entity sizes, are compared. On average the "small" data set achieves a better performance by about 28.8% on all SMOs in comparison to the "big" data set. The biggest differences from 36–42.5% are shown by *add, rename* and *move*. Since both data sets have the same number of entities as well as the same relationship sets, there are no differences between both data sets regarding migration costs (see Fig. 7). With a view on performance, it was not surprisingly at all to note that *move* is slower than *copy* for the "big" data set. The reverse is true for the "small" one.

These surprising results call for further investigation in the implementation of the Schema Evolution System used. First results of these investigations and improvements to the system are presented in Sect. 5.3.

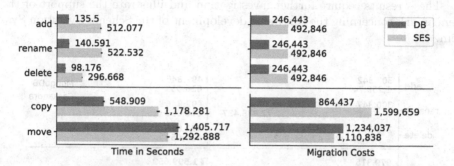

Fig. 6. Comparison between SES-side and DB-side migration – both on MongoDB and the "big" data set of *UniBench*.

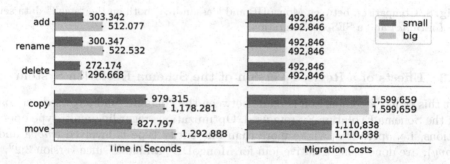

Fig. 7. Comparison between the "small" and the "big" data set of *UniBench* – both on MongoDB and a SES-side migration.

5.2   Comparison Between MongoDB and Cassandra

At this point the behaviour of the Schema Evolution System using two different database systems was considered.

Configuration: In contrast to the first experiment, the different behaviour between MongoDB and Cassandra is shown. Since a DB-side migration led to problems with the use of Cassandra, a SES-side migration using the "small" data set is considered here.

Results: It should be noted that this is a SES-side migration and the first tests of the Schema Evolution System of this kind using Cassandra. Figure 8 shows on average 90.6% better performance with MongoDB compared to Cassandra. Although the migration costs for single-type operations are identical, as expected, large performance differences are noted for Cassandra. Here *rename* shows the worst performance followed by *delete*. For the multi-type operations *copy* and *move*, it is obvious that *move* has very high migration costs and corresponding poor performance with the Schema Evolution System using Cassandra.

These results require further investigation and illustrate the support of the benchmark concerning the continued development of the Schema Evolution System.

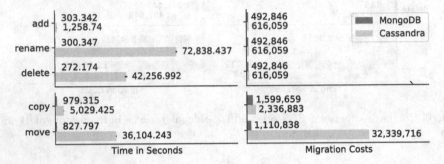

Fig. 8. Comparison between MongoDB and Cassandra – both on the "small" data set of *UniBench* and a SES-side migration.

5.3 Effects of a Revised Version of the Schema Evolution System

At this point, a comparison is made between the "default" and a revised version of the Schema Evolution System used. Optimizations regarding multi-type operations, i.e. operations where more than one entity type is involved (*move* and *copy*), are done using a native join for MongoDB[8] available since version 3.2[9].

Data Sets: The "big" data set of the *UniBench* scenario (see Sect. 4.1) were used.

Configuration: Since the changes in the revised version are mainly related to the use of a native join in the case of MongoDB, the measurements are performed with MongoDB and therefore only the *copy* and *move* SMOs from Table 3 are considered.

Results: In the first experimental setup (see Sect. 5.1) it was found that, against the expectations, *copy* had higher migration costs than *move* in case of a SES-side migration. The revised version shows the expected behaviour (see Fig. 9). An average performance improvement of 71.5% can be observed. *Copy* shows a performance gain of 78.4% and *move* of 64.6%.

---

[8] https://docs.mongodb.com/manual/reference/operator/aggregation/lookup/.

[9] https://www.mongodb.com/blog/post/joins-and-other-aggregation-enhancements-coming-in-mongodb-3-2-part-1-of-3-introduction.

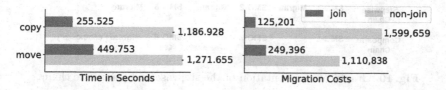

Fig. 9. Comparison between the default SES (non-join) and a revised version (join) – both on MongoDB with the "big" data set of *UniBench* and a SES-side migration.

5.4   Differences Between Stepwise and Composite

In this setup the difference between a stepwise and a composite migration is considered using a "real" scenario. In general, when migrating data to the latest schema version, all SMOs are executed stepwise. It can however be useful to "merge" SMOs where possible. For example, if an attribute is moved to another entity type (`move A.y to B.y`) and then renamed (`rename B.y to z`), these two commands can be merged into one to achieve a better performance (`move A.y to B.z`) [7].

Data Sets: The original MediaWiki *pages-articles* data set from 2018-06-20 is used (see Sect. 4.1).

Configuration: For all measurements MongoDB and a SES-side migration with the revised version of the Schema Evolution System were used. In version 1.5 of MediaWiki[10], attributes were moved from the entity type *Page* to the newly added entity type *Revision*. The 6 SMOs used here describe a part of the reverse process (see Table 4). Two benchmark chains are defined to compare a stepwise and a composite migration. In the stepwise chain, a data migration is performed after the execution of each of the 6 SMOs. In contrast, the composite chain performs a data migration only once at the end of the chain. This migration call then uses the "composite" parameter of the Schema Evolution System to compose the SMOs where possible. Figure 10 illustrates the configuration of both chains. The *composer* [7] of the Schema Evolution System used can then integrate these 6 SMOs into the 3 SMOs shown in Table 5.

Table 4. The 6 SMOs used to compare a stepwise and a composite migration.

SMO-1:	`move revision.rev_user to page.rev_user` `where revision.rev_page = page.page_id`
SMO-2:	`move revision.rev_user_text to page.rev_user_text` `where revision.rev_page = page.page_id`
SMO-3:	`copy revision.rev_timestamp to page.rev_timestamp` `where revision.rev_page = page.page_id`
SMO-4:	`rename page.rev_user to page_user`
SMO-5:	`rename page.rev_user_text to page_user_text`
SMO-6:	`rename page.rev_timestamp to page_timestamp`

---

[10] https://releases.wikimedia.org/mediawiki/.

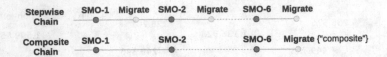

Fig. 10. Graphical representation of the stepwise and composite chain.

Table 5. The SMOs from Table 4 after the composition.

SMO-1:	`move revision.rev_user to page.page_user` `where revision.rev_page = page.page_id`
SMO-2:	`move revision.rev_user_text to page.page_user_text` `where revision.rev_page = page.page_id`
SMO-3:	`copy revision.rev_timestamp to page.page_timestamp` `where revision.rev_page = page.page_id`

Results: Since the *composer* was able to merge the 6 SMOs into 3, in Fig. 11 a performance improvement of 14.2% can be observed compared to a stepwise migration.

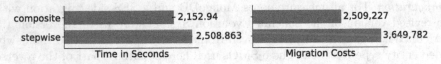

Fig. 11. Comparison between composite and stepwise – both on MongoDB using the real MediaWiki data set, a SES-side migration and the optimized version of the SES.

5.5 Comparison of a Real and a Synthetic Data Set

The last measurements compare a real data set with a generated one of the same scheme. The aim is to analyse how synthetically generated data sets using the data generator (see Sect. 4) perform in comparison to real data. This also addresses the problem of the availability of suitable and/or real data sets. Particularly real data sets are often not openly available for various reasons such as data protection. It may be possible that data sets are no longer available after a certain period of time. This is the case with the MediaWiki data set used here.

Data Sets: On the one hand, the original MediaWiki *pages-articles* data set from 2018-06-20 is used and on the other hand a synthetically generated data set of the same scheme (see Sect. 4.1).

Configuration: At this point the configuration of experimental setup 4 is adopted (see Sect. 5.4). The difference being that a composite migration is performed in both cases while comparing the real and generated data set.

Results: Figure 12 shows a difference in performance between the real and generated data set by 1.4%. This difference is less than the standard deviation of the repeated measurements. The measurements of the real data set have a deviation of 1.5% while those of the generated data set reflect a deviation by 1.1%. Since both data sets have the same number of entities and the same relationship sets, no differences in migration costs can be observed.

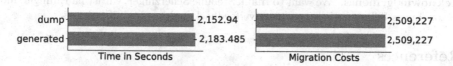

Fig. 12. Comparison between the real and the generated MediaWiki data set – both on MongoDB using a SES-side and composite migration.

6 Conclusion and Future Work

We presented the design and implementation of the first benchmark for NoSQL Schema Evolution Systems. A very easy to use and set up benchmark system was introduced which does not require the installation and configuration of complex software stacks. This is due to the use of containerization with Docker. It also addresses the problem of the reproducibility of measurements made long ago or published by others. Using Docker containers with pre-filled and configured databases also deals with the problem of the availability of data sets.

Furthermore, a data generator was provided which can be used both for the generation of individual data sets and the reconstruction of real data sets whose schema is known. Through a variety of existing functions for the generation of attribute values, high flexibility is created and realistic data can be generated. Through extensions of the library used, 1:1, n:1 and m:n relationships can also be modelled. Also, JSON schema files will be created automatically.

With the help of sample experiments presented in this work, the flexibility and applicability of the benchmark as well as the data generator were demonstrated.

To be able to reproduce our measurements, a detailed description is available on GitHub[11]. The generic Docker containers with the benchmark and the data generator as well as the containers for MongoDB and Cassandra pre-filled with the different data sets are also available on Zenodo[12].

In future we shall consider read and write operations separately in terms of migration costs. This can, for example, be useful for an in-depth analysis of high migration costs for certain operations. It may also be useful to record further metrics such as memory used or CPU load. Following the comparisons between the use of Docker and native installations in [4] and [14], we also want

---

[11] https://github.com/dbishagen/evobench-proof-of-concept/tree/master.
[12] https://doi.org/10.5281/zenodo.4993636.

to perform measurements for comparison to determine the overhead due to the use of Docker containers.

Currently, the expected state of the database after migration must be verified manually. Therefore, we want to enhance the benchmark with capabilities to automatically verify the correctness of the execution of the SMOs by the Schema Evolution System used.

Acknowledgements. We want to thank Stefanie Scherzinger, Christina Ehlinger and Edson Lucas Filho for their constructive feedback and inspired discussions.

References

1. Bermbach, D., Kuhlenkamp, J., Dey, A., Sakr, S., Nambiar, R.: Towards an extensible middleware for database benchmarking. In: Nambiar, R., Poess, M. (eds.) TPCTC 2014. LNCS, vol. 8904, pp. 82–96. Springer, Cham (2015). https://doi.org/10.1007/978-3-319-15350-6_6
2. Braininger, D., Mauerer, W., Scherzinger, S.: Replicability and reproducibility of a schema evolution study in embedded databases. In: Grossmann, G., Ram, S. (eds.) ER 2020. LNCS, vol. 12584, pp. 210–219. Springer, Cham (2020). https://doi.org/10.1007/978-3-030-65847-2_19
3. Curino, C., Moon, H.J., Tanca, L., Zaniolo, C.: Schema evolution in Wikipedia - toward a web information system benchmark. In: ICEIS 2008 (2008)
4. Felter, W., Ferreira, A., Rajamony, R., Rubio, J.: An updated performance comparison of virtual machines and Linux containers. In: ISPASS 2015. IEEE (2015)
5. Hillenbrand, A., Levchenko, M., Störl, U., Scherzinger, S., Klettke, M.: MigCast: putting a price tag on data model evolution in NoSQL data stores. In: SIGMOD 2019. ACM (2019)
6. Hillenbrand, A., Störl, U., Levchenko, M., Nabiyev, S., Klettke, M.: Towards self-adapting data migration in the context of schema evolution in NoSQL databases. In: ICDE 2020 (2020)
7. Klettke, M., Störl, U., Shenavai, M., Scherzinger, S.: NoSQL schema evolution and big data migration at scale. In: ICBD 2016. IEEE (2016)
8. Möller, M.L., Berton, N., Klettke, M., Scherzinger, S., Störl, U.: jHound: Large-Scale Profiling of Open JSON Data. In: BTW 2019. GI (2019)
9. Möller, M.L., Klettke, M., Störl, U.: EvoBench - a framework for benchmarking schema evolution in NoSQL. In: ICBD 2020. IEEE (2020)
10. Möller, M.L., Scherzinger, S., Klettke, M., Störl, U.: Why it is time for yet another schema evolution benchmark. In: Herbaut, N., La Rosa, M. (eds.) CAiSE 2020. LNBIP, vol. 386, pp. 113–125. Springer, Cham (2020). https://doi.org/10.1007/978-3-030-58135-0_10
11. Scherzinger, S., Cerqueus, T., de Almeida, E.C.: ControVol: a framework for controlled schema evolution in NoSQL application development. In: ICDE 2015. IEEE (2015)
12. Scherzinger, S., Klettke, M., Störl, U.: Managing schema evolution in NoSQL data stores. In: DBPL 2013 (2013)
13. Scherzinger, S., Sidortschuck, S.: An empirical study on the design and evolution of NoSQL database schemas. In: Dobbie, G., Frank, U., Kappel, G., Liddle, S.W., Mayr, H.C. (eds.) ER 2020. LNCS, vol. 12400, pp. 441–455. Springer, Cham (2020). https://doi.org/10.1007/978-3-030-62522-1_33

14. Shirinbab, S., Lundberg, L., Casalicchio, E.: Performance evaluation of containers and virtual machines when running Cassandra workload concurrently. Concurr. Comput. Pract. Exp. **32**, e5693 (2020)
15. Störl, U., et al.: Curating variational data in application development. In: ICDE 2018. IEEE (2018)
16. Wevers, L., Hofstra, M., Tammens, M., Huisman, M., van Keulen, M.: A benchmark for online non-blocking schema transformations. In: DATA 2015. SciTePress (2015)
17. Zhang, C., Lu, J.: Holistic evaluation in multi-model databases benchmarking. Distrib. Parallel Databases **39**(1), 1–33 (2019). https://doi.org/10.1007/s10619-019-07279-6
18. Zhang, C., Lu, J., Xu, P., Chen, Y.: UniBench: a benchmark for multi-model database management systems. In: Nambiar, R., Poess, M. (eds.) TPCTC 2018. LNCS, vol. 11135, pp. 7–23. Springer, Cham (2019). https://doi.org/10.1007/978-3-030-11404-6_2

Everyone is a Winner: Interpreting MLPerf Inference Benchmark Results

Miro Hodak[✉], David Ellison, and Ajay Dholakia[✉]

Lenovo, Infrastructure Solutions Group, Morrisville, NC, USA
{mhodak,dellison,adholakia}@lenovo.com

Abstract. MLPerf Inference benchmark suite version 1.0 was recently released. It is a third release and the version number along with minor changes from the previous version indicate a maturity of the suite. With 33 benchmarks and almost 2,000 results it provides a wealth of data on Artificial Intelligence (AI) performance, but the large amount makes it difficult for users to fully comprehend the results. At the same time, it gives opportunity for most of the submitters to claim a leadership in certain aspects of AI Inference. To clarify the situation, here we present analysis of the benchmark suite from both users and submitters perspective. We also describe ways of improving the suite going forward.

Keywords: Artificial Intelligence · Inference · MLPerf · Deep learning · GPU · Performance

1 Introduction

Explosive growth in Artificial Intelligence (AI), and Deep Learning (DL) especially, has fueled demand for performance benchmarking in this area. After a few early attempts [1, 2], key players in the industry have coalesced around the MLPerf benchmark [3]. After initially not having a formal organization developing the benchmark, MLPerf is now developed and published by MLCommons [4] established in 2020. The key advantage of MLPerf appears to be a buy-in of organizations with large AI teams (Google, Facebook, Nvidia, etc.) that have expertise to develop and maintain representative benchmarks. This is because AI benchmarking, unlike other areas, requires knowledge of the complex math underpinning of AI methods in addition to computer science and hardware skills. Furthermore, AI is a quickly developing field and benchmarks have to adjust to reflect the latest practice.

There are two major branches of MLPerf benchmark: Training and Inference, covering the major areas of current AI practice. Training is the process of determining correct weights for an AI model requiring computationally demanding operations over a long time: hours or days - depending on the model complexity and computational resources available. In other words, AI training is a highly intensive computer application that can benefit from hardware acceleration. On the other hand, AI Inference is how AI is deployed and runs as a service responding to the queries as needed. This makes it more

R. Nambiar and M. Poess (Eds.): TPCTC 2021, LNCS 13169, pp. 50–61, 2022.
https://doi.org/10.1007/978-3-030-94437-7_4

complex to benchmark as other factors beyond computational throughput need to be considered.

This work is concerned with AI Inference benchmark [5], whose latest round, version 1.0, was released on April 21st 2021 [6]. The version indicates maturity of the benchmark as well as the first release under the MLCommons organization. Compared to previous release, v0.7, the changes are very minor and limited to small adjustments of existing benchmarks without introducing major new features.

The motivation for this work is that despite the great progress that MLPerf has achieved, the large amount of benchmark results across different accelerators and servers combined with sub-optimal presentation of the results allows each submitter to claim leadership in some way making the effort less useful. Here, we attempt to clarify the situation by pointing out most relevant results and trends while also proposing areas for future improvements.

This paper is organized as follows: Sect. 2 describes the MLPerf Inference benchmarking suite, Sect. 3 looks at the results from users' point of view, while Sect. 4 gives our own insights from the latest performance data. Section 5 gives winners of the latest benchmarking round, Sect. 6 summarizes our experience as an MLPerf Inference submitter, Sect. 7 lists a few areas of future improvements and, finally, Sect. 8 gives Summary and Conclusions.

2   MLPerf Inference Benchmark Suite

Benchmarking AI inference is a complicated task. Rather than being an application running on its own, inference is a service receiving and responding to outside input. MLPerf Inference uses a concept of LoadGen, a load generator, that simulates input data sent to the inference process and makes inference benchmarking work within a single machine. LoadGen supports four scenarios:

1. **Offline:** LoadGen sends a single query containing sample data IDs to process. This is the simplest scenario covering batch processing applications and the metric is throughput in samples per second.
2. **Server:** LoadGen sends queries according to a Poisson distribution. A benchmark-specific latency bound is defined and only a small number of queries (such as 1% for vision) can exceed it. The metric is the Poisson parameter representing queries per second that can be processed while meeting the latency bound requirement. This scenario mimics a web service receiving queries from multiple clients.
3. **Single Stream:** LoadGen sends a single query to the system under test (SUT) and waits for a response. Upon a response, completion time is recorded, and a new query is generated. The metric is 90th percentile latency. This scenario mimics systems where responsiveness is a critical factor such as offline AI queries performed on smartphones.
4. **Multiple Stream:** This benchmark reflects systems that process input from multiple sensors. The metric is maximum number of inferences that the system can support while satisfying a task-specific latency constraint. An example would be a server connected multiple sensors or cameras. The resulting metric would indicate a maximum number of sensors (or cameras) that the server can handle.

MLPerf Inference is a benchmark suite covering multiple AI use cases and scenarios. Submissions are further divided into Datacenter and Edge categories, each of these cover specific tasks, scenarios, and inference accuracies although there is a significant overlap between the two.

Version 1.0 includes the following tasks:

1. Image Classification using ResNet-50 v1.5 model, ImageNet dataset
2. Object Detection using SSD-Large model, COCO dataset
3. Object Detection using SSD-Small model, COCO dataset (Edge only)
4. Medical Imagining using 3D-UNET model, BRaTS 2019 data
5. Speech-to-text using RNN-T model, LibriSpeech dataset
6. Natural Language Processing using BERT model, SQuAD v1.1 dataset
7. Recommendation DLRM model, 1TB Click Logs dataset (Datacenter only)

Table 1 gives details for submissions to Datacenter and Edge categories.

Table 1. AI tasks for datacenter and edge categories in MLPerf inference v1.0

Task	Dataset	Model	Datacenter scenarios	Datacenter accuracy	Edge scenarios	Edge accuracy
Image classification	ImageNet	Resnet50 v1.5	Server, Offline	99.0	Single stream, multiple stream, offline	99.0
Object detection (small)	COCO	SSD-MobileNet v1			Single stream, multiple stream, offline	99.0
Object detection (large)	COCO	SSD-ResNet-34	Server, offline	99.0	Single stream, multiple stream, offline	99.0
Medical imaging	BraTS 2019	3D-Unet	Offline	99.0, 99.9	Single stream, offline	99.0, 99.9
Speech-to-text	LibriSpeech	RNN-T	Server, offline	99.0	Single stream, offline	99.0
Natural language processing	SQuAD v1.1	BERT	Server, offline	99.0, 99.9	Single stream, offline	99.0
Recommendation	1TB Click Logs	DLRM	Server, offline	99.0, 99.9		

Furthermore, each submission can either be Closed or Open. The former specifies rules that need to be adhered to, which ensures that the results are comparable between submissions. The discussion here focuses on that type of submission. The Open division gives submitters much more freedom, for example, they can change the model or use different metrics, in other words they can present a different approach to solving the tasks. Open submissions are not reviewed.

Based on availability at the submission date, entries can be either classified as Available, Preview or Research. Note that this covers both hardware and software, which means that submissions cannot use a pre-release software stack. Only Available submissions are reviewed. Preview submissions cover hardware that will ship soon and obligates submitters to resubmit as Available in the next round, while Research carries no such obligation. From benchmarking perspective, the Closed and Available submissions are of most interest as they are reviewed and adhere to the Inference specifications thus making them comparable.

A new feature in Inference v1.0 is power measurement. To do this MLPerf has adopted the industry standard SPEC PTDaemon power measurement interface. The power data are optional additions to the performance data and are reported on a separate results spreadsheet.

The evolution of the MLPerf Inference is shown in Fig. 1, which shows the number of all benchmark results and number of submitters for each version of MLPerf Inference released so far. A large number of results in version v1.0 (almost a half of the total) was submitted by one submitter, Krai. Most of these submissions are in Open category and use small consumer hardware such as Raspberry Pi and thus we do not use these contributions in this analysis.

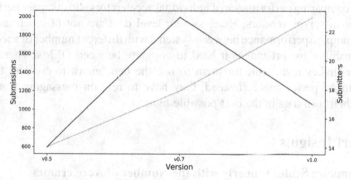

Fig. 1. Numbers of submitters and submissions for each version of MLPerf inference.

3 MLPerf Inference from Users Perspective

A weak point of MLPerf Inference Suite is the presentation to the end users. What users are shown is an online spreadsheet with many data points that cannot be downloaded or re-sorted. This makes it very difficult to gain insights from the data. By default, the results are ordered according to submitters names in alphabetical order. Each row represents a system for which at least one score is submitted. While this makes sense from the publication perspective, it makes it difficult for users to make head-to-head comparisons for systems with similar hardware or to extract performance data for different accelerators.

Another issue is that it is difficult to find out who did well in the benchmark or see who the winner is. In the effort to be independent, there is no official comment on who got the best score or what is the most relevant metric. This is left to the users, submitters, or technical press. However, the data is often impenetrable for casual users and submitters have their own agenda each touting leadership performance in some aspects of the benchmark. Technical press covers the benchmark to some degree and provides some good analysis of the benchmark, for example [7–9]. However, with many different benchmarks in the suite, the published articles can only focus on a few highlights such as GPU vs CPU or the overall best performance, while most of the results remains unexplored.

Another potentially confusing issue is that while MLPerf Inference is billed as a benchmark, in reality it functions as a competition. Submitters have no incentive to benchmark as many systems as possible, instead they submit on systems that have a chance of posting the best scores. This can be achieved by using a server with as many accelerators as possible (MLPerf Inference is a one system benchmark) and thus the published scores are heavily slanted towards massively scale-up machines, while mid-size servers which may of more interest to general enterprises and provide more flexibility are underrepresented.

One of the groups that would benefit from MLPerf data is IT managers making purchasing decisions on behalf of their data science and AI teams. These users want an easy way of comparing performance of individual accelerators and compare performance across different server vendors. Here, system level data are not of much use as it is difficult to compare performance between systems with different number of accelerators. Similarly, inability to sort makes it hard to compare between OEMs. Therefore, the current state makes it difficult for them to use the benchmark to conduct their own research into AI performance. Instead, they have to rely on messaging from OEMs presenting their own data in the best possible light.

4 MLPerf Insights

4.1 Performance Scales Linearly with the Number of Accelerators

MLPerf Inference is a system level benchmark, but because each accelerator performs inference independently, the scaling over accelerators is linear. This makes the benchmark a great resource for evaluating accelerator performance in AI tasks. This is demonstrated in Fig. 2 where per-GPU scores for Nvidia PCIe A100 GPUs are shown. Even though the numbers of GPUs range from 3 to 10, the per-GPU scores are very close with the difference between the top and lowest scores is 9%.

4.2 (Almost) Same Relative Performance Across All the AI Tasks

MLPerf Inference contains multiple benchmarks that differ in datasets and models. For example, Image Recognition uses a 26 million parameter model trained on images, while

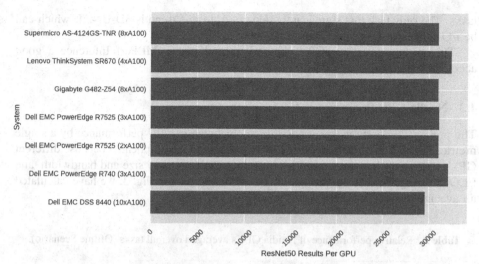

Fig. 2. Per-accelerator performance for ResNet50 inference on Nvidia A100 PCIe servers (Offline scenario).

Natural Language Processing uses a 340 million parameter BERT model that is trained on text. Surprisingly, we find that the relative performance of GPUs between those very different tasks is almost the same. This is shown in Fig. 3 for Offline scenario across all

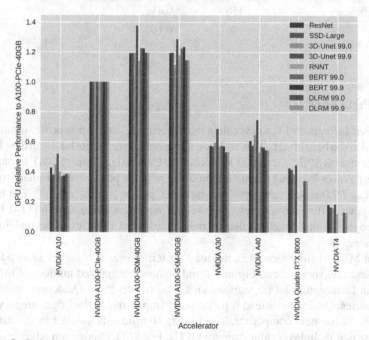

Fig. 3. Relative performance of GPUs (vs A100 PCIe) across multiple workloads.

tasks. The only task that significantly departs from this trend is 3D-UNET, which can be I/O constrained on some configurations.

This greatly simplifies GPU comparison and makes MLPerf Inference a good accelerator performance evaluation tool.

4.3 Nvidia GPU Performance Comparison

The previous property makes it possible to characterize GPU performance by a single metric. This is a great help because GPU comparison is complicated because different GPUs specs vary in many categories including TDP, memory size and bandwidth, and FLOPS ratings at different precisions. Based on the data in Fig. 3, we have calculated an average relative performance, which is given in Table 2.

Table 2. Relative performance of Nvidia GPUs averaged over all tasks (Offline Scenario).

GPU	TDP	Performance relative to A100 PCIe
Nvidia A100 PCIe-40 GB	250	1.00
Nvidia A100 SXM-40 GB	400	1.22
Nvidia A100 SXM-80 GB	400	1.19
Nvidia A40	300	0.59
Nvidia A30	165	0.58
Nvidia A10	150	0.41
Nvidia T4	70	0.16

4.4 MLPerf Power

With MLPerf Inference v1.0, a new category of metrics related to power measurement has been added to the benchmark. This addition to the benchmark suite has been developed in collaboration with SPEC (Standard Performance Evaluation Corporation). In particular, the MLPerf Power Working Group adapted the popular power measurement tools and APIs such as *PTDaemon* developed by the SPECpower committee [10]. The need for including power efficiency and related measurements was articulated in [11–13] where it was recognized that practical use of benchmark data often goes beyond just peak performance.

Within MLPerf Inference v1.0, the total system power is reported as an additional data in a separate spreadsheet. Figures 4 and 5 show normalized number of inferences per Watt in Datacenter and Edge categories. The results show Qualcomm dominating both categories. Qualcomm's lead is particularly impressive in the Edge category, where it is almost 4x the next competitor. The lead is significantly smaller in the datacenter category, which includes Nvidia Ampere GPUs. For SSD, Qualcomm advantage over a A100 system is only about 15%.

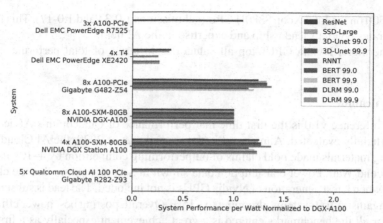

Fig. 4. Inference per Watt for Datacenter submissions.

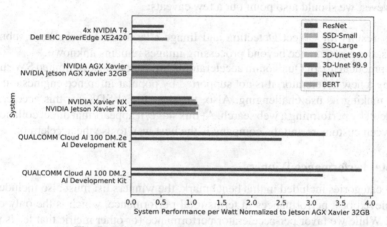

Fig. 5. Inference per Watt for Edge submissions.

5 MLPerf Inference Winners

5.1 Nvidia

Most scores in MLPerf Inference v1.0 have been generated on Nvidia GPUs: In the Datacenter category 89% of results are from Nvidia accelerators while in the Edge the ratio is 87%. This demonstrates dominance of Nvidia in the AI field. The reason for this is not just excellence in hardware, but critically also Nvidia's software stack. Because accelerators are difficult to program, providing an accessible way to use them is important for general purpose computing. Nvidia has done that with CUDA, which is integrated in many AI and scientific codes, which makes the using of Nvidia GPUs easy.

Nvidia has even pushed into the CPU territory. For the first time in version 1.0, Nvidia has made CPU submissions by making their inference engine Triton run on CPU as well. Impressively, Nvidia was able to beat Intel by posting 4800 inferences/sec vs

Intel's 4500 on the Intel Xeon 8380H CPU (submissions 1.0-34 and 1.0-17). This further demonstrates Nvidia's leadership and expertise in the AI field.

Furthermore, Nvidia GPUs top all categories in terms of total performance, see Sect. 5.3.

5.2 Qualcomm

MLPerf Inference v1.0 is the first time that performance of Qualcomm's AI accelerators is officially evaluated. Announced in the second part of 2020, the AI Cloud A100 marketing materials made bold claims of outperforming competition by 4–10x in inferences/second/Watt. Power consumption data shown in Sect. 4.4 shows that the claim is credible when latest generation of Nvidia GPUs is not included. The lead is substantially smaller against A100 systems, dropping to ~15%. Overall, posting best power efficiency results for all the benchmarks entered is a great achievement especially as a first-time submitter.

However, we should also point out a few caveats:

1. Only results for Object Detection and Image Classification have been submitted. Thus, the performance beyond processing images remains unknown.
2. The practical use of Qualcomm accelerator is limited because of limited SW support. Being a new accelerator, it is not supported by popular inference engines out of the box making its use challenging. Also, finding official SDK for this accelerator is difficult by performing a web search. At this stage, it appears that direct collaboration between customers and the company is the best way to use the accelerator.

5.3 Total Performance Winners

With 33 categories included in this benchmark, the winners list must also include those that achieved best performances in terms total performance, which is the only official metrics. While we favor per-accelerator performance (or other metric that leads to balanced performance), here we list the overall winners because they were able to navigate the existing rules the best. To account for all categories, we award one point for best performance in a benchmark and split the point in case of a tie. The results are given in Table 3 and once again show Nvidia being on top followed by Nvidia OEMs. Notably, all the top scores were generated on Nvidia GPUs.

In terms of systems, only a handful systems account for top scores. In the datacenter category, most winning systems had 8xA100 SXM 80 GB, the most performant HGX board from Nvidia. Dell EMC was also able to score some wins with 10x PCIe A100 server. In the Edge category, Inspur got most top scores because it was the only submitter to have a server with 2x PCIe A100.

These results demonstrate that the way to win MLPerf Inference as currently designed is to bundle most of the top end GPUs into a server.

6 Our MLPerf Inference Experience

Lenovo has submitted to the two most recent releases of MLPerf Inference benchmarks, versions 0.7 and 1.0. Our submissions have targeted both Datacenter and Edge categories

Table 3. Number of wins in MLPerf Inference benchmarks per submitting organization. In case of a tie, a point is divided among the submitters.

Submitter	Wins
NVIDIA	13.33
Inspur	11.33
DellEMC	6.00
Supermicro	2.00
GIGABYTE	0.33

and we have strived to submit all possible benchmarks for all our target systems. We have, however, not submitted to the power benchmarks due to insufficient time when preparing the v1.0 submission. The following are some of the most important observations from our efforts.

6.1 Work Closely with Chip Manufacturer

MLPerf Inference is a system-level benchmark, but the code needs to run on accelerators with maximum efficiency. This expertise resides with chip vendors and thus close cooperation is necessary for a competitive submission. We have worked with Nvidia and in the weeks prior to the submission and were able to obtain pre-release code and get technical help needed for a competitive submission. We expect that other submitters working with Nvidia (Dell, HPE, Inspur, etc.) have the same experience.

6.2 Use the Server with the Most Accelerators

The main Inference metric is total throughput and thus servers with the most GPUs achieve the best scores. Our datacenter entries relied on our 4-GPU server ThinkSystem SR670, which could not compete for the top overall scores despite consistently achieving one of the best per-GPU scores – the competition was using 8 and 10 GPU servers. This uncovers an additional weakness of the current MLPerf Inference setup: It pushes submitters to benchmark most GPU-dense servers, which can only be utilized at large scale while the rest of the use cases are not being adequately covered.

6.3 A Small Performance Difference Can Have Large Consequences

While the need for maximum optimization is a given for any type of benchmark, it is critical for MLPerf Inference. Because the performance is largely determined by accelerators the results for comparable systems are very close. Often, the differences are within 1% between submissions. Therefore, a minor performance gain can be a difference between a top score and an average one. For our submissions, we have not only optimized software parameters, but have tried several firmware versions and carefully monitored thermals and other accelerator metrics to achieve the best possible scores.

6.4 Results Review

After the results are submitted, they are evaluated during the review period of several weeks. This only applies to Closed and Available submissions - Open, Preview or Research submissions are not reviewed. With many results being close, one would expect a lot of challenges, but that is not the case. This is because there are no specific rules on hardware, firmware, or other system-level settings (the only exception is GPU ECC memory that needs to be enabled). The existing rules focus on AI implementation and with OEMs sharing the code developed by the accelerator makers there are not many challengeable issues beyond the wrong configuration of the provided code.

6.5 MLCommons Membership is Expensive

Submitting to an MLPerf benchmark requires an MLCommons membership. There are currently 41 members (as of June 2021). The membership cost is not publicly disclosed, but it is significantly more than those of other benchmarking organization such as SPEC or TCP. The justification is that MLCommons is about much more than AI benchmarking. Its primary mission, as stated on its website, is "to accelerate machine learning innovation and increase its positive impact on society" and to "help grow machine learning from a research field into a mature industry through benchmarks, public datasets and best practices". Thus, benchmarking is only one of the activities of the group. Other projects include People's Speech, an open speech recognition dataset in multiple languages and MLCube, "a set of best practices for creating ML software that can just "plug-and-play" on many different systems".

7 Improvements to MLPerf Inference

The most needed improvement is presentation so that data can be communicated to users clearly. While the spreadsheet giving all the performance data is a great resource, it itself needs to be improved. First, there needs to be an easy way to download it for an offline use in a spreadsheet application of user's choice. Second, the web spreadsheet should be editable, so that results can be re-sorted quickly according to whatever criteria the user desires. Additionally, having an online visualization of the results would also help to understand them. For example, the ability to quickly select all platforms with A100 PCIe and compare their performance or compare different types of accelerators would be useful to users.

Also, users would benefit from a better official description of the results so that interpreting does not requires in-depth understanding of the benchmark. While Offline scenario is the easiest to understand, the others are much harder to grasp. Part of it is due to the inherent complexity of benchmarking a service but providing a few examples might be a way to make the situation better.

Another area of improvement would be an easy way to reproduce the results. The results should be reproducible, but the instructions written by submitters are hard to follow and often require additional insight. As it stands, it is very difficult for new users to pick up the code and reproduce the results without prior experience with the benchmark.

8 Summary and Conclusions

This paper presented an in-depth evaluation of MLPerf Inference v1.0 benchmark suite. As indicated by the version, the benchmark is reaching maturity and it provides a good set of tools for evaluating AI inference across several commonly used tasks. Despite this, the results are published only as large spreadsheets which are hard for users to understand while many submitters claim performance leadership. Our work shows how the published data can be used to extract new insights into performance at the accelerator level and who the real winners are. We have also presented our experience in executing these benchmarks on Nvidia GPUs-based systems.

In conclusion, the benchmark as currently designed works well for submitters and MLCommons (the MLPerf organization), but it needs improvements from the point of view of users. The large amount of performance data without any visualization or other analysis tools is hard to grasp and hopefully will be improved going forward.

References

1. Bench Research: Deep Bench. https://github.com/baidu-research/DeepBench
2. Coleman, C.A., et al.: DAWNBench: an end-to-end deep learning benchmark and competition. In: Proceedings of the 31st Conference on Neural Information Processing Systems (NIPS 2017) (2017)
3. MLPerf. https://www.mlperf.org/
4. MLCommons. https://mlcommons.org/en/
5. Reddy, V.J., et al.: MLPerf inference benchmark. arXiv preprint arXiv:1911:02549 (2019)
6. [29] MLCommons™ Releases MLPerf™ Inference v1.0 Results with First Power Measurements. https://mlcommons.org/en/news/mlperf-inference-v10/
7. NVIDIA. https://blogs.nvidia.com/blog/2020/10/21/inference-mlperf-benchmarks/
8. NVIDIA. https://developer.nvidia.com/blog/extending-nvidia-performance-leadership-with-mlperf-inference-1-0-results/
9. Qualcomm. https://www.qualcomm.com/news/onq/2021/05/14/qualcomm-cloud-ai-100-delivers-top-marks-mlperf-10-tests
10. SPECpower working group. https://www.spec.org/power/
11. Hodak, M., Gorkovenko, M., Dholakia, A.: Towards power efficiency in deep learning on data center hardware. In: 2019 IEEE International Conference on Big Data, pp. 1814–1820 (2019). https://doi.org/10.1109/BigData47090.2019.9005632
12. Hodak, M., Dholakia, A.: Challenges in distributed MLPerf. In: Nambiar, R., Poess, M. (eds.) TPCTC 2019. LNCS, vol. 12257, pp. 39–46. Springer, Cham (2020). https://doi.org/10.1007/978-3-030-55024-0_3
13. Hodak, M., Ellison, D., Dholakia, A.: Benchmarking AI inference: where we are in 2020. In: Nambiar, R., Poess, M. (eds.) TPCTC 2020. LNCS, vol. 12752, pp. 93–102. Springer, Cham (2021). https://doi.org/10.1007/978-3-030-84924-5_7

CH2: A Hybrid Operational/Analytical Processing Benchmark for NoSQL

Michael Carey[✉], Dmitry Lychagin, M. Muralikrishna, Vijay Sarathy, and Till Westmann

Couchbase, Inc., Santa Clara, CA, USA
mike.carey@couchbase.com

Abstract. Database systems with hybrid data management support, referred to as HTAP or HOAP architectures, are gaining popularity. These first appeared in the relational world, and the CH-benCHmark (CH) was proposed in 2011 to evaluate such relational systems. Today, one finds NoSQL database systems gaining adoption for new applications. In this paper we present CH2, a new benchmark – created with CH as its starting point – aimed at evaluating hybrid data platforms in the document data management world. Like CH, CH2 borrows from and extends both TPC-C and TPC-H. Differences from CH include a document-oriented schema, a data generation scheme that creates a TPC-H-like history, and a "do over" of the CH queries that is more in line with TPC-H. This paper details shortcomings that we uncovered in CH, the design of CH2, and preliminary results from running CH2 against Couchbase Server 7.0 (whose Query and Analytics services provide HOAP support for NoSQL data). The results provide insight into the performance isolation and horizontal scalability properties of Couchbase Server 7.0 as well as demonstrating the efficacy of CH2 for evaluating such platforms.

Keywords: Benchmarks · NoSQL · HTAP · HOAP

1 Introduction

In today's online world, organizations are becoming ever more reliant on real-time information and its analysis to steer and optimize their operations. Historically, operational (OLTP) and analytical (OLAP) processing were separate activities, with each running on their own separate infrastructures; periodic ETL processes served to bridge these worlds in the overall architecture of a typical enterprise [13]. Today, database system architectures with hybrid data management support – referred to as HTAP (Hybrid Transactional/Analytical Processing [24]) or HOAP (Hybrid Operational/Analytical Processing [1]) support – are appearing on the scene and gaining traction in both industry and research in order to address the pressing need for timely analytics. Originating in the relational world, hybrid platforms are commonly linked to other concurrent high-end

© Springer Nature Switzerland AG 2022
R. Nambiar and M. Poess (Eds.): TPCTC 2021, LNCS 13169, pp. 62–80, 2022.
https://doi.org/10.1007/978-3-030-94437-7_5

server technology trends; columnar storage and main-memory data management are two of the technologies that are often assumed to be part of that picture.

While relational databases still dominate the enterprise IT landscape, today's applications demand support for millions of interactions with end-users via the Web and mobile devices. Traditional relational database systems were built to target thousands of users. Designed for strict consistency and data control, relational database systems tend to fall short of the agility, flexibility, and scalability demands of today's new applications. This has led to the emergence of the new generation of data management systems known as NoSQL systems [21]; our focus here will be on its sub-category of document databases. Examples of such systems include Couchbase Server [3] and MongoDB [8]. NoSQL systems aim to scale incrementally and horizontally on clusters of computers as well as to reduce the mismatch between the applications' view of data and its persisted view, thus enabling the players – ranging from application developers to DBAs and data analysts as well – to work with their data in its natural form.

Given this state of affairs, a natural question arises: Is the NoSQL world HOAPless[1], particularly document databases? The answer is no, as the need to combine operational and analytical capabilities for timely analytics is very much required in the NoSQL world as well. Thus, NoSQL vendors are beginning to focus on providing their enterprise customers with HOAP and are including HOAP-ful messages in their marketing materials. One such vendor, one whose document data management technology we will benchmark here, is Couchbase; the Couchbase Server platform introduced HOAP with its addition of Couchbase Analytics [2]. Our benchmark is not specific to Couchbase, however. It can be implemented and executed on HOAP-ful configurations of other NoSQL databases as well – and that, in fact, is the point of this paper: We propose a new benchmark for evaluating HOAPfulness in the world of document data management.

In the relational world, the problem of evaluating platform performance under hybrid OLTP/OLAP workloads has attracted attention in recent years. One example is the mixed workload CH-benCHmark [5] (CH) proposed by a stellar collection of database query processing and performance experts and now used by others to assess the performance of new HTAP systems [20]. The same is not yet true in the NoSQL world; there has yet to be a benchmark proposed to assess HOAP for scalable NoSQL systems. This paper proposes such a benchmark based on extending and improving CH in several important ways.

The remainder of this paper is organized as follows: Sect. 2 briefly surveys related work on HTAP systems as well as past SQL and NoSQL benchmarks. Section 3, the main event, describes our CH2 proposal for a HOAP-for-NoSQL benchmark. As an example of a HOAPful document store, Sect. 4 provides an overview of Couchbase Server and its approach to supporting HOAP. As a demonstration of CH2's potential to serve as an effective hybrid workload benchmark for NoSQL systems, Sect. 5 presents a first collection of results from

---

[1] We prefer the term HOAP over HTAP in the context of NoSQL, as it seems less tied to strict ACID transactions and columnar, main-memory technology presumptions.

running CH2 on a Couchbase server cluster in AWS under different service configurations. Section 6 summarizes the CH2 proposal and initial results.

2 Related Work

We briefly review related work on HTAP/HOAP and database benchmarks.

2.1 HTAP (HOAP)

As mentioned in the Introduction, the relational database world has witnessed an emergence of HTAP capabilities in a number of vendors' systems in recent years as well as growing research interest related to HTAP. Notable HTAP offerings today include such systems as HyPer [9] (born in research, but now owned by and used in Tableau) and SAP-HANA [12]. Other significant commercial relational HTAP offerings include DB2 BLU from IBM [19], Oracle's dual-engine main-memory database solution [10], and the real-time analytical processing capabilities now found in Microsoft's SQL Server [11]. As an example on the research side, a recent paper introduced and explored the concept of adaptive HTAP and how to manage the core and memory resources of a powerful (scale-up) many-core NUMA server running a mixed main-memory workload [20].

Stepping back, one sees that R&D in the relational HTAP world has focused heavily on in-memory scenarios for relatively "small" operational databases. Now that multi-core servers with very large main memories are available, and given the degree of compression enabled by columnar storage, it is possible for main memory to hold much or even all of an enterprises' operational business data. As a result, most current HTAP database offerings rely on main-memory database technology. And, as would be expected, the focus of these offerings is on single-server architectures – i.e., on scaling up rather than scaling out.

In contrast, providing HOAP for scalable NoSQL document databases brings different problems that require different solutions. To scale document databases while providing HOAP, the focus needs to be on Big Data – and flexible, schemaless data. In addition, NoSQL systems and applications tend to have different transactional consistency needs [21]. Data timeliness is equally important in the NoSQL world, but there is less of a need to focus on the reduction or elimination of ACID transaction interference and more of a need to focus on the successful provision of performance isolation at the level of a cluster's physical resources.

2.2 Benchmarks

Many benchmarks have been developed to evaluate the performance of relational database systems under various application scenarios [7]. The most notable are the TPC-x benchmarks developed by the Transaction Processing Council (TPC). These include TPC-C [18] for a typical transaction processing workload as well as TPC-H [16] and TPC-DS [17] for decision support and analytics. There has also been a variety of benchmarks proposed and employed in the NoSQL world, including YCSB [6] for key-value store workloads, BigFUN [14] for Big Data management platform operations' performance, MongoDB's recent adaptation of TPC-C to evaluate NoSQL transactional performance [8], and a philosophically similar NoSQL adaptation [15] of TPC-H to evaluate Big Data analytics performance, to name a handful of the NoSQL and Big Data benchmarks.

To evaluate HTAP systems, a particularly noteworthy effort was the proposal of the mixed workload CH-benCHmark [5]. This benchmark resulted from a Dagstuhl workshop attended by a group of database query processing and performance experts drawn from a variety of companies and universities. The CH-benCHmark combines ideas and operations from the TPC-C and TPC-H benchmarks in order to bridge the gap between the established single-workload benchmark suites of TPC-C, for OLTP, and TPC-H, for OLAP, thereby providing a foundation for mixed workload performance evaluation. The original paper included first results from applying the benchmark to PostgreSQL with all data being in memory and a read-committed isolation level. The CH-benCHmark appears to have gained some traction for HTAP use, having recently been used to assess the performance of a new HTAP system and its scheduling ideas [20].

To the best of our knowledge, our paper represents the first mixed workload benchmark proposed to assess HOAP for scalable NoSQL systems. A first exploratory step was reported in [23], where performance isolation in Couchbase Server (6.6) was investigated by mixing concurrent TPC-C NewOrder transactions with a stream of join/group-by/top-K queries. The effort reported here was suggested as future work at the end of that paper.

3   CH2 Benchmark Design

When we undertook the effort reported here, our goal was to explore several key aspects of NoSQL platforms' support for HOAP, including (1) their effectiveness at providing performance isolation between the OLTP and OLAP components of a mixed workload, and (2) the effectiveness of their query engines for handling OLAP-style queries. These were of particular interest because most NoSQL systems were designed to scale out horizontally on shared-nothing clusters and their initial design points for query processing have been OLTP-oriented, i.e., they were generally built to support high-concurrency/low-latency operational workloads as opposed to more complex data analytics.

Our first instinct was to design a new benchmark involving a mix of operational and analytical operations. Soon, with a healthy appreciation of the difficulty of coming up with a new schema, data, and workload, we found ourselves attracted to what MongoDB did in extending TPC-C to evaluate their new NoSQL transactional support [8]; in a project of our own we had followed a similar path by extending TPC-H for a comparative study of Big Data platform performance [15]. We decided to follow MongoDB's path for the operational side of the workload but to design our own analytical queries over the TPC-C schema for the analytical side of the mix in [23]. We then came across the mixed workload CH-benCHmark [5] for relational systems and were pleased to find that it took a similar approach. We then decided that the next step should be to "lightly" adapt the original CH-benCHmark to the document database world, but we quickly encountered a number of issues that required more extensive changes. The rest of this section details CH2, the benchmark proposal that we landed on by attempting to adapt the original CH-benCHmark (henceforth referred to simply as CH) to the NoSQL document world.

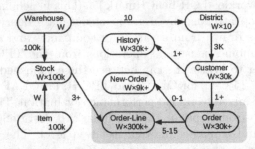

Fig. 1. TPC-C schema (NoSQL modification highlighted)

3.1   Benchmark Schema

The bulk of the schema for CH2 is MongoDB's adaptation [8] of the TPC-C schema. Figure 1 summarizes the 9 tables and relationships of the standard relational TPC-C schema. This schema models businesses which "must manage, sell, or distribute products or services" [18] and it follows a continuous scaling model. The benchmark database size is scalable based on the number of warehouses (W), and the figure includes the scaling factors for each of the tables in the TPC-C schema. MongoDB's NoSQL adaptation of this schema involves 8 collections instead of 9, because in a non-1NF-limited NoSQL world, an order would naturally embed its line items as nested data. Figure 1 highlights the affected region of the TPC-C schema. No other nesting changes were made to the TPC-C schema, as in our view doing so would involve over-nesting and would be a poor database design for such use cases [8,15].

In addition to adopting the nested order modification and TPC-C's scaling rules, the CH2 benchmark adopts CH's approach of borrowing 3 TPC-H tables as additional CH2 collections to support the adaptation of TPC-H's queries for the analytical side of a mixed workload. Following CH, CH2 borrows Supplier and Region, both unchanged, from the TPC-H schema, along with a slightly modified version of Nation. Supplier has a fixed number of entries (10,000), and an entry in Stock is associated with its Supplier through the CH relationship Stock.s_i_id × Stock.s_w_id *mod* 10,000 = Supplier.su_suppkey. A Customer's Nation is identified by the first character of the field Customer.c_state. In TPC-C this character can have 62 different values (upper-case letters, lower-case letters and numbers), so CH chose 62 nations to populate Nation (vs. 25 nations in TPC-H) and CH2 follows suit. The Nation.n_nationkey values are chosen so that their associated ASCII values are letters or numbers. Region then contains the five regions of these nations. Linkages between the new relations are modeled via the foreign key fields Nation.n_regionkey and Supplier.su_nationkey.

Table 1. CH2 collections and example sizes with 1,000 warehouses.

Collection	Collection size (W = 1000)
Warehouse	1,000
District	10,000
History	30,000,000
NewOrder	9,000,000
Stock	100,000,000
Customer	30,000,000
Orders (orderline)	30,000,000 (300,000,000)
Item	100,000
Supplier	10,000
Nation	62
Region	5

Table 1 lists the CH2 collections and gives an example of their scaling by listing their 1,000-warehouse cardinalities. Orders are nested with an average of 10 Orderline items in each. The line separates the modified TPC-C collections (top) from the three CH (and CH2) additions (bottom).

3.2 Benchmark Data

To populate the CH2 database, we first tried using the generator from the original CH effort, but found that it had significant problems – being literally based on TPC-C's data generation rules – in terms of generating data for the analytical queries. Its main problem can be described as "TPC-C's big bang" – all of the date fields in the initial CH database had the current date (i.e., the date when the benchmark is run) as their value, so there were no date ranges to be found in the data. (TPC-H queries are designed to operate on a 7-year history.) Thus, while CH's queries were purportedly based on TPC-H, many of the CH query predicates returned either nothing, everything, or something run-date-dependent as a result. In a nutshell, the CH queries in their original form were not meaningful when combined with the CH data generator's data; a "do-over" was necessary.

To address the aforementioned problems, we created a new database generator by modifying the TPC-C data generator from the publicly available py-tpcc benchmarking package from CMU to (i) generate the orders with nested items (the MongoDB NoSQL change) and (ii) carefully control the values generated for the fields used in query predicates on the analytical side of the benchmark (the CH2 data/query change). Regarding (ii), we introduced a RUN_DATE parameter to seed the data generation; RUN_DATE then leads to derivative parameters START_DATE and END_DATE that are similar to the date range in TPC-H. RUN_DATE controls the historical characteristics of the data by determining when the benchmark's past should end and when the operational workload's life should begin, i.e., START_DATE = RUN_DATE - 7 years and END_DATE = RUN_DATE - 1 day. In the process, we also fixed the dates in the data generator based on TPC-H, added the Supplier, Nation, and Region collections (as a change relative to py-tpcc, ported from the CH generator), and then (as will discuss shortly) fixed the date ranges and predicate ranges in the analytical workload's queries to conform to the TPC-H predicate selectivities and the TPC-H query business semantics. In all, the fields involved in these changes were: Customer.c_since, Orders.o_entry_d, Orders.ol.ol_delivery_d, History.h_date, and also Supplier.su_nationkey (value generation changed to avoid skew).

3.3   Benchmark Operations

The operational workload of TPC-C models the transactions of a typical production order processing system that works against this schema. Its transactions are a specified mixture of five read-only and update-intensive business transactions, namely NewOrder, Payment, OrderStatus, Delivery, and StockLevel. CH2, like CH, uses TPC-C's transaction mix as its operational workload. Also, like TPC-C and CH, CH2's performance reporting focuses on just one of the five transactions from TPC-C, namely NewOrder. NewOrder represents a business transaction that enters a new order with multiple nested orderlines into the database. A NewOrder transaction touches most of the TPC-C schema's tables and consists of both read-only queries and updates. Details of all five TPC-C transactions' logic as well as the workload's prescribed mix percentages can be found in the official TPC-C specification [18]. One CH2 change that we made to py-tpcc's out-of-the-box TPC-C operation implementation was that we chopped the Delivery operation, which does delivery processing for 10 orders, into 10 per-order transactions rather than grouping them as a single transaction. This is closer to the implementation prescribed in the specification (see Sect. 2.7 in [18]) and follows best practices for picking transaction boundaries [22]. Interestingly, py-tpcc also deviates from the TPC-C specification in that the specification states that Delivery should be handled as an asynchronous request. We did not alter that aspect of the py-tpcc implementation, so CH2 is non-compliant (by design) in that respect as it processes the Delivery operations synchronously.

   CH2's operational performance is reported, as for CH (and TPC-C), in terms of the throughput and response times for the NewOrder operations.

3.4   Benchmark Queries

For the analytical side of CH2's workload, we started with the 22 queries from the original CH effort, which in turn were inspired by the 22 queries of TPC-H. We then modified the CH queries one-by-one to operate meaningfully against the historical CH2 data with TPC-H-like predicate selectivity characteristics. This included replacing baked-in constants in predicates with controllable randomly generated values and carefully inspecting and modifying query predicates to yield a set of 22 queries that are much more aligned with TPC-H's query characteristics. (The full CH2 query set is at https://github.com/couchbaselabs/ch2 both in the code and in the Appendix of an extended version of this paper.) The

```
select ol_number ,                      SELECT ol.ol_number ,
sum(ol_quantity) as sum_qty ,           SUM(ol.ol_quantity) as sum_qty ,
sum(ol_amount) as sum_amount ,          SUM(ol.ol_amount) as sum_amount ,
avg(ol_quantity) as avg_qty ,           AVG(ol.ol_quantity) as avg_qty ,
avg(ol_amount) as avg_amount ,          AVG(ol.ol_amount) as avg_amount ,
count(*) as count_order                 COUNT(*) as count_order
from orderline                          FROM orders o, o.o_orderline ol
where ol_delivery_d >                   WHERE ol.ol_delivery_d >
   '2007-01-02 00:00:00.000000'            DATE_ADD_STR(' [START_DATE] ',
                                           [DAYS] ,'day')
group by ol_number                      GROUP BY ol.ol_number
order by ol_number                      ORDER BY ol.ol_number;
```

Fig. 2. Query 1 – CH (left) vs. CH2 (right)

```
select su_suppkey, su_name ,            SELECT su.su_suppkey, su.su_name ,
   n_name, i_id, i_name ,                  n.n_name, i.i_id, i.i_name ,
   su_address, su_phone ,                  su.su_address, su.su_phone ,
   su_comment                              su.su_comment
from item, supplier, stock, nation ,    FROM item i, supplier su, stock s ,
   region ,                                nation n, region r ,
   (select s_i_id as m_i_id ,              (SELECT s1.s_i_id AS m_i_id ,
      min(s_quantity) as m_s_quantity         MIN(s1.s_quantity) AS m_s_quantity
   from stock, supplier, nation ,          FROM stock s1, supplier su1 ,
      region                                  nation n1, region r1
   where mod((s_w_id * s_i_id),10000)      WHERE s1.s_w_id*s1.s_i_id MOD 10000
      = su_suppkey                            = su1.su_suppkey
      and su_nationkey = n_nationkey          AND su1.su_nationkey
                                                 = n1.n_nationkey
      and n_regionkey = r_regionkey           AND n1.n_regionkey
                                                 = r1.r_regionkey
      and r_name like 'Europ%'                AND r1.r_name LIKE ' [RNAME] %'
   group by s_i_id) m                      GROUP BY s1.s_i_id) m
where i_id = s_i_id                      WHERE i.i_id = s.s_i_id
   and mod((s_w_id * s_i_id), 10000)       AND s.s_w_id * s.s_i_id MOD 10000
      = su_suppkey                            = su.su_suppkey
   and su_nationkey = n_nationkey          AND su.su_nationkey = n.n_nationkey
   and n_regionkey = r_regionkey          AND n.n_regionkey = r.r_regionkey
   and i_data like '%b'                    AND i.i_data LIKE '%[IDATA]'
   and r_name like 'Europ%'               AND r.r_name LIKE ' [RNAME] %'
   and i_id=m_i_id                         AND i.i_id=m.m_i_id
   and s_quantity = m_s_quantity          AND s.s_quantity = m.m_s_quantity
order by n_name, su_name, i_id          ORDER BY n.n_name, su.su_name, i.i_id
                                        LIMIT 100;
```

Fig. 3. Query 2 – CH (left) vs. CH2 (right)

queries are expressed in N1QL (a.k.a. SQL++ [4]), a SQL-like query language that handles nested data. Note that other potential implementations of CH2 will necessarily use different languages for their versions of the benchmark due to a lack of NoSQL query standards.

Figures 2 through 4 show the first three of the 22 CH2 queries (on the right in each figure) along with the corresponding original relational CH queries (on the left). The key differences are highlighted. In Query 1 one can see changes due to the nesting of orderlines within orders as well as the replacement of a (meaningless) constant date with a TPC-H-inspired parameterized date range. In Query 2 one can see the replacement of several constants with randomly generated parameters, again akin to those of TPC-H, as well as the addition of a LIMIT clause, also akin to that of the corresponding TPC-H query. Query 3 has

```
select ol_o_id, ol_w_id, ol_d_id,         SELECT o.o_id, o.o_w_id, o.o_d_id,
  sum(ol_amount) as revenue,                  SUM(ol.ol_amount) AS revenue,
  o_entry_d                                    o.o_entry_d
from customer, neworder,                    FROM customer c, neworder no,
  orders, orderline                            orders o, o.o_orderline ol
where c_state like 'A%'                     WHERE c.c_state LIKE '[CSTATE]%'
  and c_id = o_c_id                            AND c.c_id = o.o_c_id
  and c_w_id = o_w_id                          AND c.c_w_id = o.o_w_id
  and c_d_id = o_d_id                          AND c.c_d_id = o.o_d_id
  and no_w_id = o_w_id                         AND no.no_w_id = o.o_w_id
  and no_d_id = o_d_id                         AND no.no_d_id = o.o_d_id
  and no_o_id = o_id                           AND no.no_o_id = o.o_id
  and ol_w_id = o_w_id                         -- o and ol are implicitly joined
  and ol_d_id = o_d_id                         -- as ol is nested within o
  and ol_o_id = o_id
  and o_entry_d >                              AND o.o_entry_d < '[O_YEAR]-[O_MONTH]'
    '2007-01-02 00:00:00.000000'                 || '-[O_DAY] 00:00:00.000000'
group by ol_o_id, ol_w_id, ol_d_id,         GROUP BY o.o_id, o.o_w_id, o.o_d_id,
  o_entry_d                                      o.o_entry_d
order by revenue desc, o_entry_d            ORDER BY revenue DESC, o.o_entry_d
                                            LIMIT 10;
```

Fig. 4. Query 3 – CH (left) vs. CH2 (right)

similar changes, plus it shows how the order/orderline join from the relational CH query becomes a simple unnesting (of o.o_orderline, where o ranges over orders) in the FROM clause. In a few queries we also added an additional predicate, inspired by their TPC-H cousins, to better align the two queries' business semantics. Similar changes were needed and made for all of the CH SQL queries in order to arrive at CH2's 22-query collection.

CH2's analytical performance is reported, as for CH and TPC-H, in terms of the geometric mean ("power") of the response times of the 22 CH2 queries.

4   A First Target: Couchbase Server

To illustrate the utility of CH2, we have tested the HOAP capabilities of Couchbase Server 7.0, a scalable document database system [3]. With a shared-nothing architecture, it exposes a fast key-value store with a managed cache for submillisecond data operations, secondary indexing for fast querying, and (as we will see) two complementary query engines [2] for executing declarative SQL-like N1QL[2] queries.

Data   Query   Indexing   Analytics   Full-Text Search   Eventing

Fig. 5. Major couchbase server components

Figure 5 lists Couchbase Server's major components. Architecturally, the system is organized as a set of services that are deployed and managed as a whole

---

[2] N1QL is short for Non-1NF Query Language.

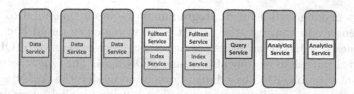

Fig. 6. Multi-Dimensional Scaling (MDS)

on a Couchbase Server cluster. Nodes can be added or removed through a rebalance process that redistributes the data across all nodes. This can increase or decrease the CPU, memory, disk, or network capacity of a cluster. The ability to dynamically scale the cluster and map services to sets of nodes is referred to as Multi-Dimensional Scaling (MDS). Figure 6 shows how MDS might enable a cluster to have 3 nodes for its Data Service, 2 shared by its Index and Full-Text Search Services, 1 for the Query Service, and 2 for the Analytics Service.

A key aspect of Couchbase Server's architecture is how data changes are communicated across services. An internal Database Change Protocol (DCP) notifies all services of changes to documents managed by the Data Service.

The Data Service lays the foundation for document management. It provides caching, persistence, and inter-node replication. The document data model is JSON, and documents live in containers called buckets. A bucket contains related documents, akin to a database in a relational DBMS. There is no explicitly defined schema, so the "schema" for documents is based on the application code and captured in the structure of each stored document. Developers can add new objects and properties at any time by deploying new application code that stores new JSON data without having to also make and deploy corresponding changes to a static schema. As of Couchbase Server 7.0, documents within a bucket reside in collections (similar to RDBMS tables) that can be grouped together logically using scopes (similar to RDBMS schemas).

The Indexing, Full-Text Search, and Query Services coordinate via DCP to provide document database management functionality that supports low-latency queries and updates for JSON documents. The Indexing Service provides global secondary indexing for the data managed by the Data Service, and the Full-Text Search service adds richer text indexing and search. The Query Service ties this all together by exposing Couchbase Server's database functionality through N1QL, a declarative, SQL-based query language that relaxes the rigid 1NF and strongly-typed schema demands of the relational SQL standard. As of Couchbase Server 7.0, N1QL supports SQL-style, multi-document, multi-statement transactions using a combination of optimistic and pessimistic concurrency control. A series of N1QL DML statements can be grouped into an atomic transaction whose effects span the Query, Indexing, and Data Services.

The Analytics Service complements the Query Service by supporting more expensive ad-hoc analytical queries (e.g., large joins and aggregations) over JSON document collections. Figures 7(a) and 7(b) show its role in Couchbase Server. The Data and Query Services provide low-latency key-value-based and query-based access to their data. Their design point is operational; they support many users making well-defined, programmatic requests that tend to be small and inexpensive. In contrast, the Analytics Service focuses on ad hoc and analytical requests; it has fewer users posing larger, more expensive N1QL queries against a real-time shadow copy of the same JSON data. The Query service has a largely point-to-point/RPC-based query execution model; the Analytics Service employs partitioned parallelism under the hood, using parallel query processing to bring all of the resources of the Analytics nodes to bear on each query [2].

The Eventing Service provides an Event-Condition-Action based framework that application developers can use to respond to data changes in real time.

So what about HOAP? As Figs. 7(a) and 7(b) try to indicate, operational data in Couchbase Server is available for analysis as soon as it is created; analysts always see fresh application data thanks to DCP. They can immediately pose questions about operational data, in its natural data model, reducing the time to insight from days or hours to seconds. There are several differences between this approach and HTAP in the relational world. One is scale: The Analytics Service can be scaled out horizontally on a shared-nothing cluster [2], and it can be scaled independently (Fig. 6). It maintains a real-time shadow copy of operational data that an enterprise wants to analyze; the copy is because Analytics is deployed on its own nodes with their own storage to provide performance isolation for the operational and analytical workloads. Another difference relates to technology: Couchbase Analytics is not an in-memory solution. It is designed to handle a large volume of NoSQL documents – documents whose individual value and access frequency would not warrant the cost of a memory-resident solution, but whose aggregated content can still be invaluable for decision-making.

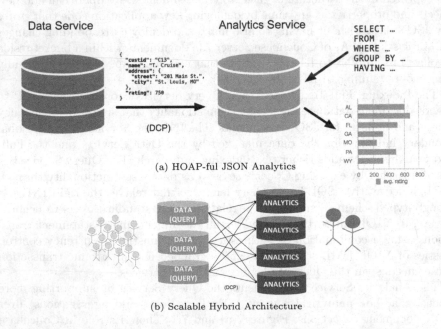

(a) HOAP-ful JSON Analytics

(b) Scalable Hybrid Architecture

Fig. 7. Couchbase analytics service in couchbase server

5   Benchmark Results

In this section we present preliminary results from implementing and running CH2 on an AWS cluster running Couchbase Server 7.0.

5.1   Benchmark Implementation

The CH2 data was stored in a scope called *ch2* in a bucket called *bench* in the Data Service. Data Definition 1.1 shows the N1QL statements for creating the CH2 benchmark's collections. The *bench* bucket was the target for the operational queries and updates and was indexed to support them. Data Definition 1.2 shows the N1QL statements used to create these indexes. For the analytical workload, shadow collections were created in the Analytics Service for each of the aforementioned Data Service collections. Data Definition 1.3 shows the N1QL statements to create these shadow collections in Analytics. Hybrid performance trends were the main focus of this exercise, not absolute performance, so little effort was made to tune the indexing choices or queries. In fact, the Analytics Service queries were run without any indexing for these initial experiments.

```
CREATE SCOPE bench.ch2;
CREATE COLLECTION bench.ch2.customer;
CREATE COLLECTION bench.ch2.district;
... (etc.)
```

Data Definition 1.1. Query Service Collection DDL

```
CREATE INDEX cu_w_id_d_id_last
          ON bench.ch2.customer(c_w_id, c_d_id, c_last) USING GSI;
CREATE INDEX di_id_w_id
          ON bench.ch2.district(d_id, d_w_id) USING GSI;
CREATE INDEX no_o_id_d_id_w_id
          ON bench.ch2.neworder(no_o_id, no_d_id, no_w_id) USING GSI;
CREATE INDEX or_id_d_id_w_id_c_id
          ON bench.ch2.orders(o_id, o_d_id, o_w_id, o_c_id) USING GSI;
CREATE INDEX or_w_id_d_id_c_id
          ON bench.ch2.orders(o_w_id, o_d_id, o_c_id) USING GSI;
CREATE INDEX wh_id
          ON bench.ch2.warehouse(w_id) USING GSI;
```

Data Definition 1.2. Query Service Index DDL

```
ALTER COLLECTION bench.ch2.customer ENABLE ANALYTICS;
ALTER COLLECTION bench.ch2.district ENABLE ANALYTICS;
... (etc.)
```

Data Definition 1.3. Analytics Service Collection DDL

As mentioned earlier, to drive the benchmark's mixed workload we started with the py-tpcc benchmarking package from CMU, the same package recently used by MongoDB [8], modified its data generator following the earlier description, and added a CH2 driver for Couchbase Server to meet our modified schema and mixed workload requirements.[3] Each operational or analytical user is simulated by a thread running on a client node of the cluster under test. Each thread consistently sends query requests to the system. Up to 128 threads send TPC-C operations to the Query Service, with 0 or 1 threads sending analytical queries to the Analytics Service. These thread counts simulate a typical business model with many front-end users but just a few data analysts (in this case one).

5.2   Benchmark Configuration(s)

Our goal here is to use CH2 to explore several key characteristics of HOAP-ful platforms for NoSQL, including (1) their effectiveness at providing performance isolation between the OLTP and OLAP components of a mixed workload, and (2) the scalability of their architectures when faced with either a need to support more operational users or a need to perform faster analytics.

To this end, we ran our CH2 benchmark implementation on a cluster consisting of 5–17 nodes that we configured in the AWS cloud. Hardware-wise, the cluster was comprised of 4–16 m5d.4xlarge instances, each with 16 vCPUs, 64 GB of memory, 2 300 GB NVMe SSDs, and up to 10 Gbps of network bandwidth, forming the Couchbase Server cluster, plus one m5d.24xlarge instance with 96 vCPUs, 384 GB of memory, 2 900 GB NVMe SSDs, and up to 25 Gbps of network bandwidth that was used to run the client workload driver. The AWS nodes running a Data, Index, and Query Service combination utilized one of the SSD drives for data and the other for indexes, while the nodes running the Analytics Service utilized both drives uniformly for enhanced query parallelism.

We configured Couchbase Server clusters in five different ways, as shown in Fig. 8. In the first configuration, the 4 Query + 4 Analytics case (4Q+4A), 4 nodes are configured to have the Data Service, Index Service, and Query Service, forming the operational subcluster. The other 4 nodes have the Analytics Service, forming the analytical subcluster. In each subcluster the CH2 data is hash-partitioned across the subcluster's nodes. Operational N1QL requests from the CH2 driver are directed to the Query Service's API endpoints, while Analytical N1QL requests are directed to the Analytics Service's endpoint. In the second configuration, the 8 Query + 4 Analytics case (8Q+4A), the operational subcluster is doubled. Symmetrically, in the third cluster configuration, the 4 Query + 8 Analytics case (4Q+8A), the analytical subcluster is instead doubled relative to its initial size. In the fourth configuration, the 8 Query + 8 Analytics case (8Q+8A), both subclusters are twice their initial size. Finally, for "extra credit", we also included a fifth configuration, the 8 Query + 2 Analytics case (8Q+2A), to test a configuration that has a scaled-up operational subcluster paired with a scaled-down analytical subcluster. Note that the Analytics Service is always given a set of nodes to itself, in all configurations, in order to provide performance isolation for the operational workload.

Data-wise, the operational data resides in the *ch2* scope of the *bench* bucket in the Data Service (in JSON document form). For these experiments we gener-

---

[3] The software artifacts associated with this paper's benchmark can be found at https://github.com/couchbaselabs/ch2.

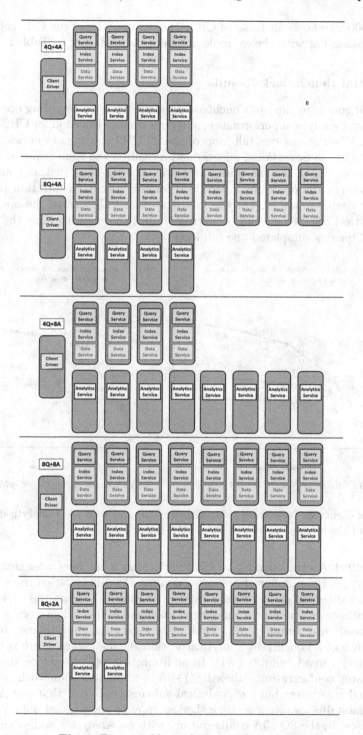

Fig. 8. Five couchbase cluster configurations

ated a 1,000 warehouse instance of CH2. The cardinalities of the CH2 collections are thus consistent with the example numbers shown earlier in Table 1.

5.3   Initial Benchmark Results

Our initial goal is to explore Couchbase Server's behavior regarding operational performance, analytical performance, and performance isolation for CH2's mixed workload. We first ran one full loop of the 22 CH2 analytical queries in isolation (i.e., with no operational clients) and measured the time required for each configuration. Then, for the purely operational CH2 runs (without analytical clients), we ran the operational workload for this measured duration (rounded up to the nearest minute). For the mixed workload CH2 runs, the operational and analytical clients were run concurrently until the client running the 22 CH2 analytical queries completed one full loop.

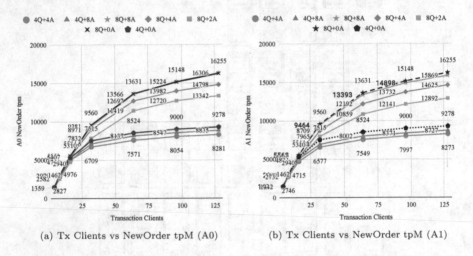

(a) Tx Clients vs NewOrder tpM (A0)   (b) Tx Clients vs NewOrder tpM (A1)

Fig. 9. Tx clients vs. NewOrder tpM, without (A0) and with (A1) analytical queries, for different cluster configurations

Figure 9 shows the operational CH2 performance, in NewOrder transactions per minute, as the number of operational client threads is varied from 4 to 128 for the five different cluster configurations. Figure 9(a) shows the performance results without a concurrent analytical workload – i.e., when zero analytical query threads are running (A0). Figure 9(b) shows the performance results in the presence of a concurrent analytical workload – i.e., when there is one analytical query thread running (A1). In addition, Fig. 9(a) shows results for one extra cluster configuration, labeled 8Q+0A – a configuration with an 8-node operational subcluster but *no* analytical subcluster. Recall that the Analytics service maintains its own real-time shadow copy of operational data for analysis purposes. In the 8Q+0A configuration, with no Analytics nodes, *no* shadow collections are being maintained, while in the five other 8Q (A0) configurations, with Analytics nodes, shadow collections are being kept up-to-date (via DCP)

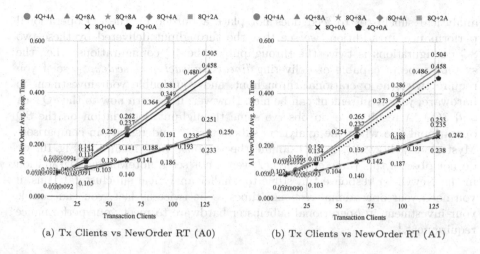

(a) Tx Clients vs NewOrder RT (A0)   (b) Tx Clients vs NewOrder RT (A1)

Fig. 10. Tx clients vs. NewOrder response time, without (A0) and with (A1) analytical queries, for different cluster configurations

in real-time even though there are no concurrent analytical queries making use of them. Figures 10(a) and (b) show the response time results for NewOrder transactions corresponding to Fig. 9's throughput results.

There is a great deal of information packed into Fig. 9, so let us proceed to unpack it and see what we can glean from the results shown there. First of all, for all configurations, with or without concurrent analytical queries, we can see that the system delivers textbook performance – i.e., the curve shapes are as expected for throughput under a closed workload, first increasing linearly and then reaching a plateau when the system's resources are saturated – so the system is *well-behaved* and exhibits no thrashing. A second observation is that if we compare the system's A0 vs. A1 throughputs in Figs. 9(a) and (b), we see *effective performance isolation*. The throughput trends and levels achieved for a given configuration in Fig. 9(b), where the CH2 analytical query workload is constantly running, are only slightly less those in Fig. 9(a) where there are no concurrent queries. These observations are borne out by the response time results in Fig. 10 as well. The response times are initially flat and then slowly become linearly proportional to the client thread count once the system becomes saturated – textbook behavior – and the corresponding response times in Figs. 9(a) and (b) are essentially pairwise identical.

Continuing with our analysis, let us now examine the throughput results (Figs. 9(a) and (b)) *within* a given operational subcluster size (Q) but with different analytical subcluster sizes (A). Let us first look at the 4Q subcluster configurations, 4Q+4A and 4Q+8A. What we see is that their operational performance is essentially the same, i.e., the system's 4Q operational performance is unaffected by the analytical subcluster size, so feeding the real-time operational updates to the analytical subcluster is not a problem here. Next let us look at the 8Q subcluster configurations. There we see that the performance for 8A+0A and 8Q+8A are also identical to one another, so having an 8-node analytical subcluster to feed does not place a burden on the 8Q operational performance. In addition, we see that the throughput delivered by these two 8Q configurations is twice the throughput of the 4Q configurations – i.e., the system appears capable of delivering *linear transactional scaleup* – so if you require twice the operational throughput, and you double your investment in hardware, your requirement can be met. However, if we turn now to the 8Q+4A and 8Q+2A results, we do observe some throughput degradation on the 8Q operational side when the analytical subcluster is "undersized" in comparison. Mysteriously, however, if we examine the response time results in Fig. 10, we do not observe this same effect – i.e., we do not see a noteworthy degradation in the NewOrder response times due to smaller analytical subclusters. Thus, if you need your operational response times to be twice as fast, you can double your investment in operational subcluster hardware to meet your performance requirement.[4]

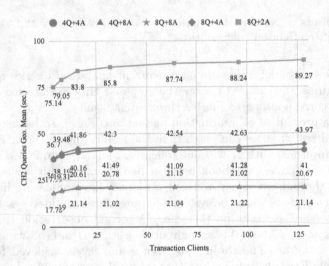

Fig. 11. Tx clients vs. power (geometric mean of analytical query times)

Let us now turn our attention to what the CH2 benchmark can reveal about Couchbase Server's analytical query performance. Figure 11 shows the geometric mean of the 22 queries' average response times (query power) for the five different cluster configurations versus the number of operational client threads. There are two key take-aways that are evident in this figure. First, we see the flip side of Couchbase Server's largely successful delivery of operational performance isolation (HOAP) – the analytical workload's performance is not overly affected as the number of concurrent operational client threads is increased on the

---

[4] The reason why we see some NewOrder throughput impact for the smaller 8Q configurations, but apparently without a corresponding NewOrder response time impact, is currently a bit of a performance mystery that running CH2 has revealed. We have several theories and we are currently investigating this behavior in order to further enhance Couchbase Server's performance isolation and scaling characteristics.

x-axis. Queries initially slow down somewhat as the operational subcluster begins generating more updates to be ingested, i.e., as the number of clients grows, because ingestion "steals" some of the analytical subcluster's query processing capacity, but query performance then levels out and is unaffected once the operational subcluster is saturated. Second, we see the very successful delivery of *linear query speedup* – i.e., when the number of nodes given to the Analytics service is doubled, the CH2 query execution times are essentially cut in half. Thus, to have your analytical queries run twice as fast, you can simply double your investment in the analytical subcluster's hardware.

6 Conclusion

Systems that provide hybrid workload support (i.e., HTAP or HOAP) first arose in the relational world, where they are often linked to server technology trends such as columnar storage and memory-rich, many-core, scale-up servers. Our focus here is on hybrid NoSQL platforms. We introduced CH2, a benchmark for evaluating hybrid platforms in the document database world. Like CH, its inspiration, the CH2 benchmark borrows from and extends both TPC-C and TPC-H. Differences from CH include a document-oriented schema, a data generation scheme that provides a TPC-H-like history for meaningful analytics, and a "do over" of the CH queries that is more aligned with TPC-H. We detailed the shortcomings that we found in CH, described the design of CH2, and shared preliminary results from running CH2 against Couchbase Server 7.0. These initial results provide insight into the performance isolation and horizontal scalability of Couchbase Server 7.0 as well as showing the value of CH2 for evaluating HOAP-ful NoSQL platforms.

Acknowledgments. The authors wish to thank the Couchbase Query Service team, especially Sitaram Vemulapalli and Kamini Jagtiani, for assisting us with the new 7.0 N1QL transaction support, and Michael Blow and Ian Maxon from the Couchbase Analytics Service team, for invaluable assistance in setting up the AWS clusters used for the experiments.

References

1. 451 Research: Hybrid processing enables new use cases (business impact brief) (2018). https://www.intersystems.com/isc-resources/wp-content/uploads/sites/24/Hybrid_Processing_Enables_New_Use_Cases-451Research.pdf. Accessed 19 Oct 2020
2. Al Hubail, M., et al.: Couchbase analytics: NoETL for scalable NoSQL data analysis. PVLDB **12**(12), 2275–2286 (2019)
3. Borkar, D., et al.: Have your data and query it too: from key-value caching to big data management. In: Proceedings of ACM SIGMOD Conference, pp. 239–251. ACM (2016)
4. Chamberlin, D.: SQL++ for SQL Users: A Tutorial. Couchbase, Inc. (2018). Amazon.com

5. Cole, R.L., et al.: The mixed workload CH-benCHmark. In: Proceedings of Fourth International Workshop on Testing Database Systems, DBTest 2011, Athens, Greece, 13 June 2011, p. 8. ACM (2011)
6. Cooper, B.F., et al.: Benchmarking cloud serving systems with YCSB. In: Proceedings of 1st ACM Symposium on Cloud Computing, SoCC 2010, Indianapolis, Indiana, USA, 10–11 June 2010, pp. 143–154. ACM (2010)
7. Gray, J. (ed.): The Benchmark Handbook for Database and Transaction Systems, 1st edn. Morgan Kaufmann, Burlington (1991)
8. Kamsky, A.: Adapting TPC-C benchmark to measure performance of multi-document transactions in MongoDB. PVLDB **12**(12), 2254–2262 (2019)
9. Kemper, A., Neumann, T.: HyPer: a hybrid OLTP&OLAP main memory database system based on virtual memory snapshots. In: 2011 IEEE 27th International Conference on Data Engineering, pp. 195–206 (2011)
10. Lahiri, T., et al.: Oracle database in-memory: a dual format in-memory database. In: 2015 IEEE 31st International Conference on Data Engineering, pp. 1253–1258 (2015)
11. Larson, P., et al.: Real-time analytical processing with SQL server. PVLDB **8**(12), 1740–1751 (2015)
12. May, N., Böhm, A., Lehner, W.: SAP HANA - the evolution of an in-memory DBMS from pure OLAP processing towards mixed workloads. In: Proceedings of BTW 2017, 17. Fachtagung des GI-Fachber. DBIS, März 2017, Stuttgart, Germany (2017)
13. Özsu, M.T., Valduriez, P.: Principles of Distributed Database Systems, 4th edn. Springer, Cham (2020). https://doi.org/10.1007/978-3-030-26253-2
14. Pirzadeh, P., Carey, M., Westmann, T.: BigFUN: a performance study of big data management system functionality. In: 2015 IEEE International Conference on Big Data, pp. 507–514 (2015)
15. Pirzadeh, P., Carey, M., Westmann, T.: A performance study of big data analytics platforms. In: 2017 IEEE International Conference on Big Data, pp. 2911–2920 (2017)
16. Pöss, M., Floyd, C.: New TPC benchmarks for decision support and web commerce. SIGMOD Rec. **29**(4), 64–71 (2000)
17. Pöss, M., et al.: TPC-DS, taking decision support benchmarking to the next level. In: Proceedings of ACM SIGMOD Conference, pp. 582–587. ACM (2002)
18. Raab, F.: TPC-C - the standard benchmark for online transaction processing (OLTP). In: Gray, J. (ed.) The Benchmark Handbook for Database and Transaction Systems, 2nd edn. Morgan Kaufmann (1993)
19. Raman, V., et al.: DB2 with BLU acceleration: so much more than just a column store. PVLDB **6**(11), 1080–1091 (2013)
20. Raza, A., et al.: Adaptive HTAP through elastic resource scheduling. In: Proceedings of ACM SIGMOD Conference, pp. 2043–2054. ACM (2020)
21. Sadalage, P.J., Fowler, M.: NoSQL Distilled: A Brief Guide to the Emerging World of Polyglot Persistence. Addison-Wesley, Upper Saddle River (2013)
22. Shasha, D.E.: Database Tuning - A Principled Approach. Prentice-Hall, Hoboken (1992)
23. Tian, Y., Carey, M., Maxon, I.: Benchmarking HOAP for scalable document data management: a first step. In: 2020 IEEE International Conference on Big Data, pp. 2833–2842 (2020)
24. Wikipedia contributors: Hybrid transactional/analytical processing – Wikipedia, the free encyclopedia (2020). https://en.wikipedia.org/w/index.php?title=Hybrid_transactional/analytical_processing&oldid=981969658. Accessed 19 Oct 2020

Orchestrating DBMS Benchmarking in the Cloud with Kubernetes

Patrick K. Erdelt[✉]

Beuth Hochschule fuer Technik Berlin, Luxemburger Strasse 10,
13353 Berlin, Germany
patrick.erdelt@beuth-hochschule.de

Abstract. Containerization has become a common practise in software
provisioning. Kubernetes (K8s) is useful in deploying containers in clusters, in managing their lifecycle, in scheduling and resource allocation.
The benchmarking process requires the interaction of various components. We propose a way to organize benchmarking in the Cloud by
looking at typical components in the process and ask if they could be
managed by K8s as containerized Microservices. We aim at scalability
for the process, parallelized execution and minimized traffic I/O from
and into the Cloud. This supports planning a series of experiments to
investigate a high-dimensional parameter space and avoiding complex
installations. This also provides a way for Cross-Cloud comparison.

In this article we discuss 1. how objects of K8s can match components
of a benchmarking process, 2. how to orchestrate the benchmarking workflow in K8s. We also present an implementation. We show this approach
is feasible, relevant, portable and scalable by designing and inspecting a
basic profiling benchmark on TPC-DS data handled by 13 DBMS at two
private Clouds and five commercial Cloud providers.

Keywords: Database Management Systems · Performance
Evaluation · Benchmarking · Virtualization · Docker · Cloud-based
systems · Kubernetes · Microservices · Tools · Amazon Web Services ·
Google Cloud Platform · IBM Cloud · Microsoft Azure · Oracle Cloud
Infrastructure

1 Introduction

Typical activities in a benchmarking process are schema creation, data loading,
data indexing, maintenance updates and query execution in a number of parallel
and sequential streams. We collect information about durations and resource
consumptions of (some of) the single steps and compute metrics to quantify the
overall quality. A software that drives a benchmark should have components
matching these steps and execute the activities in a predefined order. We are
asking for a way to integrate a benchmarking framework into the Cloud almost
completely. We propose a benchmarking system should follow the same principles
as a benchmark, so in the spirit of Gray [11] we assume the following guiding
principles:

© Springer Nature Switzerland AG 2022
R. Nambiar and M. Poess (Eds.): TPCTC 2021, LNCS 13169, pp. 81–97, 2022.
https://doi.org/10.1007/978-3-030-94437-7_6

P1 Relevance: The benchmarking framework should cover typical operations, like running DDL statements, loading, and query execution in a number of parallel and sequential streams.

P2 Portability: The benchmarking framework should cover many different systems, that is a variety of DBMS, of loading mechanisms, of workloads and datasets, and of Cloud providers.

P3 Scalability: The benchmarking framework should allow to scale the number of parallel experiments and put as much as possible and sensible into the Cloud.

P4 Simplicity: The benchmarking framework should automate as much as possible, allow to set a variety of parameters while at the same time take DBMS and Clouds as provided by vendors without having to change much.

We assume that these principles can be achieved if we consider the relevant components of a benchmarking framework as independent Microservices, put some components into Docker containers and let Kubernetes manage these containers.

1.1   Contribution

In this article we review some typical components of a benchmarking workflow and some important components of Kubernetes (K8s). We discuss how these basic components and native abilities of K8s, like naming and labeling, shell execution, setting environment variables and copying file, can be used to orchestrate the workflow as a distributed system of Microservices. We design a basic data profiling benchmark based on TPC-DS data that can also be used as preparation for statistical or machine learning tasks or to verify the end of an ETL or ELT process. We use the benchmark to test data import, as a data validity check and for performance measures. Moreover, to show that guiding principles P1-P4 are being followed, we inspect 14 publically available Docker images of DBMS at seven Clouds and try to run the benchmark in a parallized process of different scales.

1.2   Related Work

In [6] the authors list important components for benchmarking, like Benchmark Coordinator, Measurement Manager, Workload Executor. They plead for a benchmarking middleware to support the process, to "*take care of the hassle of distributed benchmarking and managing the measurement infrastructure*". This is supposed to help the benchmark designer to concentrate on the core competences: specifying workload profiles and analyzing obtained measurements. Other authors point out the need for a framework to support the process [7,9,15], too. In [10] we motivate and introduce a framework of two Python packages to support repetition and evaluation in the process of Cloud-based DBMS performance benchmarking. DBMS and monitoring metrics collector are deployed as a black box pod into a K8s cluster on a single node and everything else is fixed outside of the cluster on the same machine. We use the same packages here in particular for evaluation. In this article we desire to integrate not only the DBMS in K8s, but also other components. This yields higher automation of the benchmarking processes itself, but also of related processes like load check, configuration optimization, testing and debugging in parallel executions.

Much research about benchmarking in the Cloud on an IaaS level has been done. In [13] the authors review previous work and give principles for reproducible performance evaluation, like supplementing aggregated values with variations, precise description of the experimental setup and of how many repetitions with the same configuration have been done. Moreover the cost model is essential. We do a comparative Cloud experiment in this article, but for demonstration purposes, so we do not display all details. TPC benchmarks have been used to compare Clouds. In [3] for example the authors use HammerDB to run MySQL against TPC-C to compare Cloud Providers. In [17] the authors use TPC-H to compare DBMS and storage solutions at AWS. There is some research about Cloud-Orchestration-Tools (COT) [5,20,22]. These are supposed to help to avoid a vendor lock-in and to build Multi-Cloud and Cross-Cloud applications. In [16] for example the authors present a framework to compare availability of DBMS in Clouds using COT. These tools manage the Cloud itself, on an IaaS level for example, while we consider the shape of the Cloud fixed here.

The performance of containerization [4] and also of K8s is subject to research. In [8] for example the authors inspect scalability of K8s in a one-to-three host situation. In [19] the authors propose a method for Kubernetes autoscaling. In [14] the authors use experimental evaluations of containers to monitor the behaviour of system resources including CPU, memory, disk and network. They compare a baseline of a manually deployed K8s cluster to preinstalled K8s services like the ones we use, to benchmark their performance. We here take the preinstalled K8s services and Docker containers as given.

1.3 Motivation

Running applications in the Cloud is appealing due to scalability, elasticity and a "pay as you go" model. It is natural, when using DBMS in the Cloud, to ask for performance and cost metrics and what is a suitable product. One option is to use Database-as-a-service (DBaaS). This promises an easy setup and benefit from the Cloud architecture. There are native Cloud DBMS and adopted versions. For the usage of a non-native Cloud DBMS, we may use Infrastructure-as-a-Service (IaaS). This provides much more flexibility than DBaaS. We can choose virtual or baremetal, shared or dedicated machines in detail and build up a system from a very basic setup. However this is much more complicated than DBaaS, since we have to care for installation and scale by ourselves. Somewhat inbetween SaaS and IaaS is Platform-as-a-Service (PaaS). The primary focus is developing and launching applications of a certain kind and supporting processes by providing preinstalled and preconfigured services.

Kubernetes[1] (K8s) is an open source platform for managing containerized applications in a Cloud environment. It is a project of the Cloud Native Com-

---

[1] https://github.com/kubernetes/kubernetes.

puting Foundation (CNCF). K8s is offered as a preinstalled service by some major Cloud providers: Amazon Web Services[2], Google Cloud[3], IBM Cloud[4], Microsoft Azure[5] and Oracle Cloud[6]. It can also be installed on a local machine or a single-host system by using Docker Desktop[7] or Kubernetes Minikube[8]. However, in it's self description [18], K8s claims to be none of the above as-a-Service kinds. It provides operations on a container level and not on the host system itself. It does not provide application-level services and does not limit the types of applications supported. Also, since *the technical definition of orchestration is execution of a defined workflow* [18], K8s claims not to be an orchestration software; we think of it as more like a platform to build orchestration platforms.

Apparently not being strictly defined, we want to use the phrases as follows: A *Process* is a set of activities that interact to produce a result. A *Workflow* is the planned and automated execution of processes. *Orchestration* governs the workflow, i.e. the process automation, from a central managing instance. *Choreography* is an ordered sequence of system-to-system message exchanges between two or more participants. In choreography, there is no central controller, responsible entity, or observer of the process [1].

There has been a trend from monolith to Microservice-organized software, closely related to using automated containers [12]. The idea is a separation of concerns into modular containers similar to the idea behind object-oriented and service-oriented architectures. Besides support for distributed development, this is supposed to help scalability and, last but not least, better resource usage.

We tend to focus on the final benchmark run, the one that produces results ready for publication, the benchmark run that takes place under optimal conditions, having optimal configuration and best suitable hardware, in an exclusively reserved cluster for example. However this is only the last process in a collection of processes. Other related processes are: Prepare and provide a data source. Install DBMS. Configure DBMS. Validate loading. Adjust the workload. Tune parameter. Tune configuration. Debug. In particular the process of designing a new benchmark - or revising or adapting an existing one - is very iterative and not only conceptual, but also requires a number of practical tests.

We are looking for a way to orchestrate workflows related to DBMS benchmarking. In a heterogenous cluster, this supports repetition of experiments with different hardware configurations. In a homogenous cluster, this can speed up processes in parallel and independent experiments. In addition, we want to re-run everything to statistically check the results and isolate dependencies on parameters. Moreover, this is supposed to help in Cross-Cloud comparison.

---

[2] https://aws.amazon.com/de/kubernetes/.
[3] https://cloud.google.com/kubernetes-engine.
[4] https://www.ibm.com/cloud/kubernetes-service.
[5] https://azure.microsoft.com/de-de/services/kubernetes-service/.
[6] https://www.oracle.com/cloud-native/container-engine-kubernetes/.
[7] https://www.docker.com/products/kubernetes.
[8] https://minikube.sigs.k8s.io/docs/.

2   Designing Benchmark Experiments in Kubernetes

A DBMS *Configuration* γ is a set of hardware and software parameters of a DBMS instance. We define an *Experiment* E to consist of a fixed dataset D and workload W, that is executed by a set $C = \{\gamma_1, \ldots, \gamma_n\}$ of DBMS configurations. Each configuration might execute the workload several times. Each execution yields a corresponding result r_i, that can consist of received result sets and information about timing and resource consumption. The goal of an experiment is to obtain performance data per execution.

2.1   Components of Cloud-based Benchmarking Experiments

We identify the following components of a benchmarking experiment:
An `Orchestrator`, that has cluster management tools and access rights and allows high level control of the workflow. A `Master`, that is a DBMS and attached (hardware) monitoring functionality. `Workers`, that are optional parts of the DBMS in a shared nothing architecture. A `Monitor` that fetches and stores monitoring information. A `Data Source` that contains the raw data to be loaded. A `Loader` that triggers loading this data into the DBMS. Loading itself is done in general via some shell command. A `Data Storage` that contains the data loaded into the DBMS, the database. A `Maintainer` that triggers updating the database and is similar to the `Loader`. A `Query Executor` that runs the workload queries. Execution itself is done in general via some TCP-based connection to a DBMS server. The `Query Executor` simulates a client and stores timing information on the client-side and hardware metrics coming from the monitoring. A `Result Storage` that contains the results of the experiments. An `Evaluator` to inspect results.

2.2   Objects in Kubernetes

Kubernetes is not bound to Docker for containerization, but in the following we think of it as fixed. A `Pod` is a collection of containers that share host, storage and network space. It is the smallest deployable unit in Kubernetes. We can connect to a `Pod` from outside the cluster by using `Execute` for running shell commands inside a container of a `Pod`. Similarly we can `Copy` files to a container. We can also put information into a container at startup by using environment variables (`ENV`). A `Replica Set` makes sure a given number of identical `Pods` is running. For example, when a cluster node is lost, a failed `Pod` is brought up again. A `Deployment` is almost the same as a `Replica Set`, but it has better management abilities (for example when an image must be updated). It is considered to be the default choice for persistently running pods. A `StatefulSet` launches a list of `Pods` having a fixed ordering and uniqueness. It is useful for stateful applications, since it helps matching new pods to lost ones. `Replica Set`, `Deployment` and `StatefulSet` are for permanently running workloads that are terminated only by deliberate deletion. A `Job` on the other hand runs `Pods` that terminate on their own. We can specify a fixed number of identical copies of the Pod we want to have and how many of them should run in parallel.

K8s has sophisticated network abilities. A Service attaches a name to the network space of Pods independent of the node they are running on. We can access a Pod from outside the cluster using Port Forwarding from a localhost port to a Service port. Ingress provides a way to make a TCP port accessable from outside of the cluster. A Volume basically is a directory in a container. A Persistent Volume (PV) is a Volume that persists the data beyond the life of containers. It can have an Access Mode, in particular ReadWriteMany (the volume can be mounted as read-write by many Pods). Most Kubernetes objects[9] are grouped into Namespaces. Typically a user or a user group has access rights for only one Namespace. Each object has a Name attribute and optionally a set of Labels. These are key-value pairs. Labels are a very powerful concept. For example a Service finds suitable Pods using a Label selector. The nodes of the cluster can have Labels and we can govern the node selection by requesting nodes to have certain Labels like CPU type. Besides Labels, the basic concept to allocate resources (CPU, GPU and RAM) is by using Requests (guaranteed minimum) and Limits (allowed maximum).

2.3   Matching Components of Benchmarking to Kubernetes Objects

In the following we discuss how K8s objects can be used to match the components of a benchmarking experiment, Fig. 1. We always consider the Data Source to be inside of the cluster on a PV. The benchmarking process is organized as a distributed system, so we have to think about the communication between the components. Containers are agnostic to the cluster infrastructure. Since containers do not see the cluster or their Pod Labels, we send information to containers using environment variables or by copying files.

The Orchestrator controls the orchestration of components. It is located outside of the cluster and has cluster administration abilities, that means it can start other components, query the status of K8s objects, fetch logs from containers and processes etc. The main purpose is to control the workflow, c.f. Sect. 2.5. The Master can be very diverse and we want to keep it as schematic as possible. It is (at least) a Deployment with a Service. The Pod contains a container running a DBMS server and at least one container for collecting monitoring metrics. We additionally may use a PV as a Data Storage that is mounted in the Master to store the database persistently. The Service offers a JDBC compatible DBMS port and ports providing monitoring metrics. One way to achive a shared nothing architecture is by using a StatefulSet for the workers. Master and Worker Pods find each other by the name of their Services. We decide to design the Loader as an asynchronously started thread inside the Orchestrator. From outside the cluster, and having cluster administration rights, we can Copy DDL statements to the Master and Execute opening a shell in each container to start an import since this is part of the philosophy of

---

[9] https://kubernetes.io/docs/home/.

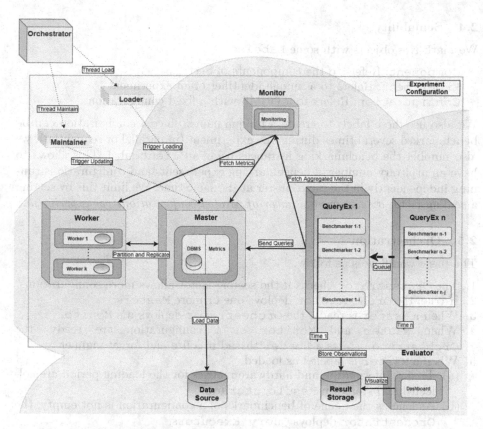

Fig. 1. Components of a benchmark experiment in kubernetes

containerization. Moreover the Loader puts Labels on the Master and it's PV when loading is completed to mark they are ready. The Maintainer is treated similarly to the Loader. The Monitor is a deployment having a Service. It has a container that fetches, stores and aggregates metrics. It finds the Master to be monitored by the Master's Service name. The Monitor's Service provides a port, where we can query metrics via an HTTP API. The Query Executor is a Pod that is controlled by a Job. It finds the Master and the Monitor using their Service's names. Measured times and hardware metrics are stored in the Result Storage, which is a PV in the distributed file system in ReadWriteMany mode. We use setting a starting time to synch Pods belonging to the same job via ENV and we use Copy to inject the workload queries as a file. Here, we use a Query Executor as a representative for a single client. Evaluation takes place in an Evaluator, that is a Deployment with a Service, that can be adressed from outside the cluster via a Dashboard or an API. It makes the Result Storage accessible.

2.4 Scalability

We mark K8s objects with some Labels:

– Component: Refers to the components of Sect. 2.3
– Experiment: Refers to a unique identifier of an experiment
– Configuration: Refers to a DBMS with a fixed configuration

We also use these labels to create a unique name. Since a configuration can be benchmarked several times during one experiment (in parallel or sequential), we also number the benchmarking instances using a Client label. This allows to have an arbitrary number of benchmarking experiments and configurations running independently in the same cluster at the same time. We limit this by setting a scaling factor σ: *maximum number of parallel configurations per experiment.*

2.5 Orchestration

The basic workflow is as follow:

1. The Orchestrator checks if the scaling factor allows more configurations.
2. If true, the Orchestrator deploys one or more Masters.
3. When a Master is ready, the Orchestrator deploys it's Monitor.
4. When Master and Monitor of a configuration are ready, the Orchestrator starts a Loader thread in a fire and forget manner.
5. When a Master is labeled as loaded
   (a) Timing information and hardware metrics for the loading period are collected and stored in Result storage.
   (b) As long as the queue of benchmarks of a configuration is not empty, the Orchestrator deploys Query Executors.
   (c) When a Job has terminated successfully, it will be deleted.
6. Orchestrator removes Master and Monitor from the cluster.

3 Experiments

In the following we present a series of experiments using several DBMS at different Clouds. As basis for the tasks we use TPC-DS data (SF=1), since it has a complex yet classical data warehouse schema and is small enough for all used DBMS versions.

Workload. We differentiate between metric attributes (INTEGER, DOUBLE, DECIMAL) and nominal attributes (others). We seek to obtain basic statistics about the attributes and we use COUNT, COUNT NULL (missing values), COUNT DISTINCT and the distribution: MIN, MAX, truncated AVG of values (metric) or of frequencies (nominal). We query for these 6 statistics per attribute and this yields 429 profiling queries. To have some statistical verification, in a stream S_n each query is executed n times before going to the next column. We install each DBMS n times and each installation has n Query Executors that run the stream S_n successively. A full workload W_n is thus given by n installations, n^2 streams and $429 \cdot n^3$ query executions.

Cloud Providers. We use several Clouds for testing and comparison. In Fig. 2 we report some basic per node characteristics. Most Clouds do not offer K8s shared folders in a distributed file system out of the box, but our concept is using it. We have to define storage in a filesystem and set an NFS mount point in a PV, optionally using a StorageClass. We do not use a PV for the database, but store the loaded data inside the container. One Cloud hides the CPU type. Another Cloud offers two different types of CPU for the two nodes. The other Clouds show the CPU type and it's the same for both nodes.

Name	Nodes	vCPU	RAM	σ	Node Type	Source Storage
Minikube	1	40	192 GiB	1		HDD
Inhouse	28	diverse	diverse	∞		SSD
Amazon EKS	2	16	128 GiB	2	r5a.4xlarge	EFS
Google GKE	2	16	128 GB	2	e2-highmem-16	FSI HDD
IBM CKS	2	16	128 GiB	2	m3c.16x128	ibmc-file-silver
MS AKS	2	16	128 GiB	2	E16as_v4	Standard_LRS
Oracle OKE	2	16	120 GB	2	VM.Standard2.8	FSS

Fig. 2. Kubernetes managed clouds

Implementation. We use Python for most of the components. The Query Executor and the Evaluator use *DBMSBenchmarker*[10], a Python3-based application-level black box benchmarking tool for DBMS. The Workload is given by a Python dict of queries with some meta data. The Orchestrator uses *Bexhoma*[11]. The Monitor uses *Prometheus*[12], a project of CNCF like Kubernetes. The metrics containers attached to the DBMS containers use *cAdvisor*[13].

DBMS. In the following we test 14 Relational DBMS and a variety of import mechanisms (Fig. 3). We only take publically available free-to-use versions or express editions (XE) of some popular systems with a minimum of changes: We derive own images for Clickhouse (change behaviour for NULL values), Exasol (install exaplus), MySQL (install tar) and OmniSci (whitelist import path) and take the others unchanged. This is a test for portability and simplicity. The DDL scripts use row-based or column-based storage engines, suitable data types, and (optionally) compressed columns, typical for the DBMS at hand. We use OmniSci in the GPU-enhanced version for tests, but the CPU version for benchmarks.

---

[10] https://github.com/Beuth-Erdelt/DBMS-Benchmarker.
[11] https://github.com/Beuth-Erdelt/Benchmark-Experiment-Host-Manager.
[12] https://prometheus.io/.
[13] https://github.com/google/cadvisor.

Name	Import Tools	XE	Image
Citus Open Source 10.0.3	`psql` and `COPY`	X	
Clickhouse 21.2.4.6	`clickhouse-client`	X	X
Exasol 7.0.5	`exaplus` and `IMPORT INTO`	X	X
IBM DB2 11.5.5.0	`db2` and `IMPORT FROM`	X	
MariaDB 10.5.8	`mysql` and `LOAD DATA INFILE`		
MariaDB Columnstore 5	`cpimport`		
MonetDB 11.39.15	`mclient` and `COPY INTO`		
MySQL CE 8.0	`mysql` and `LOAD DATA INFILE`		X
OmniSci CE 5.5	`omnisql` and `COPY`		X
Oracle Database XE-18c	`sqlplus`, `oracle_loader` and `INSERT INTO`	X	
PostgreSQL 13.1	`psql` and `COPY`		
SAP HANA XE 2.00	`hdbsql` and `IMPORT FROM`	X	
SingleStore 7.3	`memsql` and `LOAD DATA INFILE`	X	
SQL Server 2019-CU10	`bcp`	X	

Fig. 3. DBMS

3.1 Functional Tests

We want to make sure import is well configured and has been successful for all DBMS. To test this assumption, we use the hypothesis: *All DBMS produce the same result sets (i.e. column statistics) for the workload.* We set $n = 1$, so each query is executed once. We run the workload W_1 at our local Minikube with scaling $\sigma = 1$, i.e. no parallel configurations, and without monitoring.

One DBMS does not start due to the licence restrictions of the Express Edition. Docker and K8s do not hide the machine properties strictly enough and limitation does not help. We will exclude it in the following. Another three DBMS do not start because the minimum requirements of hardware quality are not fulfilled. Some DBMS do not agree with our formulation for the profiling queries and we receive errors. We need to use SQL dialects and split the workload into two versions: Subqueries in projection and subqueries in table references. We then run the workload at our Inhouse Cluster with $\sigma = \infty$, i.e. all DBMS run in parallel. We see some DBMS do not import NULL correctly and this requires special treatment. We fix this issue for all DBMS except for one. We also have to CAST to receive comparable numbers. All other DBMS produce the same statistics except for AVG (rounding issues at 4 columns), variations in COUNT DISTINCT (1 date and 1 text column) and missing values (1 text column).

3.2 Stability Tests and Metrics

We want to make sure setup is well configured and measurement is trustworth. To test this assumption, we use the hypothesis: *The same configuration yields similar performance metrics each time.* We use W_3, so each query is executed 27 times. We fix the DBMS to run in parallel ($\sigma = \infty$), but on the same node of our Inhouse cluster this time. The other components distribute in the cluster.

In Fig. 4 we see 13 blocks (i.e. DBMS) of 9 bars (i.e. streams) each. The height corresponds to the sum of all first (out of three) executions of a query of a stream. Some DBMS have 3 peaks corresponding to the 3 installations - we have to look carefully for a cold data situation. The sum is sensitive to outliers and the cardinality of the columns. One DBMS seems to tend to become better with every execution, but in general, performance seems to be very stable.

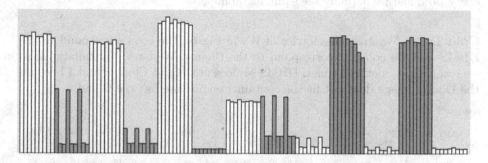

Fig. 4. Stability of sum of first execution times

To quantify cold data profiling, we will use the following metrics per installation:

Cold Data Loading Λ (the loading time)
Cold Data Profiling Σ (the sum of first execution times)
Cold Data Total $T := \Lambda + \Sigma$

We also want to have a metric that is less specific to the cardinalities and the loading situation. In Fig. 5 the height h reflects the geometric mean (per stream) of the arithmetic mean (per query) of execution times. We sometimes see the three peaks (installations) again, but overall we get a very different picture.

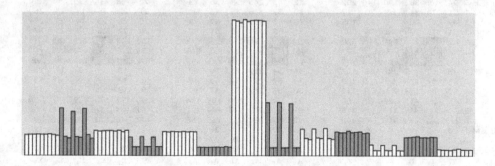

Fig. 5. Stability of geometric mean of average execution times

To quantify mixed profiling, we will use the arithmetic mean per installation:

Mixed Data Profiling : M (arithmetic mean of h)

3.3   The Benchmark: Performance of Data Profiling

We now run the profiling benchmark at our Inhouse Cloud ($\sigma = \infty$ and nodes of Master and Query Executor fixed) and the 5 public Cloud providers ($\sigma = 2$). We at first use W_1 to verify import and then run W_3 once to obtain the metrics per DBMS and Clouds. We do not want to disclose the DBMS or the Clouds, but the reader may recall that two Clouds don't guarantee the same CPU for every pod, and we actually see some instability.

Cold Data. We give the metrics of W_3 in Fig. 6. The rows correspond to the DBMS and the columns correspond to the Clouds. We have 3 installations, so we receive each metric 3 times. DBMS M does not run at Cloud 3 and 4 because the Docker image does not fit the container engine used at the Cloud.

	T_1	T_2	T_3	T_4	T_5	T_6	A_1	A_2	A_3	A_4	A_5	A_6	Σ_1	Σ_2	Σ_3	Σ_4	Σ_5	Σ_6
A-1	236	288	395	314	349	380	90	107	237	180	192	189	146	181	156	134	157	191
A-2	235	288	393	324	351	382	87	107	237	189	194	191	148	181	155	133	157	191
A-3	239	297	392	322	348	381	91	112	237	186	192	190	148	185	155	134	156	191
B-1	26	58	270	112	64	115	14	43	244	101	48	98	12	15	24	10	16	17
B-2	29	58	268	103	64	108	17	43	243	91	49	91	12	15	24	10	15	17
B-3	26	59	259	112	63	109	14	44	241	101	48	92	12	15	17	10	15	17
C-1	369	475	485	410	414	501	228	285	311	278	249	318	141	190	173	131	165	183
C-2	359	479	624	415	410	496	221	289	449	284	247	313	138	190	175	130	163	183
C-3	370	478	488	416	409	502	228	289	312	284	246	318	142	189	175	130	163	184
D-1	143	256	368	289	351	338	111	215	320	253	310	293	32	41	47	34	41	45
D-2	144	253	366	284	351	330	112	212	319	249	310	285	32	41	47	35	41	45
D-3	145	256	367	288	352	331	113	215	320	253	311	286	32	41	46	35	41	45
E-1	281	367	658	310	308	392	116	148	465	156	125	173	165	219	192	153	183	219
E-2	280	364	429	313	309	395	114	146	238	161	126	175	166	218	191	152	183	220
E-3	269	366	429	313	310	395	111	148	238	157	128	173	158	218	190	154	182	222
F-1	18	32	247	37	24	62	12	24	238	31	16	53	6	8	8	6	8	9
F-2	19	31	301	33	25	61	12	23	291	27	17	52	7	8	8	6	8	9
F-3	18	31	293	36	24	64	12	23	284	29	16	55	6	8	9	6	8	9
G-1	164	184	540	197	176	235	99	134	469	160	132	181	65	50	70	35	44	54
G-2	168	186	358	198	173	238	103	137	286	162	129	184	65	49	71	35	44	54
G-3	168	186	356	193	177	237	101	135	286	158	133	182	67	51	70	35	44	55
H-1	92	167	578	185	144	206	21	44	443	57	35	76	71	123	134	128	109	130
H-2	93	167	387	181	145	205	22	44	246	48	35	74	71	123	139	132	110	131
H-3	94	166	382	190	146	202	22	43	246	58	36	73	72	123	134	130	110	129
I-1	51	74	341	80	70	117	30	52	316	65	45	91	21	22	25	14	25	26
I-2	49	75	307	79	92	105	29	53	282	65	67	79	20	22	25	14	25	26
I-3	51	75	280	83	76	109	31	53	254	68	51	82	20	22	25	14	25	27
J-1	607	2071	1839	891	1060	890	471	1868	1419	756	877	643	136	203	420	133	183	247
J-2	597	2050	1781	909	1074	877	461	1841	1362	766	880	649	136	209	418	142	194	228
J-3	617	2084	1805	894	1064	842	475	1883	1376	754	878	647	142	201	427	140	186	195
K-1	43	67	277	86	62	102	34	54	263	75	50	89	9	13	13	9	12	13
K-2	43	67	288	85	62	102	34	54	273	74	50	89	9	13	13	9	12	13
K-3	45	66	278	83	59	112	36	53	263	73	47	99	9	13	13	9	12	13
L-1	231	282	411	326	335	364	91	105	237	196	183	184	140	177	173	129	152	180
L-2	228	279	411	317	335	370	87	105	237	186	184	191	141	174	174	129	151	179
L-3	235	282	410	316	337	368	93	106	237	188	185	188	142	176	172	128	152	180
M-1	30	48	0	0	36	79	23	40	0	0	26	67	7	8	0	0	10	12
M-2	32	47	0	0	38	78	26	39	0	0	27	66	6	8	0	0	11	12
M-3	29	48	0	0	36	78	23	40	0	0	26	66	6	8	0	0	10	12

Fig. 6. Cold data metrics [s] total, load and sum of first executions per DBMS installation (rows) and clouds (columns)

The total time T ranges from ca. 20s to ca. 2000s, that is a factor of 100.

We can see some general trends. DBMS F, I, K and M seem to be prepared best for the use case. DBMS B, H and D, G seem to be quite good at it, too. DBMS J is the slowest by far. This in particular comes from the loading itself; the profiling performance is not too bad. This DBMS seems to be particularly sensitive to the file system or network. We also can see differences in the Clouds. Cloud 2 and 3 seem to be slow at importing data. We suspect the disk usage to be the reason. It is a general observation that the performance seems to depend on the combination DBMS/Cloud. For example for DBMS H, Cloud 4 is clearly slower at profiling than Cloud 1. For DBMS G and I it is the other way around.

All in all the performance per DBMS is quite stable and we can see characteristics. The execution performance is amazingly stable. Instability arises from loading.

Mixed Data. We have 3 installations, so we receive the metric 3 times again. We report the mean and the coefficient of variation (standard deviation divided by mean) this time in Fig. 7. The rows correspond to the DBMS and the columns correspond to the Clouds again.

	μ_1	μ_2	μ_3	μ_4	μ_5	μ_6		CV-1	CV-2	CV-3	CV-4	CV-5	CV-6
A	19	29	34	26	26	31		1.98	8.44	0.99	0.0	0.75	0.62
B	11	16	27	12	16	18		0.0	1.19	29.71	0.0	2.13	0.0
C	24	34	33	25	33	33		1.61	0.0	1.02	0.77	0.0	0.58
D	12	17	18	15	19	18		3.33	4.5	1.08	0.0	0.0	0.0
E	22	34	41	28	30	37		2.27	8.57	1.64	14.31	1.26	1.36
F	9	13	12	8	12	13		2.19	1.49	0.0	0.0	1.59	0.0
G	124	68	112	49	59	74		1.73	0.56	0.75	0.39	0.0	0.0
H	22	38	48	42	39	44		0.88	0.0	2.21	2.77	0.5	0.0
I	19	24	26	16	30	30		1.04	0.8	0.74	1.24	1.95	1.1
J	22	34	60	27	32	36		2.33	0.56	1.12	3.23	2.16	0.93
K	7	11	11	7	11	11		5.41	1.73	0.0	0.0	0.0	0.0
L	17	27	24	18	24	25		2.21	7.91	0.81	1.06	0.81	1.57
M	6	8	0	0	9	12		3.15	0.0			2.11	1.62

Fig. 7. Mean [ms] and coefficient of variation [%] of mixed data metrics per DBMS (rows) and clouds (columns)

DBMS F, K and M are the fastest again. DBMS I is not obviously better than others this time. DBMS J is not the slowest this time, but rather in the middle of the field. DBMS G is slowest by far. There are less differences between the DBMS this time. The range is between 6ms and 124ms, that is a factor of about 20. In general performance is very stable (CV up to about 5%). Some individual variations are much higher, especially 14% and 30%: DBMS B runs on two different nodes in Cloud 3 and so does DBMS E at Cloud 4. The two-node issue also arises at Cloud 2 for DBMS A, B, D, E and L. It does not occur at Clouds 1, 5 and 6. Again performance seems to depend on the combination DBMS/Cloud. For example we are tempted to say Cloud 2 is about 50% slower than Cloud 1. As a rule of thumb this is ok, but it is violated dramatically at DBMS B and G. Cloud 2 and 5 seem to have about the same performances, but at DBMS I they differ about 20%.

4 Discussion

DBMS are very diverse not only in their execution engines but also the import functionality. Also the quality of Docker support varies. Some images already support a shared nothing architecture with a mounted custom data storage, others don't. Some DBMS vendors even support K8s explicitly. We have used a schematic approach here and this shows, it is feasible to put a variety of DBMS in their basic form into the same orchestration mechanism. We have also shown, this orchestration mechanism is applicable to several Clouds and can be used for comparison. This shows portability and simplicity of the approach.

To not implement the Loader as a container inside the cluster has been a hard decision. This seems to violate the principle of putting as much as possible inside the Cloud as a Microservice. However the Loader is very lightwight: Copy DDL scripts and trigger loading using a remote shell. This is very easy from outside the cluster and rather hard to implement from inside for a broad spectrum of DBMS. We have convinced ourselves parallel loading can be archieved this way with little traffic I/O and machine usage. We have decided to have a Monitoring component per configuration. Technically it is possible to use a single Monitoring instance for all DBMS running in a cluster. However dynamically adding and removing a variable number of watched instances may lead to disturbances, so this way we have more flexibility and stability. This shows scalability.

We have tested a shared nothing architecture for one DBMS at 100 GB to make sure it works, but refrain from including results here. We have had to limit the size in order to include a lot of DBMS in their Express Editions. For such a small scale dataset, sharding is not sensible. This also applies to monitoring. A 20 seconds experiment is too fast for reliable monitoring [10]. We are convinced treating the Maintainer similar to Loader is applicable, but we have not checked this. Here, we have focused on the most basic components to show relevance.

The profiling benchmark is very simple, but useful and generally applicable. We are convinced we have benchmarked querying the same data each time, although more refined statistics could have been used, too [2]. In the experiments we have found different CPUs, sometimes even in the same Cloud. Without a cost model the expressiveness is limited. To isolate dependencies on the scaling factor σ and on the node for Query Executors, more experiments are necessary. However, we think it is remarkable, that even in this mixed setting, and even when we have the same instance type and the same CPU at two nodes in a Cloud, a DBMS benchmark of column profiling on the TPC-DS dataset is still sensitive enough to detect the node most of the time.

5   Outlook

We suggest that it is worth taking a closer look at containerization and Kubernetes and using them more intensively. Containerization is a useful concept to support provision of software. Kubernetes allows containers to be deployed, distributed and combined in a cluster. This can be used to flexibly combine components from processes that accompany DBMS benchmarking. The approach is also applicable to benchmark Cloud typical features like node failure: The Orchestrator can also be used to add or remove nodes during a benchmark run. The ability to spread an arbitrary number of parallel Query Executors might be particularly interesting in concurrent, transactional workloads. Due to the widespread availability, this is possible uniformly and independently of DBMS vendors and Cloud providers. This can speed up the development or adoption of benchmarks. Having reusable and configurable components, that can be put together in automated processes that can run in parallel, we can explore many options of the benchmark and it's implementation. It can help with pure implementation problems, but also with conceptual questions such as the consistency of the workload with the data and the meaningfulness of metrics.

This is in particular relevant for a benchmark with a complicated and involving workload like TPCx-AI [21]. To have a (new) System-Under-Test to perform the tasks will surely not succeed in the first shot and it seems promising to leave the strictly sequential tests behind in an automated way by providing default containers for the components of the benchmarking as a Benchmark KIT.

6   Conclusion

Our investigations have been guided by the question whether a Microservice approach for basic benchmarking components can be applied to many DBMS and Clouds. We use an Orchestrator outside the cluster and some components as containers inside. Kubernetes is used to manage the components. Objects receive unique names and we use labels to mark the status. Resource requests and limits and node selectors can control the distribution of the components. We also introduce a scaling factor to limit the number of parallel configurations. With the exception of the DBMS themselves, we use Open Source software throughout. The approach has proven to be fruitful. We can run a variety of DBMS in a variety of Clouds and we can do so in parallel benchmarking experiments. The benchmark itself is suitable to show characteristics of DBMS and Clouds, to reveal differences in CPU and disk usage and it is sensitive to variations in the cluster nodes. The author would like to thank his colleagues at the Berlin Data Science + X Research Center and in particular Peter Tröger and his team for managing the Inhouse K8s cluster.

References

1. IEEE Guide for Terms and Concepts in Intelligent Process Automation. In: IEEE Std. 2755–2017, pp. 1–16 (2017)

2. Abedjan, Z., Golab, L., Naumann, F.: Profiling relational data: a survey. VLDB J. **24**(4), 557–581 (2015). https://doi.org/10.1007/s00778-015-0389-y
3. Avula, R.N., Zou, C.: Performance evaluation of TPC-C benchmark on various cloud providers. In: 2020 11th IEEE Annual Ubiquitous Computing, Electronics Mobile Communication Conference (UEMCON), pp. 0226–0233 (2020)
4. Bachiega, N.G., Souza, P.S.L., Bruschi, S.M., de Souza, S.D.R.: Container-based performance evaluation: a survey and challenges. In: 2018 IEEE International Conference on Cloud Engineering (IC2E), pp. 398–403 (2018)
5. Baur, D., Seybold, D., Griesinger, F., Tsitsipas, A., Hauser, C.B., Domaschka, J.: Cloud orchestration features: are tools fit for purpose? In: 2015 IEEE/ACM 8th International Conference on Utility and Cloud Computing (UCC), pp. 95–101 (2015)
6. Bermbach, D., Kuhlenkamp, J., Dey, A., Sakr, S., Nambiar, R.: Towards an extensible middleware for database benchmarking. In: Nambiar, R., Poess, M. (eds.) TPCTC 2014. LNCS, vol. 8904, pp. 82–96. Springer, Cham (2015). https://doi.org/10.1007/978-3-319-15350-6_6
7. Brent, L., Fekete, A.: A versatile framework for painless benchmarking of database management systems. In: Chang, L., Gan, J., Cao, X. (eds.) ADC 2019. LNCS, vol. 11393, pp. 45–56. Springer, Cham (2019). https://doi.org/10.1007/978-3-030-12079-5_4
8. Dewi, L.P., Noertjahyana, A., Palit, H.N., Yedutun, K.: Server scalability using kubernetes. In: 2019 4th Technology Innovation Management and Engineering Science International Conference (TIMES-iCON), pp. 1–4 (2019)
9. Difallah, D.E., Pavlo, A., Curino, C., Cudre-Mauroux, P.: OLTP-Bench: an extensible testbed for benchmarking relational databases. In: Proceedings of the VLDB Endow. 7, Dezember, Nr. 4, pp. 277–288 (2013). ISSN 2150–8097
10. Erdelt, P.K.: A framework for supporting repetition and evaluation in the process of cloud-based DBMS performance benchmarking. In: Nambiar, R., Poess, M. (eds.) TPCTC 2020. LNCS, vol. 12752, pp. 75–92. Springer, Cham (2021). https://doi.org/10.1007/978-3-030-84924-5_6
11. Gray, J.: Benchmark Handbook: For Database and Transaction Processing Systems. Morgan Kaufmann Publishers Inc., San Francisco (1992). ISBN 1558601597
12. Jamshidi, P., Pahl, C., Mendonca, N.C., Lewis, J., Tilkov, S.: Microservices: the journey so far and challenges ahead. IEEE Softw. **35**, 24–35 (2018). ISSN 1937–4194
13. Papadopoulos, A.V.: Methodological principles for reproducible performance evaluation in cloud computing. IEEE Trans. Softw. Eng. 1 (2019)
14. Pereira Ferreira, A., Sinnott, R.: A performance evaluation of containers running on managed Kubernetes services. In: 2019 IEEE International Conference on Cloud Computing Technology and Science (CloudCom), 199–208 (2019)
15. Seybold, D., Domaschka, J.: Is distributed database evaluation cloud-ready? In: Kirikova, M., et al. (eds.) ADBIS 2017. CCIS, vol. 767, pp. 100–108. Springer, Cham (2017). https://doi.org/10.1007/978-3-319-67162-8_12
16. Seybold, D., Wesner, S., Domaschka, J.: King louie: reproducible availability benchmarking of cloud-hosted DBMS. In: Proceedings of the 35th Annual ACM Symposium on Applied Computing 2020 (SAC 2020), pp. 144–153. Association for Computing Machinery, New York (2020). ISBN 9781450368667
17. Tan, J., et al.: Choosing a cloud DBMS: architectures and tradeoffs. Proc. VLDB Endow. **12**, 2170—2182 (2019). ISSN 2150–8097
18. The Kubernetes Authors: What is Kubernetes? https://kubernetes.io/docs/concepts/overview/what-is-kubernetes. Accessed 8 Apr 2021

19. Thurgood, B., Lennon, R.G.: Cloud computing with kubernetes cluster elastic scaling. In: Proceedings of the 3rd International Conference on Future Networks and Distributed Systems, (ICFNDS 2019). Association for Computing Machinery, New York (2019). ISBN 9781450371636
20. Tomarchio, O., Calcaterra, D., Modica, G.Di.: Cloud resource orchestration in the multi-cloud landscape: a systematic review of existing frameworks. J. Cloud Comput. **9**(1), 1–24 (2020). https://doi.org/10.1186/s13677-020-00194-7
21. Transaction Processing Performance Council: TPCx-AI Homepage. http://tpc.org/tpcx-ai/default5.asp. Accessed 5 Aug 2021
22. Weerasiri, D., Barukh, M.C., Benatallah, B., Sheng, Q.Z., Ranjan, R.: A taxonomy and survey of cloud resource orchestration techniques. ACM Comput. Surv. (CSUR) **50**, 1–41 (2017)

A Survey of Big Data, High Performance Computing, and Machine Learning Benchmarks

Nina Ihde[1], Paula Marten[1], Ahmed Eleliemy[2], Gabrielle Poerwawinata[2], Pedro Silva[1], Ilin Tolovski[1(✉)], Florina M. Ciorba[2], and Tilmann Rabl[1]

[1] Hasso Platner Institut, Potsdam, Germany
{pedro.silva,ilin.tolovski,tilmann.rabl}@hpi.de,
{nina.ihde,paula.marten}@student.hpi.de
[2] University of Basel, Basel, Switzerland
{ahmed.eleliemy,gabrielle.poerwawinata,florina.ciorba}@unibas.ch

Abstract. In recent years, there has been a convergence of Big Data (BD), High Performance Computing (HPC), and Machine Learning (ML) systems. This convergence is due to the increasing complexity of long data analysis pipelines on separated software stacks. With the increasing complexity of data analytics pipelines comes a need to evaluate their systems, in order to make informed decisions about technology selection, sizing and scoping of hardware. While there are many benchmarks for each of these domains, there is no convergence of these efforts. As a first step, it is also necessary to understand how the individual benchmark domains relate.

In this work, we analyze some of the most expressive and recent benchmarks of BD, HPC, and ML systems. We propose a taxonomy of those systems based on individual dimensions such as accuracy metrics and common dimensions such as workload type. Moreover, we aim at enabling the usage of our taxonomy in identifying adapted benchmarks for their BD, HPC, and ML systems. Finally, we identify challenges and research directions related to the future of converged BD, HPC, and ML system benchmarking.

Keywords: Benchmarking · Big Data · HPC · Machine Learning

1 Introduction

A benchmark refers to a process to obtain quantitative measures that enable meaningful comparison across multiple systems [19]. Such quantitative measures are essential to explore and assess the potential benefits and drawbacks of emerging software and hardware architectures. Benchmarks range from simple computational kernels, mini-apps, and proxy-apps to full applications, which are used to stress one or more components of the system under test (SUT).

In this work, we turn our attention to big data (BD), high performance computing (HPC) and machine learning (ML) systems which have been fueled

R. Nambiar and M. Poess (Eds.): TPCTC 2021, LNCS 13169, pp. 98–118, 2022.
https://doi.org/10.1007/978-3-030-94437-7_7

by modern applications that rely on complex data analytics pipelines. Besides "classic" applications such as stream processing for BD, complex simulations for HPC and neural network training for ML, we also observe a growing number of applications that belong to two or more of those domains, such as digital twins [33] or earning simulation engines in the context of Industry 4.0 [60]. Those applications require *hybrid-systems* that lie at the *convergence* between BD, HPC, and ML [26,45,59].

The state-of-the-art benchmarks that either target BD, HPC, or ML systems are rich. However, the appearance of those hybrid systems raises questions about the need for developing new benchmarks capable of evaluating them.

Our objective in this work is to review the literature on BD, HPC, ML, and hybrid benchmarks and investigate their capabilities. Hybrid systems include specific hardware and software components optimized for BD, HPC, and ML workloads. Consequently, hybrid benchmarks refer to benchmarks that can assess the performance of hybrid systems. We propose a classification of modern and widely used BD, HPC, and ML benchmarks using a *feature space* composed of *purpose, stage level, metrics,* and *convergence* which allow us to perform a unified analysis of BD, HPC, ML, and hybrid benchmarks. The features space is complemented by a high level architecture of modern *data analysis pipelines* that helps visualizing the capabilities of the evaluated benchmarks and drawing insights on improvement directions.

The rest of this article is organized as follows. In Sect. 2, we discuss some of the most representative and modern BD, HPC and ML benchmark systems. In Sect. 3, we present our classification methodology and use it to classify the work discussed in Sect. 2. In Sect. 4, we highlight certain research efforts that are closely related to the current work. In Sect. 5, we discuss our insights, present our vision on convergence, and conclude this work.

2 Background

Benchmarking refers to the process of obtaining quantitative measures that enable performance comparison across a set of target systems or components [19]. Benchmarks are critical to explore the potential benefits and drawbacks of emerging software and hardware architectures, and the vast amount of existing benchmarks/benchmark suites reflects their importance to the scientific community. HiBench [41], BigBench [36], BigDataBench [34], YCSB [27], LDBC Graphalytics [42] are examples of BD benchmarks. NPB [15], SPEC [8,10,10], HPCC [47], UEABS [11] CORAL-2 [2], and HPCG [29] are examples of HPC benchmarks. DeepBench [53], MLPerf [49], Fathom [12], LEAF [24], and CleanML [46] are examples of ML benchmarks. The point of these lists is not to be exhaustive but rather to show the exuberance of existing benchmarks, which yields several challenges regarding selecting a specific benchmark. In the following, we survey the most common and well-known benchmarks for BD, HPC, and ML systems.

2.1   Big Data Benchmarking

The main characteristics of BD systems are summarized in the "Vs" of BD, *volume*, *variety*, and *velocity*, these must be captured by workloads and metrics of BD benchmarks. Typically, BD workloads are characterized by processing large amounts of data that may be encoded in different types, such as text, semi-structured data, structured data, or binary, and may be delivered in different speeds, such as statically for batching, or streamed. The metrics are commonly related to the amount of data processed, the time taken, and the resources used for processing.

In the next paragraphs, we describe in more detail some of the most important BD benchmarks in the literature, their workloads and metrics.

2.1.1   HiBench

HiBench [39–41] is an open-source BD benchmark proposed by Intel. It focuses on offering workloads based on real-world use cases that could be representative of situations found when processing large amounts of data. Therefore, HiBench proposes 29 different workloads in 6 different categories.

Initially designed to be a benchmark for Apache Hadoop[1] in 2010, HiBench would originally support four MapReduce related workloads categories. Nevertheless, HiBench has been continuously updated since then and currently offers 6 workload categories: (i) external sorting and file system micro-benchmarks, (ii) machine learning (e.g., K-means and Bayesian Classification), (iii) web search (e.g., PageRank [22]), (iv) OLAP, (v) graph processing, and (vi) stream processing. The metrics considered by HiBench are resource consumption (e.g. CPU, I/O, Memory), job running time, throughput, HDFS bandwidth, and data access patterns (e.g., ratio amount of input data per amount of output data).

Finally, HiBench also has pre-configurations [41] for running sets of workloads on updated versions of Apache Hadoop and Apache Spark[2], and on old versions of the stream processing systems Apache Flink[3], Apache Storm[4], and Apache Kafka[5].

2.1.2   BigBench

BigBench [36] is an end-to-end BD benchmark and the basis of TPCx-BB [18]. It is based on TPC-DS [56], a decision support benchmark, and proposes a rich data model and a generator covering the key aspects of BD systems *volume*, *variety* and *velocity*. That is accomplished through the generation of large amounts of data that may be structured, semi-structured or unstructured at high frequencies by an extension of the Parallel Data Generation Framework [57] (PDGF) data generator.

---

[1] https://hadoop.apache.org/.
[2] https://spark.apache.org/.
[3] https://flink.apache.org/.
[4] https://storm.apache.org/.
[5] https://kafka.apache.org/.

BigBench's workload is inspired by a BD retail business analytics by McKinsey and encompasses the *collect, store,* and *analysis* steps of a BD system lifecycle. It is composed of 30 queries designed to cover different (i) *data inputs*, (ii) *processing types*, and (iii) *analytic techniques*. In terms of data input, it can generate and load structured data (database tables), semi-structured data (logs), and unstructured data (natural language reviews). The supported processing types relate to the type of paradigm that is most adapted to answering a query, and can be procedural (e.g., Map Reduce programs) or declarative (e.g., SQL). Finally, the analytic techniques define the approach for solving a query, which are statistical analysis (e.g., linear regression), data mining (e.g., clustering) or simple ad-hoc queries (e.g., simple SQL queries).

The metrics used by BigBench are based on those used by TPC-DS, and are, in summary, the partial execution times of the different steps of the benchmark. It also proposes a final metric defined as a geometric mean [18] of the partial execution times.

2.1.3   BigDataBench

BigDataBench[6] [34] is a BD and Artificial Intelligence (AI) benchmark suite mainly provided by the Institute of Computing Technology (Chinese Academy of Sciences) and the non-profit organization BenchCouncil. BigDataBench is open-source and has been actively developed since 2013 [35,38,61,64]. Most recently, version 5.0[7] was released, which covers five application domains (search engine, social networks, electronic commerce, multimedia processing, bioinformatics) and defines a workload as a pipeline of one or more so-called "data motifs". This refers to classes of units of computation that typically consume the majority of the runtime of workloads. Especially when these data motifs are used together, it should be possible to address a wide range of BD and AI workloads. So instead of applying a separate benchmark for each workload, the authors of BigDataBench suggest using data motif-based workloads, which is why they have elaborated eight data motifs, namely Matrix, Sampling, Logic, Transform, Set, Graph, Sort and Statistic computation.

BigDataBench contains a BD Generator Suite (BDGS) [51] that can generate synthetic data based on scaled real data. Both the synthetic and the additional 13 real-world data sets can be structured, semi-structured or non-structured. Moreover, they are extracted from text, graph, table, or image data to model the impact of different data types and inputs on the workload's behaviour and runtime.

Furthermore, BigDataBench offers 44 BD and AI benchmarks with respective implementations for seven workload types (online services, offline analytics, graph analytics, AI, data warehouse, NoSQL, and streaming). Three types of benchmarks are provided: (i) *micro benchmarks*, (ii) *component benchmarks*, and (iii) *end-to-end application benchmarks*. A single data motif represents a micro

---

[6] https://www.benchcouncil.org/BigDataBench/.
[7] https://www.benchcouncil.org/BigDataBench/files/BigDataBench5.0-User-Manual.pdf.

benchmark, for instance sort (offline analytics), filter (data warehouse) or connected component (graph analytics). If several data motifs are put together like for clustering or classification benchmarks, this is called a component benchmark. Several component benchmarks form an end-to-end application benchmark. Finally, BigDataBench offers a benchmark model for the examination of the hardware, software, and algorithms. Each of the models considers at least as metrics the wall clock time and energy efficiency to execute a benchmark.

2.1.4   YCSB

The Yahoo! Cloud Serving Benchmark (YCSB)[8] [17,27] is an open-source benchmark suite for cloud data serving systems started in 2010. The main components of this benchmark are the *YCSB client* for the generation of workloads and the core package of workloads. When the YCSB client decides for a operation to perform (insert, update, read, scan, or delete) or how many and which records to scan, these decisions are based on random distributions (e.g. uniform or multinomial). Accordingly, each of the 6 available workloads in the core package is defined by one or several distribution/s which is/are combined with a set of operations to perform and records to read or write. The offered workloads by the YCSB are (i) update-heavy, (ii) read-heavy, (ii) read-only, (iv) read latest, (v) read-modify-write, and (vi) short range scan. One can observe that the core package consists of related workloads that stress a wider range of the performance space than a single workload which can examine a system at one specific point in the performance space. In addition, the framework is easy expandable with new workloads that enable the benchmarking of new systems.

The YCSB mainly evaluates the performance and the scalability of the cloud data serving the system under test. For measuring the performance, the latency of requests is monitored while the throughput (i.e. the load of the database) is increased. The scalability is benchmarked with two different metrics. The first metric *scaleup* looks at how the system behaves as the amount of servers is increased. This is implemented by loading the servers with data and starting the workload. The data is then removed to add more servers, which then run the workload again with more data. The second metric *elastic speedup* does basically the same, but here the servers are added while the workload is still running.

2.1.5   LDBC Graphalytics

Linked Data Benchmark Council (LDBC) Graphalytics[9] [42] is a benchmark suite for graph analysis platforms which has been under constant development since 2014 [25,37,55]. Its construction is mainly based on the approach that a benchmark should have diversity in terms of (i) *algorithms*, (ii) *data sets*, and (iii) *metrics*. Therefore it currently consists of six algorithms, namely BFS, PageRank [23], weakly connected components, community detection using label propagation, local clustering coefficient, and single-source shortest path. The

---

[8] https://github.com/brianfrankcooper/YCSB.
[9] https://graphalytics.org/.

algorithms were selected in collaboration with the LDBC Technical User Community (TUC) and using surveys to ensure that they are the most relevant and cover a wide variety of scenarios.

Second, Graphalytics consists of synthetic and real data sets categorized into "T-shirt size" classes of different magnitudes (e.g., graphs in scale from 7.5 to 8 belong to the class "S"). The criteria for the data set choice are size, domain and characteristics. In order to make the creation of synthetic data sets possible, the LDBC Social Network Benchmark data generator (Datagen)[10] was extended.

Third, the Graphalytics benchmark suite offers a test harness which allows to run a large set of diverse experiments. Thus, scalability and performance are evaluated using deep metrics. For instance, scalability is measured in terms of whether the data set size grows when using more resources (strong vs. weak scaling). In addition, robustness of the system under test can be specified with performance variability, crash points and service-level agreement (SLA) compliance. The SLA is fulfilled if the algorithm execution for a given data set requires a maximum of one hour.

Complementary to the algorithms, data sets, and metrics that Graphalytics provides, it offers reference outputs for a standardized comparison of different platforms and reference implementations for graph analysis platforms from the community (e.g., Giraph[11]) and from the industry (e.g., PGX [6]). Industrial platforms were benchmarked by the vendors themselves. In order to constantly meet the performance requirements and general developments of graph analysis platforms, a new version of Graphalytics is published every two years, which mainly adapts the workload (i.e., the chosen data sets and algorithms).

2.2 High Performance Computing Benchmarking

The goal of HPC benchmarking is to evaluate the HPC system performance and application characteristics. HPC workloads stress different system components such as CPU, memory, I/O, network, file-system, etc. The response of these system parts is measured with different performance metrics, such as speedup, throughput, communication speed, access speed, and others. The workloads typically originate from computational science domains, such as physics, chemistry, material science, etc. The evaluation of existing systems also creates a yardstick for the design of future HPC systems. We summarize classical HPC benchmarks in the following subsections.

2.2.1 NPB

The Numerical Aerodynamic Simulation Parallel Benchmarks (NPB)[12] by NASA Ames Research Center, is a large effort to advance the state of computational aerodynamics [14]. NPB 1.0 was introduced in 1992; later another

---

[10] https://www.ldbcouncil.org/ldbc_snb_docs/ldbc-snb-specification.pdf.

[11] https://giraph.apache.org/.

[12] https://www.nas.nasa.gov/software/npb.html.

version (NPB 2.3) was introduced in 1997 [66] and included MPI implementations. NPB includes five kernels: (i) Embarrassingly Parallel (EP) that assesses the floating point computing rate. (ii) MultiGrid (MG), (iii) Conjugate Gradient (CG), (iiii) Discrete 3D Fast Fourier Transform (FT), and Large Integer Sort. (IS) which all evaluate the integer computation rate. NPB contains three pseudo applications: (i) Lower-upper Gauss-Seidel (LU) to evaluate fine-grained MPI communication [15], (ii) Block Tri-diagonal (BT) and (iii) Scalar Penta-diagonal (SP) to measure coarse-grained MPI communication [15]. NPB defines performance results in the number of floating-point operations per second (FLOP/s). NPB codes are written in Fortran-77 or C.

While NPB benchmarks exhibit fine-grained exploitable parallelism, many scientific problems require several levels of parallelism. Therefore, the NPB Multi-zone was introduced [65]. Aside from improvements were made to parallel systems including the scalability and performance, the limitations on I/O performance were evident due to access to data files. Thus, BTIO was invented based on BT benchmark using MPI-IO and were used to test the speed of parallel I/O [66]. Another benchmark called Arithmetic Data Cube (ADC) extends typical data mining operations related to Data Cube Operator in OLAP tool into a grid environment. ADC measures data movement across computational grid and across memory hierarchy of individual grid machines [32].

2.2.2 SPEC

Standard Performance Evaluation Corporation (SPEC)[13] was founded in 1988 and is a non-profit consortium that has 22 major computer vendors whose common goals are to provide the industry with performance measurement tools and educate consumers about the performance of vendors' products [48]. The development of the benchmark suites since 1994 includes obtaining candidate benchmark codes, putting these codes into the SPEC harness, testing and improving the codes' portability across many operating systems, compilers, interconnects, runtime libraries, and for correctness and scalability [52]. We consider SPEC CPU 2017 and SPEC HPC: OpenMP, MPI, OpenACC, OpenCL benchmarks are the most useful to HPC. SPEC CPU 2017 and SPEC HPC benchmarks code were written in C, C++, or Fortran.

SPEC CPU 2017 focuses on the performance of compute-intensive applications on processor, memory systems, and compilers. SPEC CPU 2017 comprises 43 benchmarks, organized into four suites: SPECspeed Integer and SPECspeed Floating Point suites both employ time (in seconds) as a metric to compute single tasks; SPECrate Integer and SPECrate Floating Point both measure the throughput or work per unit of time metric (jobs per hour) [10]. SPEC High Performance Computing consists of SPEC ACCEL measures parallel compute performance including the hardware accelerator, the host CPU, the memory transfer between host and accelerators, and the compilers [7]; SPEC MPI 2007 compares measurement of MPI-parallel, floating-point, compute-intensive performance, across the widest range of cluster and SMP hardware [9]; SPEC OMP

---

[13] https://www.spec.org/benchmarks.html.

2012 measures the performance of applications based on the OpenMP 3.1 standard for shared-memory parallel processing [8].

2.2.3   HPCC

The HPC Challenge (HPCC)[14] benchmark suite was developed for the DARPA's HPCS (High Productivity Systems) Program to provide a set of standardized hardware probes based on commonly occurring computational software kernel [43]. The suite is designed to augment the Top500 list, providing benchmarks that bound the performance of many real applications as a function of memory access. HPCC's first version was released in 2003. The HPCS program performance targets will flatten the memory hierarchy, improve real application performance, and decrease development time. The suite is composed of several computational kernels such as STREAM (PB/s), HPL (Pflop/s), matrix multiply- DGEMM, parallel matrix transpose - PTRANS, and FFT (Pflop/s), that attempt to span high and low spatial and temporal locality space [47].

2.2.4   UEABS

The Unified European Application Benchmark Suite (UEABS)[15] was released during the Partnership for Advanced Computing in Europe Second Implementation Phase (PRACE-2IP) project in 2010 [11], which consist of ALYA (See Footnote 15) that solves computational mechanics models, Code_Saturne (See Footnote 15) that is a multi-purpose CFD software, CP2K (See Footnote 15) which performs atomistic simulations, GADGET (See Footnote 15) which simulates cosmological N-body/SPH, GPAW (See Footnote 15) and Quantum Espresso (See Footnote 15) which calculates electronic structure, GROMACS (See Footnote 15) and NAMD (See Footnote 15) which simulates molecular dynamics, PFARM (See Footnote 15) which solves many-electron equation program, NEMO (See Footnote 15) which models ocean and climate sciences, QCD (See Footnote 15) which performs quantum chromodynamics, SHOC (See Footnote 15) that tests the performance and stability of systems, SPECFEM3D (See Footnote 15) which simulates seismic wave, and DeepGalaxy (See Footnote 15) using Tensorflow which performs neural-networks optimization in machine learning [11].

Each benchmark has their own test case/s and were experimented over PRACE Tier-0 and Tier-1 Systems, PRACE PCP, DEEP-ER, and Mont-Blanc 3 Prototype machines [63]. The metrics such as time(s), speedup, parallel efficiency, energy consumption (kJ), and performance in nano seconds elapsed per day (ns/day) are the output from this suite [63]. The benchmarks programming languages are as follows: ALYA, Code Saturne, QuantumEspresso, SPECFEM3D, NEMO were written in Fortran 90/95; PFARM in Fortran 2003; CP2K in Fortran 2008; Code_Saturne, GADGET, GPAW, and GROMACS were written in C; NAMD and NEMO in C++; GPAW and DeepGalaxy were written

---

[14] https://icl.utk.edu/hpcc/.
[15] https://repository.prace-ri.eu/git/UEABS/ueabs/.

in Python [11]. Parallelization using MPI is used in CP2KL, GADGET, GPAW, GROMACS, NAMD, PFARM, QCD, and SPECFEM3D. OpenMP and MPI are used in ALYA, Code_Saturne, PFARM, and QuantumEspresso; multi-threading is used in CP2K; GPU support applies to CP2K, NAMD, PFARM, GROMACS v4.6, QCD, SHOC, and DeepGalaxy; and TPUs support is provided in Deep-Galaxy [11].

2.2.5   CORAL-2
The collaboration of Oak Ridge, Argonne, and Lawrence Livermore National Laboratory (CORAL) began in late 2012 intending to deliver three systems that would each improve delivered performance as compared to the existing 20 PetaFlop Department of Energy (DOE) systems - Titan at Oak Ridge National Laboratory (ORNL) and Sequoia at Lawrence Livermore National Laboratory (LLNL) [62]. The CORAL-2 benchmarks[16] are distinguished into four categories: scalable science, throughput, data science and deep learning, and skeleton benchmarks.

The scalable science benchmarks are expected to run at full scale of the CORAL systems [2], and include CORAL-2 HACC, Nekbone, LAMMPS (atom-timesteps/s), and QMCPACK (samples/s). The throughput benchmarks (metric: total number of unknowns (across all MPI tasks)/(sec/iter)) represent large ensemble runs, and applications include CORAL-2 AMG, Kripke, Quicksilver, and PENNANT.

The data science and deep learning benchmarks contain machine learning (TB/s) with K-Means, PCA, and SVM; and deep learning algorithms (batch/s) with Convolutional Neural Networks (CNN) and Recurrent Neural Network (RNN). Lastly, skeleton benchmarks investigate various platform characteristics including performance on network, threading overheads, I/O, memory, system software and programming models [2].

2.2.6   HPCG
The High-Performance Conjugate Gradient (HPCG) benchmark[17] performs a fixed number of multigrid preconditioned (using a symmetric Gauss-Seidel smoother) conjugate gradient (PCG) iterations using double precision (64-bit) floating point values [3]. High Performance Linpack (HPL)[18] solves a (random) dense linear system in 64-bit arithmetic on distributed-memory computers [4] and measures the sustained floating-point rate (GFLOP/s). HPCG has been released as a complement to the FLOPs-bound HPL [58].

In 2019, the High Performance Linpack-Artificial Intelligence (HPL-AI)[19] benchmark seeks to highlight the emerging convergence of HPC and AI workloads [5]. The development of HPL-AI is to experiment HPC simulations on new

---

[16] https://asc.llnl.gov/coral-2-benchmarks.
[17] https://www.hpcg-benchmark.org/index.html.
[18] https://www.netlib.org/benchmark/hpl/.
[19] https://icl.bitbucket.io/hpl-ai/.

accelerator hardware [44]. HPL-AI strives to unite modern algorithms and contemporary hardware while connecting its solver formulation to the decades-old HPL framework [5]. Some of the machines on the TOP500 have been benchmarking with HPL-AI, such as RIKEN's Fugaku supercomputer which HPL-AI achieved 2 EFLOP/s, while HPL achieved 0.442 EFLOP/s [5].

2.3 Machine Learning Benchmarking

ML systems are characterized by the usage of complex ML models for specific ML inference tasks, such as classification or regression. Those models are often *trained* using large amounts of data which commonly have to be pre-processed first. Therefore, we can delineate *data preparation*, *training*, and *inference* as the most common stages of ML systems and the main targets of modern ML benchmarks. The workload of each of those stages vary, as well as their performance metrics. Data preparation is usually a processing intensive step involving transforming data into a format that can be exploited by other stages, hence, resource consumption and execution time are common performance metrics. Training is also a very processing intensive stage, however, the objective is often to achieve a certain model accuracy, thus metrics related to time-to-accuracy are an addition to resource consumption and execution time. In the inference stage, the accuracy of the model with unseen data and its latency to calculate solutions are the main performance indicators.

In the next paragraphs we analyze some of the main ML benchmarks in the state-of-the-art and discuss in more details stages, workloads and metrics considered by them.

2.3.1 DeepBench

[53] is a ML benchmark designed by Baidu Research with an open source implementation[20]. It measures the performance of hardware systems on basic operations necessary for deep neural network training and inference. It was first released in 2016 and extended a year later to account for broader operation types and to include inference [54].

DeepBench benchmarks four different operations: Matrix multiplications, convolutions, recurrent layers and all-reduce. It allows for the transposition of matrices and supports vanilla, long short term memory or gated recurrent unit architecture for convolutions [53] DeepBench provides a selection of numerical data that the operations are run on, all varying in size (See Footnote 20). It allows the evaluation of these operations on dense and sparse matrices and vectors in order to also evaluate systems with regards to sparse neural network training and inference [54]. The minimum precision for all accumulating operations is 32 bits, for multiplication in training and inference operations the precision has to be at least 16 and 8 bits respectively. The performance for each operation is measured in TeraFLOPS and milliseconds. For sparse operations the speedup in comparison to the same operation on dense matrices is also provided.

---

[20] https://github.com/baidu-research/DeepBench.

2.3.2   MLPerf

MLPerf [49] is a benchmark suite that can measure a system's performance for training and inference in ML pipelines. The suite offers customized benchmarks for both cases under different hardware configurations, suitable for proof-testing embedded and mobile devices, single nodes, and distributed data centers.

The MLPerf suite covers five different ML area: image classification, object detection, translation, reinforcement learning and recommendation. One data set is provided for each task besides the reinforcement learning task, where the data is generated in training. The data set used for the recommendation task is the only synthetic set. Systems can be compared in two versions of MLPerf: In the closed division the benchmark specifies which model to use on which task, only for object detection and translation it is possible to choose between two models, which are fit for different applications and represent a broader collection of ML models. The open division of the benchmark allows free model choice [50].

MLPerf training uses time-to-train to a defined accuracy as a performance metric [50]. This end-to-end metric provides a combined measurement of the speed and accuracy of a system. The goal-accuracy chosen for each model is slightly beneath the state-of-the-art to, show adverse effects of speed optimizations on the quality of a model, and reduce run-to-run variations while still being able to achieve the goal-accuracy in each run. MLPerf perform many runs of the tasks in order to reduce the effects of run-to-run variance. However, certain parts of the training process are excluded from the timing: System initialization, model creation and initialization taking up to 20 min and data reformatting, including organizing the data in databases or changing file formats. In the inference benchmarks, MLPerf measures the throughput of queries and samples per second, with respect to latency constraints. Multiple latency constraints can be imposed when evaluating distributed or multistream systems. By implementing the latency constraints in their inference benchmarks, MLPerf can proof-test systems in varying conditions adapted for specific use cases.

All implementations benchmarked must be mathematically equivalent to the reference implementation, which are provided either in PyTorch or Tensor Flow[21]. Adjustment of the hyper-parameters are only allowed inside of a defined frame. These rules should ensure that the actual system performance is measured and not any user optimization or hyper-parameter exploration abilities.

2.3.3   Fathom

Fathom [12] is a collection of reference workloads of deep learning models. It includes open source implementations of seven ML models, all representatives of the state-of-the-art in deep learning, offering a diverse set of characteristics and influential to deep learning research. All open source implementations of the workloads[22] are provided in TensorFlow and were either adapted, translated from a different language or re-implemented to fit their description in the original paper. Pre- or post-processing steps and extra logging was removed from the

---

[21] https://github.com/mlcommons/training.

[22] https://github.com/rdadolf/fathom.

original implementations. The implementation also provides a standard model interface and is compatible with Fathom's profiling tools. The workloads are either run on the data used in the original implementation of the model or on an open source alternative which is widely used for the type of model. Fathom includes recurrent neural networks, memory networks, auto-encoders, residual networks, convolutional networks and deep reinforcement learning models. To asses the performance of the hardware and system running the model the execution time of primitive operations during training and inference is measured. These operations, including matrix multiplies and tensor exponentiations, are the smallest schedulable unit in TensorFlow and make up up to 99% of the runtime. Measuring their execution time can not only offer insight into the time spent on a certain operation, but also show similarities between workloads, effects of parallelism and the correlations and ratios between different types of operations. Using this data the qualities and trade offs of hardware and systems developed for ML can be understood and compared.

2.3.4   LEAF

LEAF [24] is an open source ML benchmark suite for federated learning[23]. LEAF imitates a federated learning scenario, where models are trained on data produced by Edge devices in a decentralized fashion [20]. LEAF's data sets satisfy three conditions to represent realistic federated data sets: All data is keyed with an ID linking it to the device and user that produced it, generated in a large network of thousands to millions of devices and the distribution of data points is skewed across all devices in the network [24]. LEAF includes six data sets in total, five real world, and one synthetic data set. The real world data sets offer different sizes and number of devices. The workload associated to these data sets are image classification, sentiment analysis, classification, next-word, and next-character prediction (See Footnote 23). LEAF also includes instructions for creating synthetic data sets, which let users specify the number of devices and is designed to create highly variable multi centered data sets [24]. Reference implementations using the federated learning algorithms SGD, FedAvg and Mocha are provided.

The metrics proposed in LEAF include measurements of the performance at the 10th, 50th and 90th percentile, an evaluation of the accuracy distribution across devices and data on the performance divided by the hierarchies in the data. This means that, for example for image classification on a set of pictures of handwritten characters, the accuracy across devices for each letter is measured. To not only capture a realistic picture of the performance distribution but to also measure the resources used on each device the number of FLOPS and bytes uploaded and downloaded on each device are included in the metrics as well.

---

[23] https://github.com/TalwalkarLab/leaf.

2.3.5 CleanML

CleanML [46] is a joint ML and data cleaning benchmark with an open source implementation[24]. It explores the influence of a set of error types and corresponding data cleaning methods on the quality of different ML models. CleanML provides 13 real world data sets with a combination of inconsistencies, duplicates, missing values and outliers, some of them with mislabeled data injected synthetically. For each error type one or more detection and repair methods are provided. It also specifies seven classification algorithms to train the models with: logistic regression, KNN, decision tree, random forest, Adaboost, XGBoost and naive Bayes.

The workloads are based on training on cleaned or dirty data and testing on cleaned data as well as testing a model trained on cleaned data with either cleaned or dirty test data. The effects of data cleaning on the quality of the model is evaluated for each combination of data set, data cleaning methods and model as well as for the best model and for the combination of the best cleaning method with the best model. A comparison of the accuracy or F1 score of the different models determines if the model quality was affected positively, negatively or insignificantly by the data cleaning, this result is the main metric of CleanML.

3 Methodology

In this section we analyze the benchmarks presented in Sect. 2 under the light of four *dimensions*: *purpose, analytics pipeline stage, metrics,* and *convergence,* which compose a benchmarking *feature space*. Furthermore, we propose an *integrated data analytics* (IDA) architecture to illustrate the reach of current benchmarks and identify research opportunities.

3.1 Benchmarking Dimensions

Purpose relates to the aspects of the benchmark that will be used to stress the SUT. It is usually associated to data sets, application domain, kernels, or workloads. It is common that benchmarks have *multiple* purposes in order to stress a wider spectrum of characteristics of the SUT. Examples of purposes are a BD workload that performs external sorting on a large file [40], an HPC kernel that calculates matrix transposition [47], and a ML image classification application [49].

Stages refer to the different *stages* of the SUT that are stressed by the benchmark. As BD, HPC, and ML systems are often represented as *pipelines* composed by multiple stages, e.g., data processing, computation, and training, the pipeline stage dimension specifies which of those stages are stressed. For example, BigBench [36] is an *end-to-end* benchmark, stressing all levels (data collection, analysis, and storage) of the SUT in the data processing stage, while DeepBench [53] focuses only the training and inference stages of a ML pipeline.

---

[24] https://github.com/chu-data-lab/CleanML.

Metrics are used to measure the performance of a SUT for given purposes and stages. For example, the FFT kernel of HPCC [47] is measured in PFLOP/s and stresses the computation stage, while BigBench's [36] MapReduce workloads are measured in seconds and stress the data processing stage.

Convergence defines the intersection between two or more of the benchmarking domains studied in this work, i.e., BD, HPC, and ML. That intersection may happen in the purpose or pipeline stage dimensions, or both, and reflect a trend observed on current BD, HPC, and ML systems. HPL-AI [5], for example, is at the convergence of HPC and ML since it has kernels based on both higher and lower precision floating pointing operations that replicate modern HPC and ML systems, respectively.

3.2   Integrated Data Analytics Pipelines

As discussed in Sect. 2, several benchmarks exist to assess BD, HPC, ML systems, and individual components. Figure 1 shows an abstraction of the ecosystem for an integrated data analytics (IDA) pipeline. This abstraction includes components from BD, HPC, ML systems. The stages of the IDA pipeline: *computation*, *data processing*, and *training*, correspond to the HPC, BD, and ML domains, respectively. We will use this abstraction in later section of this work to explore which of the existing benchmarks can cover multiple components of the three systems, and consequently, be used as a benchmark for such an IDA ecosystem.

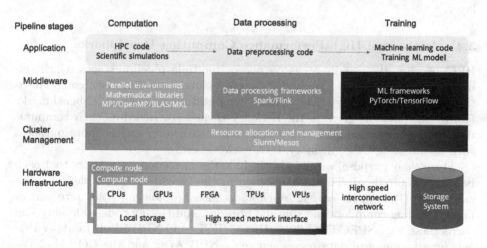

Fig. 1. Ecosystem for an integrated data analytics pipeline

3.3   Analysis of Big Data Benchmarks

BD systems commonly have three distinct steps: data collection, data analysis, and data storage. The *data analysis step* concentrates most efforts of current BD benchmarks, since that step is the focus of state-of-the-art BD systems, such as, stream processing, graph processing or MapReduce-based systems. Among the benchmark systems evaluated in Sect. 2.1, HiBench, BigBench, BigDataBench, and Graphalytics propose data analysis benchmarking.

The *data collection step* is explored by BigBench and Graphalytics, and, the *data storage step*, by BigBench and YCSB. Note that, while work like Graphalytics takes into consideration two of the three steps, end-to-end BD benchmarks, i.e., benchmark systems that consider all three data processing steps, such as BigBench, are still seldom in the literature.

In terms of *purpose*, the evaluated BD benchmark systems are all multi-purpose and very diverse, making them complementary. For the *metrics*, resource management and execution time are the most used, in particular for data analysis stages. For the data collection and storage levels, throughput and latency are also used.

Finally, the evaluated benchmarks describe some degree of convergence reflecting a trend observed in current production systems. Both BigBench and BigDataBench have ML purposes and benchmarking tasks based on performing statistical computations that simulate ML model training. The metrics related to those purposes, however, do not reflect ML performance.

Under the light of the Integrated Data Analytics pipeline (c.f., Sect. 3.2), the targets of the evaluated benchmark systems lie in the data processing pipeline stage and are part of Application and Middleware layers. In terms of converged benchmark systems, BigBench and BigDataBench, cover only the Application layer.

3.4   Analysis of High Performance Computing Benchmarks

HPC benchmarks usually focus on one or multiple pipeline stages which can involve parallel computation and data processing (including data communication and/or data storage). The parallel computation stage for HPC benchmarks follows the patterns given in the Berkeley Dwarfs [1]. Based on their computation pattern and workload, the benchmarks can involve one or more purposes such as targeting CPU, memory, I/O, network, etc.

From their purpose, we can also include the measurement metrics that each benchmark produces. Thus, we distinguish the benchmarks into the following categories: (i) *compute-centric benchmarks* measure floating point rate performance, testing compilers and runtime libraries, and testing code scalability and correctness, e.g., SPEC CPU 2017, HPCG/HPL, and NPB EP, (ii) *data-centric benchmarks* measure data movement, e.g., NPB ADC and the CORAL-2 Big Data benchmark which measures the data workload per sec, (iii) *network-centric benchmarks* measure communication performance between processing units, e.g., NPB FT and SPEC MPI, (iv) *memory-centric benchmarks* measure memory bandwidth, e.g., Coral-2 Memory Benchmark, HPCC STREAM, and UEABS NEMO, (v) *I/O-centric benchmarks*, e.g., CORAL-2 I/O Suite and NPB BTIO, and (vi) *a mix of the above categories* with overlapping problem interest, e.g. SPEC MPI.

We also observed certain research efforts towards benchmark convergence. HPL-AI highlights the emerging convergence of HPC and AI workloads. Unlike HPC benchmarks that mostly rely on 64-bit floating point operations accuracy, HPL-AI uses lower floating-point precision formats such as 16-bit which fit ML needs and offer better processing performance. Nevertheless, the metrics measured by these applications do not relate to ML accuracy but rather to measuring the execution time.

Another example is MLPerf's HPC benchmark[25], which is a step towards an end-to-end benchmark as the measured time does not include the training time only. Nevertheless, it captures the time of data staging from parallel file systems into accelerated and/or on-node storage systems.

3.5   Analysis of Machine Learning Benchmarks

ML systems are often composed of three main steps: data preparation, training, and inference. The purposes and metrics of those steps are usually disjoint, with data preparation involving purposes related to data cleaning and metrics such as execution time; training involves model training and time-to-accuracy related metrics; and inference involves model inference and time consumption metrics. This behavior is also observed in the evaluated benchmarking systems.

As the training step is usually the bottleneck of ML systems, we observe that all of the highlighted benchmark systems in Sect. 2.3 with exception of CleanML focus on the training step. They have multiple purposes spanning from matrix multiplication to sentiment analysis, but they all share time-to-accuracy and execution time metrics. DeepBench, in particular, also measures CPU consumption in teraflops and, together with MLPerf, has purposes associated to the inference stage. CleanML is the only of the evaluated benchmark systems that focuses on the preparation stage. It has purposes related to data cleaning, such as, duplicate detection, mislabeled data detection, and missing value correction. Its performance metric is the difference between the accuracy of a model training with data cleaned by the system under test and with cleaned data.

When analyzing the evaluated ML benchmarking systems in regards to the Integrated Data Analytics pipeline (c.f., Sect. 3.2), with the exception of Deep-Bench and MLPerf, the benchmarking systems mostly cover mostly the training part of Application and Middleware levels. DeepBench and MLPerf have purposes related to GPU training, hence, they also target the hardware infrastructure. CleanML also covers the data processing part of Integrated Data Analytics pipeline in spite of not considering the *volume* aspect of BD systems. Therefore, CleanML is the only of the evaluated benchmark systems to have convergence aspects.

4   Related Work

Many research efforts conducted extensive surveys to get deeper insights into the existing BD, HPC, and ML benchmarks. For instance, an early research

---

[25] https://mlcommons.org/en/training-hpc-07/.

effort introduced the Berkeley dwarfs [13], representing common computational patterns in HPC applications. These patterns span from linear algebra to graphical models, and finite state machine, and are important for understanding the breadth of the applications that a given benchmark can cover.

Another research effort introduced the BD ogres [30,31], which defines certain views/dimensions that capture common characteristics of BD applications. The views are not as simple as the computational patterns of the Berkeley dwarfs, with one view having many facets and covering several application characteristics.

The literature also comprises several surveys on benchmarks that focus on isolated stage levels (c.f., Sect. 3.1) of BD, HPC, and ML systems [16,21,28,67]. However, to the best of our knowledge, no other surveys focus on benchmarking of hybrid systems or systems covering two or more stages of the integrated data analysis pipeline (c.f., Sect. 3.2).

5   Conclusion

In this work, we discussed the state-of-the-art of BD, HPC, and ML benchmarks. We summarized a representative selection of some of the classic and most used benchmarks in the state of the art and classified them under the light of a feature space composed of purpose, stage, metric, and convergence, as well as from the perspective of a proposed Integrated Data Analysis architecture.

Through this classification, we observed that the evaluated benchmarking systems cover a wide range of purposes and stages of BD, HPC, and ML systems. However, even if modern hybrid-systems become more common, benchmarking systems are still not fully capable of targeting those data analytics systems.

We believe that a unified environment for benchmarking the performance of hybrid data analytics systems is a promising direction to explore in the future. We observed such behavior in a few benchmark systems. Nevertheless, we consider that such unified benchmarking environment could go *more broadly cover the three domains and more deeply capture the ecosystem layers* of the integrated data analysis (IDA) architecture, and hence, support *end-to-end converged benchmarking systems*.

Based on these observations, we argue that it would be possible to analyze features that are often ignored, in particular, middleware and software connections between systems from different domains (e.g., connection between the results of an HPC simulation and an ML training system). That position does not imply that "classic" kernel benchmarks are not needed, but that converged and end-to-end benchmark systems are needed and can open new dimensions for analyzing the performance of hybrid systems.

Acknowledgement. This project has received funding from the European Union's Horizon 2020 research and innovation programme under grant agreement No 957407 as DAPHNE. This work has also been supported through the German Research Foundation as FONDA.

References

1. Computer architecture is back - the Berkeley view on the parallel computing landscape. https://web.stanford.edu/class/ee380/Abstracts/070131-BerkeleyView1.7.pdf. Accessed 18 Aug 2021
2. Coral procurement benchmarks. https://asc.llnl.gov/sites/asc/files/2020-06/CORALBenchmarksProcedure-v26.pdf. Accessed 30 June 2021
3. High performance conjugate gradient benchmark (HPCG). https://github.com/hpcg-benchmark/hpcg/. Accessed 04 July 2021
4. High performance conjugate gradient benchmark (HPCG). http://www.netlib.org/benchmark/hpl/. Accessed 04 July 2021
5. HPCG benchmark. https://icl.bitbucket.io/hpl-ai/. Accessed 06 July 2021
6. Parallel graph analytix (PGX). https://www.oracle.com/middleware/technologies/parallel-graph-analytix.html. Accessed 01 July 2021
7. SPEC ACCEL: Read me first. https://www.spec.org/accel/docs/readme1st.html#Q13. Accessed 29 June 2021
8. SPEC OMP 2012. https://www.spec.org/omp2012/. Accessed 07 July 2021
9. SPECMPI. https://www.spec.org/mpi2007/. Accessed 07 July 2021
10. Standard performance evaluation corporation, SPEC CPU (2017). https://www.spec.org/cpu2017/Docs/overview.html#suites. Accessed 29 June 2021
11. Unified European applications benchmark suite. https://repository.prace-ri.eu/git/UEABS/ueabs. Accessed 29 June 2021
12. Adolf, R., Rama, S., Reagen, B., Wei, G.Y., Brooks, D.: Fathom: reference workloads for modern deep learning methods. In: 2016 IEEE International Symposium on Workload Characterization (IISWC), pp. 1–10. IEEE (2016)
13. Asanovic, K., et al.: A view of the parallel computing landscape. Commun. ACM **52**(10), 56–67 (2009)
14. Bailey, D., et al.: The NAS parallel benchmarks. Technical report, RNR-94-007, NASA Ames Research Center, Moffett Field, CA, March 1994 (1994)
15. Bailey, D., Harris, T., Saphir, W., van der Wijngaart, R., Woo, A., Yarrow, M.: The NAS parallel benchmarks 2.0. Technical report, RNR-95-020, NASA Ames Research Center, Moffett Field, CA, March 1995 (1995)
16. Bajaber, F., Sakr, S., Batarfi, O., Altalhi, A., Barnawi, A.: Benchmarking big data systems: a survey. Comput. Commun. **149**, 241–251 (2020). https://doi.org/10.1016/j.comcom.2019.10.002. https://www.sciencedirect.com/science/article/pii/S0140366419312344
17. Barata, M., Bernardino, J., Furtado, P.: YCSB and TPC-H: big data and decision support benchmarks. In: 2014 IEEE International Congress on Big Data, pp. 800–801. IEEE (2014)
18. Baru, C., et al.: Discussion of BigBench: a proposed industry standard performance benchmark for big data. In: Nambiar, R., Poess, M. (eds.) TPCTC 2014. LNCS, vol. 8904, pp. 44–63. Springer, Cham (2015). https://doi.org/10.1007/978-3-319-15350-6_4
19. Bienia, C., Kumar, S., Singh, J.P., Li, K.: The PARSEC benchmark suite: characterization and architectural implications. In: Proceedings of the 17th International Conference on Parallel Architectures and Compilation Techniques, pp. 72–81 (2008)
20. Bonawitz, K., et al.: Towards federated learning at scale: system design. arXiv preprint arXiv:1902.01046 (2019)

21. Bonifati, A., Fletcher, G., Hidders, J., Iosup, A.: A survey of benchmarks for graph-processing systems. In: Fletcher, G., Hidders, J., Larriba-Pey, J. (eds.) Graph Data Management. DSA, pp. 163–186. Springer, Cham (2018). https://doi.org/10.1007/978-3-319-96193-4_6

22. Brin, S., Page, L.: The anatomy of a large-scale hypertextual web search engine. Comput. Netw. ISDN Syst. **30**(1), 107–117 (1998). https://doi.org/10.1016/S0169-7552(98)00110-X. https://www.sciencedirect.com/science/article/pii/S016975529800110X. Proceedings of the Seventh International World Wide Web Conference

23. Brin, S., Page, L.: The anatomy of a large-scale hypertextual web search engine. Comput. Netw. ISDN Syst. **30**(1–7), 107–117 (1998)

24. Caldas, S., et al.: Leaf: a benchmark for federated settings. arXiv preprint arXiv:1812.01097 (2018)

25. Capotă, M., Hegeman, T., Iosup, A., Prat-Pérez, A., Erling, O., Boncz, P.: Graphalytics: a big data benchmark for graph-processing platforms. In: Proceedings of the GRADES 2015, pp. 1–6 (2015)

26. Cheng, P., Lu, Y., Du, Y., Chen, Z.: Experiences of converging big data analytics frameworks with high performance computing systems. In: Yokota, R., Wu, W. (eds.) SCFA 2018. LNCS, vol. 10776, pp. 90–106. Springer, Cham (2018). https://doi.org/10.1007/978-3-319-69953-0_6

27. Cooper, B.F., Silberstein, A., Tam, E., Ramakrishnan, R., Sears, R.: Benchmarking cloud serving systems with YCSB. In: Proceedings of the 1st ACM Symposium on Cloud Computing, pp. 143–154 (2010)

28. Czarnul, P., Proficz, J., Krzywaniak, A., Weglarz, J.: Energy-aware high-performance computing: survey of state-of-the-art tools, techniques, and environments. Sci. Program. **2019** (2019). https://doi.org/10.1155/2019/8348791

29. Dongarra, J., Luszczek, P., Heroux, M.: HPCG technical specification. Sandia National Laboratories, Sandia Report SAND2013-8752 (2013)

30. Fox, G.C., Jha, S., Qiu, J., Ekanazake, S., Luckow, A.: Towards a comprehensive set of big data benchmarks. Big Data High Perform. Comput. **26**, 47 (2015)

31. Fox, G.C., Jha, S., Qiu, J., Luckow, A.: Ogres: a systematic approach to big data benchmarks. Big Data Extreme-scale Comput. (BDEC) 29–30 (2015). Barcelona, Spain

32. Frumkin, M.A., Shabanov, L.: Arithmetic data cube as a data intensive benchmark. Technical report, NAS-03-005, NASA Ames Research Center, Moffett Field, CA, March 2003 (2003)

33. Fuller, A., Fan, Z., Day, C., Barlow, C.: Digital twin: enabling technologies, challenges and open research. IEEE Access **8**, 108952–108971 (2020)

34. Gao, W., et al.: BigDataBench: a scalable and unified big data and AI benchmark suite. arXiv preprint arXiv:1802.08254 (2018)

35. Gao, W., et al.: BigDataBench: a big data benchmark suite from web search engines. arXiv preprint arXiv:1307.0320 (2013)

36. Ghazal, A., et al.: BigBench: towards an industry standard benchmark for big data analytics. In: Proceedings of the 2013 ACM SIGMOD International Conference on Management of Data, SIGMOD 2013, pp. 1197–1208. Association for Computing Machinery, New York (2013). https://doi.org/10.1145/2463676.2463712

37. Guo, Y., Varbanescu, A.L., Iosup, A., Martella, C., Willke, T.L.: Benchmarking graph-processing platforms: a vision. In: Proceedings of the 5th ACM/SPEC International Conference on Performance Engineering, pp. 289–292 (2014)

38. Han, R., et al.: BigDataBench-MT: a benchmark tool for generating realistic mixed data center workloads. In: Zhan, J., Han, R., Zicari, R.V. (eds.) BPOE 2015. LNCS, vol. 9495, pp. 10–21. Springer, Cham (2016). https://doi.org/10.1007/978-3-319-29006-5_2

39. Huang, S., Huang, J., Dai, J., Xie, T., Huang, B.: The HiBench benchmark suite: characterization of the MapReduce-based data analysis. In: 2010 IEEE 26th International Conference on Data Engineering Workshops (ICDEW 2010), pp. 41–51. IEEE (2010)

40. Huang, S., Huang, J., Liu, Y., Yi, L., Dai, J.: HiBench: a representative and comprehensive Hadoop benchmark suite. In: Proceedings of the ICDE Workshops, pp. 41–51 (2010)

41. Intel: Hibench (2021). https://github.com/Intel-bigdata/HiBench

42. Iosup, A., et al.: LDBC graphalytics: a benchmark for large-scale graph analysis on parallel and distributed platforms. Proc. VLDB Endow. 9(13), 1317–1328 (2016)

43. Jack Dongarra, P.L.: HPC Challenge: Design, History, and Implementation Highlights, chap. 2. Chapman and Hall/CRC (2013)

44. Dongarra, J., Heroux, M., Luszczek, P.: BOF HPCG benchmark update and a look at the HPL-AI benchmark (2021)

45. Kambatla, K., Kollias, G., Kumar, V., Grama, A.: Trends in big data analytics. J. Parallel Distrib. Comput. 74(7), 2561–2573 (2014)

46. Li, P., Rao, X., Blase, J., Zhang, Y., Chu, X., Zhang, C.: CleanML: a benchmark for joint data cleaning and machine learning [experiments and analysis]. arXiv preprint arXiv:1904.09483, p. 75 (2019)

47. Luszczek, P., et al.: Introduction to the HPC challenge benchmark suite, December 2004

48. Dixit, K.M.: Overview of the SPEC benchmark. In: Gray, J. (ed.) The Benchmark Handbook, chap. 10, pp. 266–290. Morgan Kaufmann Publishers Inc. (1993)

49. Mattson, P., et al.: MLPerf training benchmark. arXiv preprint arXiv:1910.01500 (2019)

50. Mattson, P., et al.: MLPerf: an industry standard benchmark suite for machine learning performance. IEEE Micro 40(2), 8–16 (2020)

51. Ming, Z., et al.: BDGS: a scalable big data generator suite in big data benchmarking. In: Rabl, T., Jacobsen, H.-A., Raghunath, N., Poess, M., Bhandarkar, M., Baru, C. (eds.) WBDB 2013. LNCS, vol. 8585, pp. 138–154. Springer, Cham (2014). https://doi.org/10.1007/978-3-319-10596-3_11

52. Müller, M., Whitney, B., Henschel, R., Kumaran, K.: SPEC Benchmarks, pp. 1886–1893. Springer, Boston (2011)

53. Narang, S.: Deepbench. https://svail.github.io/DeepBench/. Accessed 03 July 2021

54. Narang, S., Diamos, G.: An update to deepbench with a focus on deep learning inference. https://svail.github.io/DeepBench-update/. Accessed 03 July 2021

55. Ngai, W.L., Hegeman, T., Heldens, S., Iosup, A.: Granula: toward fine-grained performance analysis of large-scale graph processing platforms. In: Proceedings of the Fifth International Workshop on Graph Data-Management Experiences & Systems, pp. 1–6 (2017)

56. Poess, M., Nambiar, R.O., Walrath, D.: Why you should run TPC-DS. a workload analysis. In: Proceedings of the 33rd International Conference on Very Large Data Bases, VLDB 2007, pp. 1138–1149. VLDB Endowment (2007)

57. Rabl, T., Frank, M., Sergieh, H.M., Kosch, H.: A data generator for cloud-scale benchmarking. In: Nambiar, R., Poess, M. (eds.) TPCTC 2010. LNCS, vol. 6417, pp. 41–56. Springer, Heidelberg (2011). https://doi.org/10.1007/978-3-642-18206-8_4

58. Radulovic, M., Asifuzzaman, K., Carpenter, P., Radojković, P., Ayguadé, E.: HPC benchmarking: scaling right and looking beyond the average. In: Aldinucci, M., Padovani, L., Torquati, M. (eds.) Euro-Par 2018. LNCS, vol. 11014, pp. 135–146. Springer, Cham (2018). https://doi.org/10.1007/978-3-319-96983-1_10

59. Reed, D.A., Dongarra, J.: Exascale computing and big data. Commun. ACM **58**(7), 56–68 (2015)

60. von Rueden, L., Mayer, S., Sifa, R., Bauckhage, C., Garcke, J.: Combining machine learning and simulation to a hybrid modelling approach: current and future directions. In: Berthold, M.R., Feelders, A., Krempl, G. (eds.) IDA 2020. LNCS, vol. 12080, pp. 548–560. Springer, Cham (2020). https://doi.org/10.1007/978-3-030-44584-3_43

61. Tian, X., et al.: BigDataBench-S: an open-source scientific big data benchmark suite. In: 2017 IEEE International Parallel and Distributed Processing Symposium Workshops (IPDPSW), pp. 1068–1077. IEEE (2017)

62. Vazhkudai, S.S., et al.: The design, deployment, and evaluation of the coral pre-exascale systems. In: SC18: International Conference for High Performance Computing, Networking, Storage and Analysis, pp. 661–672 (2018)

63. Lioen, W., et al.: Evaluation of accelerated and non-accelerated benchmarks (2019)

64. Wang, L., et al.: BigDataBench: a big data benchmark suite from internet services. In: 2014 IEEE 20th International Symposium on High Performance Computer Architecture (HPCA), pp. 488–499. IEEE (2014)

65. van der Wijngaart, R., Jin, H.: NAS parallel benchmarks, multi-zone versions. Technical report, NAS-03-010, NASA Ames Research Center, Moffett Field, CA, March 2003 (2003)

66. Wong, P., van der Wijngaart, R.: NAS parallel benchmarks i/o version 2.4. Technical report, NAS-03-020, NASA Ames Research Center, Moffett Field, CA, March 2003 (2003)

67. Zhang, Q., et al.: A survey on deep learning benchmarks: do we still need new ones? In: Zheng, C., Zhan, J. (eds.) Bench 2018. LNCS, vol. 11459, pp. 36–49. Springer, Cham (2019). https://doi.org/10.1007/978-3-030-32813-9_5

Tell-Tale Tail Latencies: Pitfalls and Perils in Database Benchmarking

Michael Fruth[1]([envelope]) [iD], Stefanie Scherzinger[1], Wolfgang Mauerer[2,3] [iD], and Ralf Ramsauer[2]

[1] University of Passau, 94032 Passau, Germany
{michael.fruth,stefanie.scherzinger}@uni-passau.de
[2] Technical University of Applied Sciences Regensburg, 93058 Regensburg, Germany
{wolfgang.mauerer,ralf.ramsauer}@othr.de
[3] Siemens AG, Corporate Research, Otto-Hahn-Ring 6, 81739 Munich, Germany

Abstract. The performance of database systems is usually characterised by their average-case (*i.e.*, throughput) behaviour in standardised or de-facto standard benchmarks like TPC-X or YCSB. While tails of the latency (*i.e.*, response time) distribution receive considerably less attention, they have been identified as a threat to the overall system performance: In large-scale systems, even a fraction of requests delayed can build up into delays perceivable by end users. To eradicate large tail latencies from database systems, the ability to faithfully record them, and likewise pinpoint them to the root causes, is imminently required. In this paper, we address the challenge of measuring tail latencies using standard benchmarks, and identify subtle perils and pitfalls. In particular, we demonstrate how Java-based benchmarking approaches can substantially distort tail latency observations, and discuss how the discovery of such problems is inhibited by the common focus on throughput performance. We make a case for purposefully re-designing database benchmarking harnesses based on these observations to arrive at faithful characterisations of database performance from multiple important angles.

Keywords: Database benchmarks · Tail latencies · Benchmark harness

1 Introduction

Measuring performance is an essential ingredient of evaluating and optimising database systems, and a large fraction of published research (*e.g.*, [2,16,18,19,24, 25,29,33,45]) is driven by guidance from the collection of benchmarks provided by the Transaction Processing Performance Council (TPC) [50], or commercial de-facto standards like the Yahoo! Cloud Serving Benchmark (YCSB) [9].

These benchmarks usually focus on measuring *throughput* (*i.e.*, number of operations performed in a given time interval), or latency (*i.e.*, time from submitting a request to receiving the result, usually characterised by the 95th or 99th percentile of the response time distribution). However, it is known that

© Springer Nature Switzerland AG 2022
R. Nambiar and M. Poess (Eds.): TPCTC 2021, LNCS 13169, pp. 119–134, 2022.
https://doi.org/10.1007/978-3-030-94437-7_8

120   M. Fruth et al.

high latency episodes rarer than events in the 99th percentile may severely impact the whole-system performance [11], including important use-cases like interactive web search [3]—even if they do not receive much attention in standard performance evaluations. In this article, we focus on properly characterising tail latencies in database benchmarking, and unearth shortcomings in popular benchmark setups.

We find that tail latencies observed in the ubiquitous TPC-C or YCSB benchmarks for commonly used databases often fall into the (costly) millisecond (ms) range, but are caused by the benchmarking process itself. Since Barroso *et al.* [1] point out that systemic optimisation efforts require targeting microsecond (μs) latencies, aptly termed "killer microseconds", it seems evident that nonproductive perturbations that exceed such delays by three orders of magnitude make it impossible to obtain a faithful characterisation of database performance.

We show that the popular OLTPBench harness [10,12], that is, the software setting up and executing database benchmarks [34], records latencies that were actually imposed by its own execution environment, in particular garbage collection in the Java Virtual Machine (JVM). We show that significant noise is caused by the benchmark harness itself, disturbing the measurements. However, latencies must be pinpointed to their actual source before targeted improvements can unfold their impact. If measured latencies are not identified as being caused by the measurement setup, developers will inevitably fail to pin them down, and consequently, to properly address them.

Contributions. In this article, we claim the following contributions, based on measuring latencies in database query evaluation, using the popular Java-based benchmark harness OLTPBench [10,12] with two well-accepted benchmarks (YCSB and TPC-C) on mature database management systems (MariaDB and PostgreSQL), capturing throughput and tail latencies:

- We show that seemingly irrelevant technical details like the choice of Java Virtual Machine (and even the particular garbage collection mechanism) for the benchmark harness can severely distort tail latencies, increasing maximum latencies by up to several orders of magnitude, while the usually considered quantities median, 95th and 99th percentile of the observed latency distribution remain largely unperturbed.
- We carefully separate systemic noise (such as caused by the system software stack) from the noise intrinsic to the benchmarking harness and the database system. We succeed in identifying and isolating the latencies introduced by the garbage collector managing the memory for the benchmark harness.
- Based on custom-crafted dummy components, we carefully characterise upper *and* lower bounds for the influence of the measurement infrastructure on the measurement itself, enabling researchers and developers to distinguish between relevant measurement observations, and sources of non-productive perturbations caused by the measurement itself.
- We consistently rely on time-resolved measurements which, unlike established summary approaches, allow us to discover temporal relations between events caused by different components of the measurement setup.

Overall, we systematically build a case for adapting benchmarking harnesses towards faithfully capturing tail latencies.

Structure. This paper is organised as follows. We review the preliminaries in Sect. 2. We then present our experiments in Sect. 3, which we further discuss in Sect. 4. We state possible threats to validity in Sect. 5, and review related work in Sect. 6. We conclude with Sect. 7.

2 Preliminaries

2.1 Database Benchmarks

TPC-C [49], defined in 1992, is an industry-standard measure for OLTP workloads. The benchmark models order processing in warehouses.

The Yahoo! Cloud Serving Benchmark (YCSB) [9] is an established big data benchmark. YCSB handles lightweight transactions, as most operations access single records. This results in low-latency requests, compared to TPC-C.

The No Operation (NoOp) benchmark provides a simplistic baseline: To establish lower bounds on achievable latencies, it sends an empty statement (*e.g.*, the semicolon command for PostgreSQL) that only has to be acknowledged by the database system, not causing any productive internal processing. NoOp benchmarks quantify the raw measurement overhead of the benchmark harness, and can also be interpreted to represent the minimum client-server *round-trip time* of a statement.

2.2 The OLTPBench Benchmark Harness

A benchmark harness is a toolsuite that provides the functionality to benchmark a software and/or hardware system. Typically, a benchmark harness contains components that generate the payload data, execute the database workload, monitor, and collect monitoring data, and even visualise the measured results [34].

For instance, the harness OLTPBench [10,12] is a popular [23] academic open source project [39] written in Java. At the time of writing, the harness implements 19 benchmarks, including the three benchmarks introduced above. At the time of writing, Google Scholar reports over 280 citations of the full article [12] and the project is rated with over 330 stars on GitHub [39], with almost 250 forks.

2.3 JVM and Garbage Collectors

The Java Platform is the specification of a programming language and libraries. The open source OpenJDK [41] is a reference implementation since Java 7.

The *Java Virtual Machine* (JVM) is responsible for all aspects of executing a Java application, including memory management and communication with the operating system. The JVM is a specification as well [31], with different implementations; the two most common are the HotSpot JVM [41] by OpenJDK and the OpenJ9 JVM [40], an implementation maintained by the Eclipse Foundation.

The JVM utilises the concept of safepoints. While implementations differ between JVMs, in general, an executing thread is in a *safepoint* when its state is well described, that is, all heap objects are consistent. Operations such as executing Java Native Interface (JNI) code require a local safepoint, whereas others, such as garbage collection, require a global safepoint. A global safepoint is a *Stop-The-World (STW)* pause, as all threads have to reach a safepoint and do not proceed until the JVM so decides. The latency of a STW pause is the time once the first thread reaches its safepoint until the last thread reaches its safepoint, plus the time for performing the actual operation that requires an STW pause.

Java is a garbage-collected language. The *garbage collector* (GC) is a component of the JVM that manages heap memory, in particular to remove unused objects [31]. These housekeeping tasks can follow different strategies with different optimisation targets, such as optimising for throughput or low latency. The GC is configured at JVM startup, and additional tuneables can be applied to both, the JVM and the GC of choice. This allows for optimising a Java application for peak performance based on its environmental conditions, such as hardware aspects or the specific area of use. However, most GC implementations [6,7,14,42,47] require a global safepoint during their collection phases, which introduces indeterministic latencies. Azul's C4 GC [8,48] overcomes the issue of STW pauses by exploiting read barriers and virtual memory operations, provided by specialised hardware or a Linux kernel module, for continuous and pauseless garbage collection.

3   Experiments

In the following, we report on the results of our experiments with OLTPBench. As a baseline, we execute a minimalist database workload (with the NoOp benchmark), while de-facto disabling the garbage collector (using the HotSpot JVM configured with the Epsilon GC). This setup is designed to reveal latencies imposed by the benchmark harness itself on top of payload latencies. We further configure the harness with special-purpose garbage collectors designed for different scenarios, *e.g.*, which cause only low latencies, and contrast this with the default garbage collectors.

Our experiments are fully reproducible and we refer to our reproduction package[1] for inspection and reproduction. The package contains all our measurement scripts, modifications and measured data.

Experimental Setup. All experiments are performed with OLTPBench, executing the built-in benchmarks NoOp, YCSB and TPC-C against PostgreSQL and MariaDB. For Non-Uniform Memory Access (NUMA) awareness, database

---

[1] Zenodo: https://doi.org/10.5281/zenodo.5112729
GitHub: https://github.com/sdbs-uni-p/tpctc2021

server and benchmark processes are pinned to CPUs within the same NUMA node.

Benchmark Configuration. Each benchmark is configured with a ten-second warm up phase, to populate database caches, buffer pools, etc., followed by a 60-second measurement phase. The isolation level is set to serialisable, and requests are sent in a closed-loop fashion (a new request will not be sent until the response of the previous request has been received and processed). Requests are issued by ten worker threads in ten parallel connections.

TPC-C is configured with a scale factor of ten, resulting in ten independent warehouses. Each transaction relates to a specific warehouse using the warehouse ID (primary key). The warehouse IDs are distributed uniformly over all available worker threads, hence each worker thread executes transactions only on its dedicated warehouse. This leads to a distribution of one worker per warehouse. OLTPBench implements TPC-C in "good faith" and therefore deviates from the TPC-C specification in some minor details [12][2].

For YCSB[3], we use a scale factor of 1,200, resulting in a table with 1.2 million records. The workload distribution is as follows: 50% read, 5% insert, 15% scan, 10% update, 10% delete and 10% read-modify-write transactions, while all but scan access a single record based on the primary key. The primary key selection is based on a Zipfian distribution. All these settings are defaults in OLTPBench.

In the current implementation of OLTPBench, the NoOp benchmark is only supported by PostgreSQL. In case of an empty query, PostgreSQL will acknowledge the query and report successful execution. However, MariaDB reports an empty query error, which results in a Java runtime exception on the side of the benchmark, which, in turn, results in different code paths, compared to PostgreSQL. To promote comparable behaviour, we enhanced both, MariaDB and OLTPBench: In OLTPBench, we disabled explicit *commits* after transactions.[4] Additionally, we enhanced MariaDB to interpret the empty statement ";" internally as comment (--), that is, as a NoOp. The modifications are part of our reproduction package (see Footnote 1).

Java and GC Settings. To run OLTPBench, we use Java version 16.0.1 (OpenJDK). We measure with both the HotSpot JVM and OpenJ9 JVM. For the HotSpot JVM, we use the garbage collectors G1 (default) [42], Shenandoah [6], ZGC [7], and Epsilon [47]. The latter is a pseudo garbage collector, it leaves all objects in memory and performs no garbage collection at all. For OpenJ9, we used gencon (default) [14] and metronome [14]. Table 1 provides an overview of the strategies of the GCs used. We chose the default GC for HotSpot JVM and OpenJ9 JVM as they are probably the starting point for most measurements

---

[2] For example, TPC-C defines ten terminals (workers) per warehouse and each customer runs through a thinking time at one terminal, which is eliminated by OLTP-Bench.

[3] OLTPBench is built with the libraries *jaxb-api* and *jaxb-impl* in version 2.3.0, which leads to a NullPointerException with Java versions ≥ 9. This issue is resolved in the libraries with version 2.3.1, to which we updated.

[4] A commit after an empty query does not have any effects on execution.

done with a Java application. In addition, we choose all low latency GC strategies with short STW pauses for precise latency measurements.

Experiment Execution. By default, OLTPBench sets a maximum heap size of 8 GiB (JVM option -Xmx8G), which we also used for our experiments, with the exception of Epsilon GC. As the Epsilon GC does not perform garbage collection, we enlarge the heap size accordingly: In total, the Epsilon GC requires 180 GiB of heap space of which 160 GiB were pre-allocated upon startup. During the 60-second measurement, 160 GiB heap space were sufficient, so no latencies were introduced due to an increase of the heap. The remaining 20 GiB of heap space that were not pre-allocated, but reserved, were required by OLTPBench for the YCSB benchmark to create result files.

To capture latencies introduced by the JVM, and to confirm our hypothesis, we consult a second dataset. We exploit the unified logging mechanism, introduced in HotSpot JVM for Java 9 [28]. It allows for logging all safepoint events, including those for garbage collection. OpenJ9 JVM also provides unified logging, but only records garbage collection events and thus no safepoint events [13]. We mine the log for safepoint events, or in case of OpenJ9 JVM for GC events, and interpret these latencies as overhead caued by the JVM.

Table 1. Garbage collectors for the HotSpot JVM and OpenJ9 JVM, and design goals.

JVM	GC	Design
HotSpot	G1	Balance throughput and latency
	Z	Low latency
	Shenandoah	Low latency
	Epsilon	Experimental setting: No GC tasks are performed, except for increasing heap.
OpenJ9	gencon	Transactional applications with short-lived objects
	metronome	Low latency

Execution Platform. All measurements are performed on a Dell PowerEdge R640, with two Intel Gold 6248R CPUs (24 cores per CPU, 3.0 GHz) and 384 GB of main memory. To avoid distortions from CPU frequency transitions, we disable Intel®™ Turbo Boost®™, and operate all cores in the performance P-State for a permanent core frequency of 3.0 GHz. We disable simultaneous multithreading (SMT) since it causes undesired side-effects on low-latency real-time systems [32] due to resource contention.

To avoid cross-NUMA effects, OLTPBench as well as database server processes execute on 22 cores of the same NUMA node: OLTPBench and the database server (either MariaDB or PostgreSQL) each execute exclusively on eleven cores. This ensures one worker of the benchmark, which is pinned to a dedicated CPU, is connected to one worker of the database, which is pinned to a dedicated CPU as well. The remaining two cores of the NUMA node are reserved for the remaining processes of the system.

The server runs Arch Linux with Kernel version 5.12.5. The benchmark as well as the database server are compiled from source. For OLTPBench, we use the version of git hash #6e8c04f, for PostgreSQL Version 13.3, git hash #272d82ec6f and for MariaDB Version 10.6, git hash #609e8e38bb0.

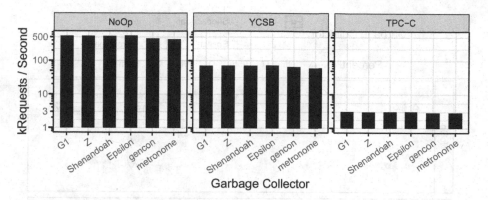

Fig. 1. Database throughput for MariaDB, in thousand requests per second for benchmarks NoOp, YCSB and TPC-C, and different JVM/GC configurations of OLTP-Bench. Throughput is affected marginally by the choice of JVM, but not the GC.

3.1 Results

Our evaluation with MariaDB and PostgreSQL shows that the results are virtually independent of the DBMS. Hence, we focus on presenting the results for MariaDB. For PostgreSQL, we refer to our reproduction package (see Footnote 1).

We follow a top-down approach: We first measure latencies on the level of single transactions, under variation of different JVM and GC configurations with the NoOp, YCSB, and TPC-C benchmarks. We then characterise the latency distributions, and systematically investigate the latency long tail.

Throughput. Figure 1 shows the throughput measured in thousand requests per second, for different benchmarks, JVMs, and GCs. For TPC-C, throughput is commonly reported as NewOrder transactions per minute (tpmC), but we deviate for a better comparability between the different benchmarks.

For all three benchmarks, Fig. 1 reports a difference in performance between the two JVMs: Compared to OpenJ9 JVM, HotSpot JVM has about 17%–28% more throughput for the NoOp benchmark, about 5%–18% for YCSB, and only about 5% more for the TPC-C benchmark (note the log-scaled vertical axis).

Naturally, the choice of JVM for OLTPBench has a stronger influence for benchmarks in which comparatively little time is spent on the database side. To put this in context: By executing the NoOp benchmark with about 500k requests per second, we spend much more time in the process of OLTPBench compared to the TPC-C benchmark with only 3k requests per second.

Latency Distribution. The distribution of latencies reported by OLTPBench is visualised by box-plots in Fig. 2. The minimum (0th percentile) and maximum (100th percentile) latencies, as well as the 95th and 99th latency percentiles, are marked separately. The absolute value of the maximum latency is also labelled.

Overall, there is little variation in the median latencies within a benchmark. Comparing the median latencies of the two JVMs for the NoOp benchmark,

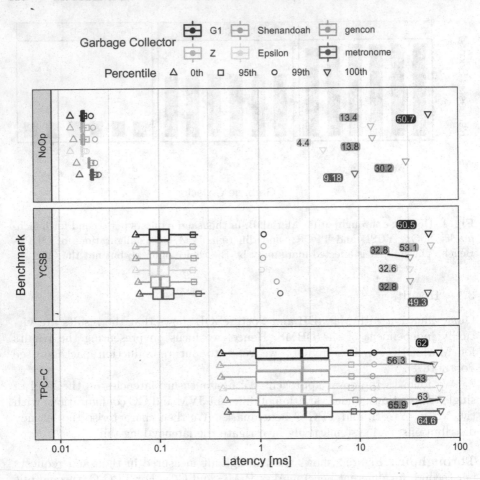

Fig. 2. The latency distributions measured by OLTPBench for three benchmarks, visualised as box plots. Key percentiles are highlighted.

we see a lower median latency for HotSpot JVM than for OpenJ9 JVM: All GCs of HotSpot JVM have a median latency of 0.017 ms, while gencon has 0.020 ms and metronome 0.021 ms, based on about 500k requests per second. As the NoOp benchmark generates only a small load on the database side, the maximum latencies reported are candidates for latencies introduced by the Java environment of the benchmark harness. As expected, Epsilon GC has the lowest maximum latency for the NoOp benchmark.

The YCSB benchmark shows strong variance in maximum latencies, depending on the garbage collector used. For GCs G1, Z and metronome, a maximum latency of around 50 ms is recorded, whereas the other GCs display a maximum latency of about 30 ms. We inspect these latencies more closely in the following. Nevertheless, the distribution of the latencies is close to uniform for all six garbage collectors, except the 99th percentile latency: Observations for OpenJ9 exceed those for HotSpot.

The different JVM/GC configurations result in near-identical latency distributions for the TPC-C benchmark: Due to the larger share of time spent on the database side (compared to the other benchmarks), the latencies introduced by the benchmark harness do not weigh in as much in comparison.

Latency Time Series. Figures 3 through 5 show time series plots for the benchmarks NoOp, YCSB, and TPC-C. Red, labelled triangles mark minimum and maximum latencies, as observed by OLTPBench. In order to prevent overplotting, we downsampled the latencies except for extreme values. Ochre dots represent sampled, normal observations. A latency is considered an extreme value and displayed as grey dot if it is outside a pre-defined range. We define benchmark-specific sampling rates and extreme value ranges, as detailed below. Latency fluctuations smoothed by a sliding window covering 1,000 data points are shown in red.

Superimposed black dots represent latencies extracted from the JVM logs. Since randomised, mixed workloads do not allow us to associate given latencies with specific queries, we visualise all JVM latencies.

The time series plots for the YCSB and TPC-C benchmark are provided for selected queries only. We refer to our reproduction package (see Footnote 1) for the full set of charts, which confirm our observations. Similarly, we do not visualise the Shenandoah GC as it behaves similar to the Z GC and metronome GC, with a similar latency pattern as gencon GC.

NoOp Benchmark. The latency time series for the NoOp benchmark is shown in Fig. 3. To arrive at meaningful visualisations, we apply a sampling strategy that avoids overplotting for "standard" observables by only using 0.001% of the recorded values in between the 0.025th and 99.975th percentile. However, we show the full collection of observations outside this interval.

OLTPBench, executed with the Epsilon GC, shows that this setup has the lowest latency possible, and the JVM is only active for a short time at the very end. This measurement shows that regular outliers in the range of about 1 ms occur regularly in the time series, and can be used as a reference for comparison with other GCs. The measurement of the GC G1 shows that the GC causes the maximum latency and the tail of the latencies. Almost each latency higher than 10 ms was introduced by the GC because the latencies reported by OLTPBench and these reported by the JVM display the same pattern and match each other.

YCSB Benchmark. We show the time series latency of the YCSB benchmark in Fig. 4. We report the latencies measured by the G1, Z, Epsilon and gencon GC and selected the two transaction types ReadRecord (read transaction) and UpdateRecord (write transaction). We used a sampling rate of 0.05% (ReadRecord) and 0.1% (UpdateRecord) for standard values and the 99.975th and 0.025th latency percentile are the limits for a latency to be marked as an extreme value.

The Epsilon GC is again the reference and except for the maximum latency, all tail latencies fall into the interval between 1 ms and 5 ms. By comparing the

128   M. Fruth et al.

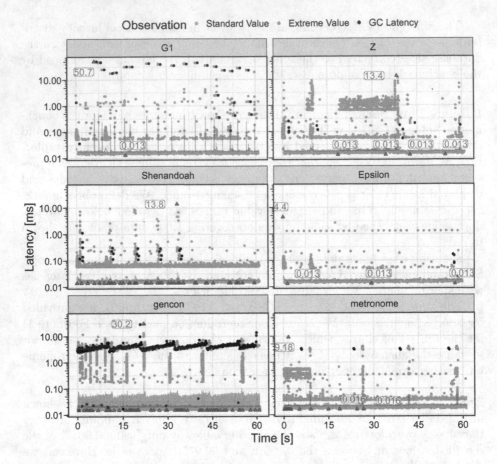

Fig. 3. Latency time series of the NoOp benchmark. Minimum and maximum latencies measured with OLTPBench are marked by red, labelled triangles. Grey dots represent extreme values, ochre dots (down-sampled) standard observations. Latencies from the JVM log file are superimposed in black. The red line shows the sliding mean window. (Color figure online)

ReadRecord latencies reported from OLTPBench and from the JVM, again the G1 GC is responsible for the tail latencies occurring in this transaction. The write transaction shows a similar behaviour, but here outliers on the database side are responsible for the maximum latency, nevertheless again the G1 GC latency defines the tail.

TPC-C Benchmark. The time series latency of TPC-C is shown in Fig. 5. The sampling rate of standard values of the NewOrder transaction is set to 0.5% and for OrderStatus to 5%. Extreme values are marked as such if they exceed the 99.75th percentile or subceed the 0.25th percentile.

For this particular benchmark, the influence of the JVM is negligible. The transactions, especially write transactions, are so heavyweight that the process-

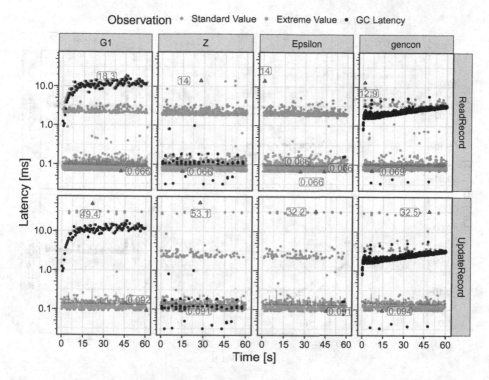

Fig. 4. Latency time series of the YCSB benchmark for read (ReadRecord) and write (UpdateRecord) transactions. Labels and colours as in Fig. 3. (Color figure online)

ing time inside the database substantially exceeds the benchmark overhead. Furthermore, due to the low number of requests per second (about 3k), only a limited amount of intermediate, temporary objects that require garbage collection are created in the first place. The same applies to read transactions.

4 Discussion

Our experiments show that for the popular benchmark harness OLTPBench, the choice of the execution environment (JVM and its GC strategy) substantially impacts (tail) latency measurements. By super-imposing the latencies extracted from JVM log files on the latency time series reported by OLTPBench, we make this connection visually apparent, and show that different GC strategies translate to different temporal patterns. By setting up a baseline experiment, with garbage collection de-facto disabled, and a minimalist database workload, we can successfully establish a lower bound on non-productive latency contributions.

Naturally, for lightweight database workloads (in our experiments, YCSB), this non-productive overhead is more noticeable in relation to the actual query execution time.

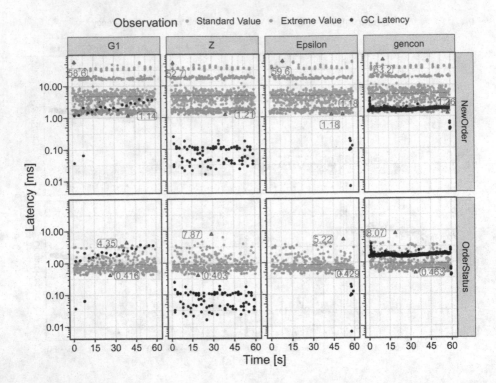

Fig. 5. Latency time series of the TPC-C benchmark for read (OrderStatus) and write (NewOrder) transactions. Labels and colours as in Fig. 3. (Color figure online)

Interestingly, while researchers and practitioners optimise latencies in the realm of microseconds [1], the latencies imposed by the benchmark harness reach the ballpark of milliseconds. Evidently, this factor of one thousand proves these effects are non-negligible, and deserve careful consideration in any evaluation, albeit most published research neglects this issue so far.

Our observations are replicable for PostgreSQL. We provide the data and full set of plots, along with a reproduction package (see Footnote 1).

5   Threats to Validity

We applied great care and diligence in analysing the garbage collector logs. Yet as the logging mechanisms differ between JVMs, we must deal with some level of uncertainty: The HotSpot JVM logs all safepoints (including, but not restricted to garbage collection events), whereas the OpenJ9 JVM logs only the garbage collection events. As the GC events dominate the logged safepoint events, we treat the reported latencies in both logs uniformly. In addition, we do not distinguish between local and global safepoints, as local safepoints can also block a thread.

Further, the latencies reported by OLTPBench and the latencies logged by the JVM are two distinct sources of data. As usual, data integration brings uncertainties, so the latencies displayed from OLTPBench and JVM might be minimally shifted in time in the time series plots. In summary, we consider the above threats to the validity of our results as minor.

One further threat to validity is that we only focus on the Java environment of the benchmark harness, but no other possible sources of systemic noise (such as caused by the hardware). We have diligently configured the execution platform to eradicate sources of noise (*e.g.*, by disabling SMT). Moreover systemic noise is typically in the range of micro seconds [1]. Since the harness-induced latencies are in the millisecond range (exceeding them by a factor of one thousand, and clearly traceable back to the harness), we may dismiss this threat.

6 Related Work

Databases, as core components of data-intensive systems, are important contributors to system-wide tail latency effects. Likewise, they have started to enjoy increasing popularity in real-time scenarios like sensor networks or IoT [16,43], where the most crucial service indicator is determinism and *maximum* latency, instead of average-case performance. Care in controlling excessive latencies must be exercised in all cases.

As modifiable open source components are increasingly used in building systems [23,44], several measures addressing software layers above, inside and below the DBMS have been suggested to this end. For instance, optimising end-to-end communications [18,35,46] tries to alleviate the issue from above. Specially crafted real-time databases [27], novel scheduling algorithms in scheduling/routing queries [24,25,45], transactional concepts [5], or query evaluation strategies [19,51], work from inside the database. Careful tailoring of the whole software stack from OS kernel to DB engine[30,33], or crafting dedicated operating systems [4,20–22,36,37] to leverage the advantages of modern hardware in database system engineering (*e.g.*, [15,29]), contribute to solutions from below the database.

In our experiments, we execute the well-established YCSB and TPC-C benchmarks, which are supported by the OLTPBench harness out-of-the-box. However, further special-purpose benchmarks have been proposed specifically for measuring tail latencies, as they arise in embedded databases on mobile devices [38]. This contribution is related to our work insofar as the authors also unveil sources of measurement error, however, errors that arise when measuring the performance of embedded databases at low throughput.

There are further benchmark harnesses from the systems research community that specifically target tail latencies. These capture latencies across the entire systems stack, while in the database research community, we benchmark the database layer in isolation. Harnesses such as TailBench [26] or TreadMill [52] define such complex application scenarios (some involving a database layer).

In its full generality, the challenge of benchmarking Java applications, including jitter introduced by garbage collection, is discussed in [17]. We follow the best practices recommended in this article, as we classify outliers as either systematic or probabilistic. We present the latency distributions clearly, and have carried out sufficiently many test runs. Different from the authors of [17], we do not apply hypothesis tests, since we are mostly interested in latencies maxima, rather than confidence in averaged values.

It has been reported that database-internal garbage collection [2,29] can also cause latency spikes, which might however be seen as part of productive operation. Our work considers the effects of garbage collection inside the test harness, rather than the database engine.

7   Conclusion and Outlook

Tail latencies in database query processing can manifest as acute pain points. To address their possible causes, we must be able to faithfully measure them. Our work shows that Java-based benchmark harnesses serve well for measuring database throughput, or 95th or 99th percentile latencies. However, these benchmarks can significantly impact the capturing of extreme tail latencies: The choice of JVM and garbage collector in the harness is a non-negligible source of indeterministic noise. For database workloads composed of low-latency queries (*e.g.*, as in the YCSB benchmark), we risk distorted measurements which can lead us to chase ghosts in database systems engineering, and prevent an accurate and faithful characterisation of important extreme events. We find that future efforts in evaluating database performance for real-time and large-scale computing scenarios should put more effort into understanding and controlling such effects.

References

1. Barroso, L.A., Marty, M., Patterson, D.A., Ranganathan, P.: Attack of the killer microseconds. Commun. ACM **60**(4), 48–54 (2017)
2. Böttcher, J., Leis, V., Neumann, T., Kemper, A.: Scalable garbage collection for in-memory MVCC systems. Proc. VLDB Endow. **13**(2), 128–141 (2019)
3. Brutlag, J.: Speed matters for google web search (2009). https://venturebeat.com/wp-content/uploads/2009/11/delayexp.pdf
4. Cafarella, M.J., et al.: DBOS: a proposal for a data-centric operating system. CoRR abs/2007.11112 (2020)
5. Chen, X., et al.: Achieving low tail-latency and high scalability for serializable transactions in edge computing. In: Proceedings of EuroSys, pp. 210–227 (2021)
6. Clark, I.: Shenandoah GC (2021). https://wiki.openjdk.java.net/display/shenandoah
7. Clark, I.: ZGC (2021). https://wiki.openjdk.java.net/display/zgc
8. Click, C., Tene, G., Wolf, M.: The pauseless GC algorithm. In: Proceedings VEE, pp. 46–56 (2005)
9. Cooper, B.F., Silberstein, A., Tam, E., Ramakrishnan, R., Sears, R.: Benchmarking cloud serving systems with YCSB. In: Proceedings of SoCC, pp. 143–154 (2010)

10. Curino, C., Difallah, D.E., Pavlo, A., Cudré-Mauroux, P.: Benchmarking OLTP/web databases in the cloud: the OLTP-bench framework. In: Proceedings of CloudDB, pp. 17–20 (2012)
11. Dean, J., Barroso, L.A.: The tail at scale. Commun. ACM **56**(2), 74–80 (2013)
12. Difallah, D.E., Pavlo, A., Curino, C., Cudré-Mauroux, P.: OLTP-Bench: an extensible testbed for benchmarking relational databases. Proc. VLDB Endow. **7**(4), 277–288 (2013)
13. Eclipse Foundation: -Xlog. https://www.eclipse.org/openj9/docs/xlog/
14. Eclipse Foundation: Garbage collection policies. https://www.eclipse.org/openj9/docs/gc/
15. Fent, P., van Renen, A., Kipf, A., Leis, V., Neumann, T., Kemper, A.: Low-latency communication for fast DBMS using RDMA and shared memory. In: Proceedings of ICDE, pp. 1477–1488 (2020)
16. Garcia-Arellano, C., et al.: Db2 event store: a purpose-built IoT database engine. Proc. VLDB Endow. **13**(12), 3299–3312 (2020)
17. Georges, A., Buytaert, D., Eeckhout, L.: Statistically rigorous java performance evaluation. In: Proceedings of OOPSLA, pp. 57–76 (2007)
18. Gessert, F.: Low latency for cloud data management. Ph.D. thesis, University of Hamburg, Germany (2019)
19. Giannikis, G., Alonso, G., Kossmann, D.: SharedDB: killing one thousand queries with one stone. Proc. VLDB Endow. **5**(6), 526–537 (2012)
20. Giceva, J.: Operating system support for data management on modern hardware. IEEE Data Eng. Bull. **42**(1), 36–48 (2019)
21. Giceva, J., Salomie, T., Schüpbach, A., Alonso, G., Roscoe, T.: COD: database/operating system co-design. In: Proceedings of CIDR (2013)
22. Giceva, J., Zellweger, G., Alonso, G., Roscoe, T.: Customized OS support for data-processing. In: Proceedings of DaMoN, pp. 2:1–2:6 (2016)
23. Hofmann, G., Riehle, D., Kolassa, C., Mauerer, W.: A dual model of open source license growth. In: Petrinja, E., Succi, G., El Ioini, N., Sillitti, A. (eds.) OSS 2013. IAICT, vol. 404, pp. 245–256. Springer, Heidelberg (2013). https://doi.org/10.1007/978-3-642-38928-3_18
24. Jaiman, V., Mokhtar, S.B., Quéma, V., Chen, L.Y., Riviere, E.: Héron: taming tail latencies in key-value stores under heterogeneous workloads. In: Proceedings of SRDS, pp. 191–200 (2018)
25. Jaiman, V., Ben Mokhtar, S., Rivière, E.: TailX: scheduling heterogeneous multiget queries to improve tail latencies in key-value stores. In: Remke, A., Schiavoni, V. (eds.) DAIS 2020. LNCS, vol. 12135, pp. 73–92. Springer, Cham (2020). https://doi.org/10.1007/978-3-030-50323-9_5
26. Kasture, H., Sánchez, D.: Tailbench: a benchmark suite and evaluation methodology for latency-critical applications. In: Proceedings of IISWC, pp. 3–12 (2016)
27. Lam, K., Kuo, T. (eds.): Real-Time Database Systems: Architecture and Techniques. Springer, Heidelberg (2001). https://doi.org/10.1007/b116080
28. Larsen, S., Arvidsson, F., Larsson, M.: JEP 158: unified JVM logging (2019). https://openjdk.java.net/jeps/158
29. Lersch, L., Schröter, I., Oukid, I., Lehner, W.: Enabling low tail latency on multi-core key-value stores. Proc. VLDB Endow. **13**(7), 1091–1104 (2020)
30. Li, J., Sharma, N.K., Ports, D.R.K., Gribble, S.D.: Tales of the tail: hardware, OS, and application-level sources of tail latency. In: Proceedings of SoCC, pp. 1–14 (2014)

31. Lindholm, T., Yellin, F., Bracha, G., Buckley, A., Smith, D.: The java virtual machine specification - Java SE 16 edition (2021). https://docs.oracle.com/javase/specs/jvms/se16/jvms16.pdf
32. Mauerer, W.: Professional Linux Kernel Architecture. Wiley, Hoboken (2010)
33. Mauerer, W., Ramsauer, R., Filho, E.R.L., Lohmann, D., Scherzinger, S.: Silentium! run-analyse-eradicate the noise out of the DB/OS stack. In: Proceedings of BTW, vol. P-311, pp. 397–421 (2021)
34. Nicolas, M.: Benchmark harness. In: Sakr, S., Zomaya, A.Y. (eds.) Encyclopedia of Big Data Technologies. Lecture Notes in Computer Science, pp. 137–141. Springer, Cham (2019). https://doi.org/10.1007/978-3-319-77525-8
35. Moehler, G., Scherzinger, S., Steinbach, T.: Performance monitoring of a computer resource (2014). US Patent US8863084B2, International Business Machines Corp
36. Mühlig, J., Müller, M., Spinczyk, O., Teubner, J.: mxkernel: a novel system software stack for data processing on modern hardware. Datenbank-Spektrum **20**(3), 223–230 (2020)
37. Müller, M., Spinczyk, O.: MxKernel: rethinking operating system architecture for many-core hardware. In: Proceedings of SFMA (2019)
38. Nuessle, C., Kennedy, O., Ziarek, L.: Benchmarking pocket-scale databases. In: Nambiar, R., Poess, M. (eds.) TPCTC 2019. LNCS, vol. 12257, pp. 99–115. Springer, Cham (2020). https://doi.org/10.1007/978-3-030-55024-0_7
39. OLTPBenchmark.com: OLTPBench. https://github.com/oltpbenchmark/oltpbench
40. eclipse openj9: OpenJ9. https://github.com/eclipse-openj9/openj9
41. OpenJDK: JDK. https://github.com/openjdk/jdk
42. Oracle: Java Platform, Standard Edition HotSpot Virtual Machine Garbage Collection Tuning Guide - 9 Garbage-First Garbage Collector (2017). https://docs.oracle.com/javase/9/gctuning/garbage-first-garbage-collector.htm
43. Paparrizos, J., et al.: VergeDB: a database for IoT analytics on edge devices. In: Proceedings of CIDR (2021)
44. Ramsauer, R., Lohmann, D., Mauerer, W.: Observing custom software modifications: a quantitative approach of tracking the evolution of patch stacks. In: Proceedings of OpenSym, pp. 1–4 (2016)
45. Reda, W., Canini, M., Suresh, P.L., Kostic, D., Braithwaite, S.: Rein: taming tail latency in key-value stores via multiget scheduling. In: Proceedings of EuroSys, pp. 95–110 (2017)
46. Scherzinger, S., Karn, H., Steinbach, T.: End-to-end performance monitoring of databases in distributed environments. In: Proceedings of BTW. LNI, vol. P-144, pp. 612–615 (2009)
47. Shipilev, A.: JEP 318: epsilon: a no-op garbage collector (experimental) (2018). https://openjdk.java.net/jeps/318
48. Tene, G., Iyengar, B., Wolf, M.: C4: the continuously concurrent compacting collector. In: Proceedings of ISMM, pp. 79–88 (2011)
49. Transaction Processing Council: TPC-C Benchmark (Revision 5.11) (2010). http://tpc.org/tpc_documents_current_versions/pdf/tpc-c_v5.11.0.pdf
50. Transaction Processing Performance Council: TPC-Homepage. http://tpc.org/
51. Unterbrunner, P., Giannikis, G., Alonso, G., Fauser, D., Kossmann, D.: Predictable performance for unpredictable workloads. Proc. VLDB Endow. **2**(1), 706–717 (2009)
52. Zhang, Y., Meisner, D., Mars, J., Tang, L.: Treadmill: attributing the source of tail latency through precise load testing and statistical inference. In: Proceedings of ISCA, pp. 456–468 (2016)

Quantifying Cloud Data Analytic Platform Scalability with Extended TPC-DS Benchmark

Guoheng Chen[✉], Timothy Johnson, and Miso Cilimdzic

Microsoft Corporation, One Microsoft Way, Redmond, WA 98052, USA
{guche,tijohnso,misoc}@microsoft.com

Abstract. In the past decade, many data analytic systems have been moved to cloud platforms. One major reason for this trend is the elasticity that cloud platforms can provide. However, different vendors describe the scalability of their platform in different ways, so there is a need to measure and compare the scalability of different data analytic platforms in a consistent way. To achieve this goal, we extend the well-known TPC Benchmark™DS (TPC-DS). The primary metrics in TPC-DS are Performance Metric, Price-Performance Metric and System availability date. We propose an additional primary metric, Scalability Metric, to evaluate the scalability of System Under Test at a given scale factor across different resource levels. We use a set of experimental performance runs to demonstrate how Scalability Metric is derived and how it measures the scalability of a cloud data analytic platform.

1 Introduction

1.1 TPC-DS Benchmark

The TPC Benchmark™DS (TPC-DS) [1] is a decision support benchmark that models several generally applicable aspects of a decision support system, including queries and data maintenance. TPC-DS first defines System Under Test (SUT), which includes hardware, software, network interface devices, etc. SUT is generally not changed during the test. TPC-DS then specifies multiple scale factors from 1 TB to 100 TB that represent different database sizes. Data size is also fixed during a test. Third, TPC-DS defines a specific workload that includes four steps: data loading, power test, throughput test and data maintenance. Although some vendors have focused on the power test, the primary performance metric, QphDS@SF, gives equal weight to the time taken for each of these steps. This metric models the challenges of business intelligence systems in which operational data is used both to support business decisions made in near real time and to direct long-range planning and exploration. In this way, it measures more completely the overall performance of a data analytic platform system.

TPC-DS run results at different scale factors, even on the same SUT, are not comparable, due to the substantially different computational challenges found at different data volumes. Similarly, TPC-DS run results from different SUT are not directly comparable, even when the tests are using the same scale factor, due to both software and hardware configuration difference. To compare across different data analytic platforms,

© Springer Nature Switzerland AG 2022
R. Nambiar and M. Poess (Eds.): TPCTC 2021, LNCS 13169, pp. 135–150, 2022.
https://doi.org/10.1007/978-3-030-94437-7_9

the price/performance metric is defined. It is worth noting that system price/performance may not scale up and down linearly with database size due to configuration changes required by changes in database size. For full details on how to compute the performance and price/performance metrics, see the TPC-DS specification.

There are many publications on various aspects of TPC-DS benchmarks in recent years. Meikel P. has reiterated the most important aspects of this benchmark. [2] Manan T and Zhenqiang C. did an in-depth analysis of some queries in this benchmark. [3] S. Yeruva et al. has shared some insights in TPC-DS in a distributed data warehouse environment [4].

1.2 Separation of Storage and Compute in Cloud Data Analytic Platform

Data analytic platforms have two main components, compute and storage, and both of these variables are important when scalability is analyzed. Originally, compute and storage were tightly coupled for most systems. In recent years, as data analytic platforms move to the cloud, compute and storage have been increasingly separated, so that compute can be scaled in and out independently on the same dataset with the same storage. With today's technology, cloud platform vendors can quickly change the hardware configuration, including the number of nodes or slices of a node and the types of nodes, with different CPU capacity, number of cores, memory, local disk, network bandwidth, etc. of a cloud data analytic platform.

As noted, TPC-DS indicates that performance metric results at the different scale factors are not comparable. But it is possible to compare the performance on different hardware configurations at the same data scale factor. Therefore, we propose to use this comparison to provide a systematic method for comparing the effectiveness of the scalability of various cloud data analytic platforms.

2 Related Work in Measuring Scalability

Quantifying scalability can be challenging. In computer architecture, Amdahl's law provides the theoretical speedup in latency of the execution of a task at fixed workload that can be expected of a system whose resources are improved. It is named after the computer scientist Gene Amdahl, and was presented at the AFIPS Spring Joint Computer Conference in 1967 [5, 6].

In Amdahl's law, a workload has two portions, one that can be executed in parallel, and one that must be serialized. If the total workload execution time with a single processor is T_1, and the serial fraction is σ, $0 < \sigma < 1$, the parallelized portion is $1 - \sigma$. The total execution time with p processors T_p is then:

$$T_p = \sigma T_1 + \frac{(1 - \sigma)T_1}{p}$$

Therefore, with p-way scale up, the speedup factor is:

$$C(p) = \frac{p}{1 + \sigma(p - 1)}$$

In the Universal Scalability Law (USL) [7], Neil Gunther extended Amdahl's law to also account for additional overhead due to inter-process communication. This can be explained using a typical database application, in which multiple server processes need to communicate with a single database. Even though each process can progress without explicit communication with other processes when reading elements from the database, they should explicitly communicate with other processes when updating the database to maintain the ACID properties of transactions. If there are p processors running in parallel, then each processor needs to communicate with p − 1 other processors. Hence on average, the number of interactions that take place is p(p − 1).

Therefore, in USL the speedup factor with p processors is:

$$C(p) = \frac{p}{1 + \sigma(p - 1) + \kappa p(p - 1)}$$

Neil Gunther later further normalizes the formula to

$$C(p) = \frac{\gamma N}{1 + \alpha(p - 1) + \beta p(p - 1)}$$

The three coefficients, α, β, γ, in this equation can be identified respectively with the three Cs:

1. CONCURRENCY or ideal parallelism (with proportionality γ), which can also be interpreted as either:

    a. the slope associated with linear-rising scalability.
    b. the maximum throughput attainable with a single load generator, i.e., $X(1) = \gamma$

2. CONTENTION (with proportionality α) due to waiting or queueing for shared resources.
3. COHERENCY or data consistency (with proportionality β) due to the delay for data to become consistent, or cache coherent, by virtue of point-to-point exchange of data between resources that are distributed.

Amdahl's law is a special case of USL when $\beta = 0$ and $\gamma = 1$ [8, 9].

Both Amdahl's law and USL give insights into why scalability can be a challenge and they provide a quantitative approach to measure system scalability. At the same time, we need a representative workload to evaluate the scalability of different systems. In this paper, we leverage some of the ideas in these two scalability laws and define a new metric in an extended TPC-DS benchmark. We also provide analysis of the TPC-DS performance metric on a cloud Data Analytic Platform.

3 Proposed Extended TPC-DS Benchmark

Our proposed TPC-DS benchmark is based on executing the same TPC-DS workload at the same scale factor against different hardware configurations. These configurations can be single-node machines or clusters of machines such as an appliance or cloud data analytic platform. The extended benchmark only requires the ability to quantify and compare the resource levels of different hardware configurations, so it can be applied to non-cloud platforms as well. But our main motivation is cloud platforms, since the separation of compute and storage makes it easy to run the same workload at the same scale against different hardware configuration.

At a high level, the proposed extended TPC-DS benchmark is created with these major steps:

- Abstract resource level of a cloud data analytic platform to run a TPC-DS workload.
- Normalize resource levels of a cloud data analytic platform.
- Execute standard TPC-DS benchmark run at different resource levels.
- Normalize TPC-DS benchmark metrics.
- Calculate scalability metric.
- Generate the extended TPC-DS benchmark report.

3.1   Abstract Cloud Data Warehouse Resource Level

The resource level of a cloud data analytic platform is defined as a combination of CPU, memory, network IO, storage IO, etc. Different vendors use different terminology to describe the resource level of their platform. For example, Microsoft Azure Synapse Analytics uses the service level objective (SLO) to define its resource level. Synapse dedicated SQL pool ranges from DW100c to DW30000c. Hardware information is not exposed in the SLO, but under the hood, a specific SLO corresponds to slices of a node or multiple nodes of a certain hardware generation [10]. AWS Redshift uses node type (RA3, DC2, DS2) and number of nodes to define its resource level [11]. Snowflake labels its resource levels as T-Shirt sizes, which correspond to servers/cluster or credits/hour, from X-Small, Small, Medium, ... to 4X-Large [12]. Google BigQuery uses the number of slots to represent its various resource levels [13].

Here are some characteristics of the abstraction of resource level of a cloud data analytic platform:

- Hardware information is mostly hidden. It can be considered as a combination of CPU, memory, network IO, storage IO, and other resources.
- The resource level is only directly comparable within the product family of a single vendor.
- Even within the same vendor, it is difficult to compare the same product on different hardware generations, unless the vendor can clearly define performance difference and how to convert between different hardware generations.
- Within the same product family and hardware generation, resource levels of different configurations are directly comparable. For example, in Azure Synapse Analytics, DW6000c can be considered as 6X of a DW1000c in terms of resource level. For AWS Redshift, a 10 ra3.16 node instance is 5X resource level of a 2 ra3.16 node instance.
- For a specific workload, there could be a minimal resource level requirement, since not all resource level instances can complete a specific workload successfully.

- Some cloud data analytic platforms can dynamically change the resource level while executing queries. But each query is still executed under a specific resource level at a certain moment.

To measure the scalability of a cloud data analytic platform, it is required to run the same TPC-DS workload against instances at different resource levels. It is up to the vendor to choose the range of resource level and data scale factor to run TPC-DS benchmark to demonstrate its scalability. In this paper, we use TPC-DS 10TB as our dataset.

To ensure that there is enough data for the extended benchmark to be meaningful, it is required to have instances with at least 6 different resource levels that can run the TPC-DS workload in the scalability test. Each TPC-DS run must be individually auditable.

For example, for Azure Synapse Analytics, the workload can run on DW1000c, DW1500c, ... DW6000c. For AWS Redshift, ra3.16xLarge can run the workload with 5 nodes, 10 nodes, 15 nodes, ..., 60 nodes, etc.

3.2 Normalize Resource Level

Assume the extended TPC-DS performance test is run against a range of resource level instances. Using Azure Synapse Analytics and AWS Redshift as an example, define the resource level as:

$$\{R_1, R_2, \ldots, R_n\} = \{DW1000c, \ DW1500c, \ DW2000c, \ DW3000c, \ DW5000c, \ DW6000c\}$$

Or

$$\{R_1, R_2, \ldots, R_n\} = \{10 \, node, \ 20 \, node, \ 30 \, node, \ 40 \, node, \ 50 \, node, \ 60 \, nodes\}$$

Since the resource level of different instances in the scalability test is comparable, we define the smallest as the base unit with normalized resource level value 1. For other resource level instance, we define the ratio against the base unit as its normalized resource level.

$$NR_i = \frac{R_i}{R_1}$$

R_1 is the resource level of the smallest resource level. So NR_1 is always 1.
The normalized resource level of the instances in the example above is:

$$\{NR_1, NR_2, \ldots, NR_n\} = \{1, \ 1.5, \ 3, \ 5, \ 6, \ 7.5\}$$

Or

$$\{NR_1, NR_2, \ldots, NR_n\} = \{1, \ 2, \ 3, \ 4, \ 5, \ 6\}$$

3.3 Normalize Benchmark Performance Metric

Assume TPC-DS 10TB benchmark is executed against all instances of different resource levels. The TPC-DS primary performance metric $QphDS@SF$ is collected for each run.

$$\{X_1, X_2, \ldots, X_n\}$$

Define the normalized performance metric of the lowest resource level instance in the scalability test as base unit with value 1. For other resource level instances, define the ratio against the base unit as its normalized performance metric.

$$NP_i = \frac{X_i}{X_1}$$

X_1 is the performance metric of the lowest resource level instance. NP_1 is always 1. The normalized performance metric of the instances used in the scalability test is:

$$\{NP_1, NP_2, \ldots, NP_n\} = (\frac{X_1}{X_1}, \frac{X_2}{X_1}, \ldots, \frac{X_n}{X_1})$$

For example, this is an experimental run with normalized data points (Table 1).

Table 1. An experimental run with normalized data points.

Normalized resource level (NR)	TPC-DS performance metric (QphDS@SF)	Normalized performance metric (NP)
1	664867	1.0000
2	1407936	2.1176
2.5	1749317	2.6311
3	2011301	3.0251
5	2899566	4.3611
6	3076677	4.6275

3.4 Scalability Factor

With normalized resource level and normalized performance metrics, we have a set of data points.

$$\{(NR_1, NP_1), (NR_2, NP_2), \ldots, (NR_n, NP_n)\}$$

We calculate the linear regression line based on this dataset, where X is the normalized resource level, and Y is the normalized performance metric.

We then define the ScalabilityFactor as the slope of the best-fit line from the linear regression [14]:

$$\text{ScalabilityFactor} = \frac{(n \times \sum_{i=1}^{n} NR_i \times NP_i) - \sum_{i=1}^{n} NR_i \times \sum_{i=1}^{n} NP_i}{n \times \sum_{i=1}^{n} NR_i^2 - (\sum_{i=1}^{n} NR_i)^2}$$

For completeness, the intercept of the linear regression is defined as

$$Intercept = \frac{\sum_{i=1}^{n} NP_i - ScalabilityFactor \times \sum_{i=1}^{n} NR_i}{n}$$

We have

$$NP = Intercept + NR \times ScalabilityFactor$$

We also define ScalabilityFactor Confidence as the R-Square of the linear regression line. This measures how reliable the ScalabilityFactor is.

$$r = \frac{n \times (\sum_{i=1}^{n} (NR_i \times NP_i)) - \sum_{i=1}^{n} NR_i \times \sum_{i=1}^{n} NP_i}{\sqrt{(n \times \sum_{i=1}^{n} NR_i^2 - (\sum_{i=1}^{n} NR_i)^2) \times (n \times \sum_{i=1}^{n} NP_i^2 - (\sum_{i=1}^{n} NP_i)^2)}}$$

$$Confidence = r^2$$

The confidence is expected to be at least 0.8 for this model to be applicable. In the scalability test, we had this normalized data set (Fig. 1, Table 2).

Table 2. Normalized performance metrics for the runs at each resource level.

Normalized resource level (NR)	Normalized performance metric (NP)
1	1.0000
2	2.1176
2.5	2.6311
3	3.0251
5	4.3611
6	4.6275

With the formulas, we get:

ScalabilityFactor = 0.7122, Intercept = 0.6459, Confidence = 0.9639,

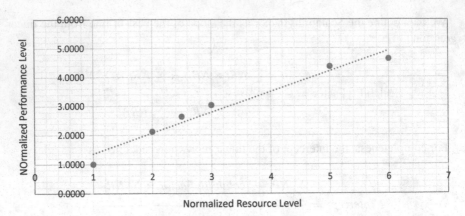

Fig. 1. Plot of normalized performance metrics for the runs at each resource level.

Therefore,

$$NP = 0.6459 + 0.7122 \times NR$$

This shows approximately how this system scales according to resource level. Note in this chart, the origin is shifted to (1, 1). This is correct because normalized resource level and normalized performance metric are being used and (1, 1) is the performance metric at the smallest resource level. The area below the x-axis and to the left of the y-axis can be considered as the configurations which are not in the scalability test and for which there is no data.

3.5 Extended TPC-DS Benchmark

We are proposing an extended TPC-DS benchmark that synthesizes this information:

- A cloud data analytic platform scales up and down with n ≥ 6 different resource levels, all running a TPC-DS workload at a specific scale factor, such as 10TB.
- At each resource level, an auditable TPC-DS benchmark report is generated.
- Normalize the resource level and TPC-DS performance metric based on these TPC-DS benchmark reports.
- Calculate the Scalability Factor and Confidence.
- Get the price information of each configuration from the TPC-DB benchmark reports.
- Combining all the information, we have this Table 3:

The extended TPC-DS benchmark has 4 metrics (with calculated value as an example):

1. Aggregated Performance Metric: This is the sum of Performance Metric of all TPC-DS runs in the scalability test.

$$AggregatedQphDS@SF = \sum_{i=1}^{n} X_i = 11,809,664(\text{QphDS@SF})$$

Table 3. A sample of a full extended TPC-DS benchmark report.

Configuration	Resource level	Normalized resource level (NR)	TPC-DS performance metric (QphDS@SF)	TPC-DS performance metric	Normalized performance metric (NP)	Price ($)
C1	R1	1	664,867	X1	1.0000	$100,000
C2	R2	2	1,407,936	X2	2.1176	$200,000
C3	R3	2.5	1,749,317	X3	2.6311	$250,000
C4	R4	3	2,011,301	X4	3.0251	$300,000
C5	R5	5	2,899,566	X5	4.3611	$500,000
C6	R6	6	3,076,677	X6	4.6275	$600,000
Sum			11,809,664			$1,950,000

C1..C6: Vendor dependent configurations name
R1..R6: Vendor dependent resource level
NR: Normalized Resource Level
Performance Metric: TPC-DS Performance Metric from benchmark report
X1..X6: Performance Metric value
NP: Normalized Performance Metric
P1..P6: Price from benchmark report (Not real price, just for demo purpose)
Sum of Performance Metric: 11,809,664(QphDS@SF)
Calculated Price Performance Metric: $1,950,000/11,809,664(QphDS@SF) = $0.165
Calculated Scalability factor: 0.7122
Calculated Confidence: 0.9639

2. Aggregated Price Performance Metric ($/AggregatedQphDS@SF): Aggregated price is the sum of the price of the system at different resource level in the scalability test. AggregatedQphDS@SF is defined above.

$$\$/AggregratedQphDS@SF = \frac{\sum_{i=1}^{n} P_i}{\sum_{i=1}^{n} X_i QphDS@SF} = \$0.165$$

3. Scalability Metric: (ScalabilityFactor, Confidence): This is calculated using simple linear regression model. ScalabilityFactor demonstrates how the system TPC-DS throughput scales according to different resource level. Confidence indicates how accurate or reliable the ScalabilityFactor is. It is expected Confidence >0.8.

$$\text{ScalabilityFactor} = \frac{(n \times \sum_{i=1}^{n} NR_i \times NP_i) - \sum_{i=1}^{n} NR_i \times \sum_{i=1}^{n} NP_i}{n \times \sum_{i=1}^{n} NR_i^2 - (\sum_{i=1}^{n} NR_i)^2} = 0.7122$$

$$r = \frac{n \times (\sum_{i=1}^{n} (NR_i \times NP_i)) - \sum_{i=1}^{n} NR_i \times \sum_{i=1}^{n} NP_i}{\sqrt{(n \times \sum_{i=1}^{n} NR_i^2 - (\sum_{i=1}^{n} NR_i)^2) \times (n \times \sum_{i=1}^{n} NP_i^2 - (\sum_{i=1}^{n} NP_i)^2)}} = 0.9639$$

$$Confidence = r^2$$

4. The Availability Date of the complete configuration of all resource level in the tests.

In summary, this is the portion of the primary metrics of the extended TPC-DS benchmark report in this example (Table 4):

Table 4. Extended TPC-DS benchmark report summary.

Aggregated total system cost	Aggregated TPC-DS throughput	Aggregated price performance	Scalability metric	System availability date
$1,950,000 USD	11,809,664 QphDS@10000 GB	$0.165 USD $/QphDS@10000 GB	(0.7122, 0.9639)	As of Publication
Dataset Size	**Database Manager**	**Operation System**	**Other Software**	**Cluster**
10000 GB	Vendor DB	Vendor OS		Yes
System configuration in the scalability Test		**Supported System Configuration**		
{C1, C2, C3, C4, C5, C6}		{C1, C2, C3, C4, C5, C6, CX1, CX2, ...CXn}		

Here are some important notes for this Extended TPC-DS benchmark:

- The extended TPC-DS benchmark is based on the original TPC-DS benchmark.
- All the TPC-DS benchmark runs are individually auditable. Each report is required to report the original TPC-DS performance metric, price performance metric, normalized resource level, and normalized performance metric for each benchmark run.
- It is required to list all the instances and their resource level in the scalability test and all the supported resource level. There must be at least 6 different configurations in the scalability test. It is up to each vendor to choose the resource configuration in the scalability test. But the vendor needs to disclose the range of supported resource configuration, so it is beneficial for vendors to use both the smallest and largest resource levels to best demonstrate scalability of their systems.
- Scalability Metric has 2 numbers, ScalabilityFactor and Confidence. This demonstrates how the system scales and how reliable the test result is.
- Aggregated TPC-DS Throughput is not comparable between two different scalability tests as it is up to the vendor to choose the resource configuration participating in the scalability test.
- Aggregated price performance metric is comparable between two different scalability tests just like the original TPC-DS benchmark.
- Scalability metric is comparable between two different tests. It is required Confidence > 0.8.
- The Availability Date metric is the availability date for all configurations in the scalability test.

4 Scalability Analysis for TPC-DS Operations

The TPC-DS benchmark has 4 different workload types, Data Load Test, Power Test, Throughput Test, Data Maintenance Test. These tests demonstrate different kinds of scalability characteristics. We can take a quick look at the Scalability Metric of each of these 4 operations by using the relative performance of each operation.

4.1 Load Operation

Normalized data set (Table 5):

Table 5. Normalized load performance per run.

Normalized resource level	Normalized load performance
1	1.000
2	2.500
2.5	3.532
3	4.327
5	6.742
6	8.071

Scalability Metric: (ScalabilityFactor = 1.3923, Confidence = 0.9934)

In this data set, loading operation in TPC-DS has good scalability (1.3923). This operation is loading data into a new table. In cloud data analytic platforms, data sources are usually organized in different data blobs, so that data can be loaded directly into backend databases by each compute unit concurrently. There is little contention among these compute units. Data consistency is also easy to achieve as it is acceptable that the table is not accessible during initial load. In the USL formula, both α and β for load operations are close to 0. Each operation also has some overhead, like data type conversation, data movement, etc. With higher resource levels, the weight of the overhead is reduced. So for data load operations, it is relatively easy to achieve linear or even super scalability.

$$C(p) = \frac{\gamma N}{1 + \alpha(p - 1) + \beta p(p - 1)}$$

One important aspect of this operation is that it is required to eventually distribute and dynamically adjust loading tasks among compute units. Depending on how the source blobs are organized, it is possible that there are some skewed loading tasks among the compute units that eventually slow down the whole operation.

To improve load performance, the system needs better distribution of tasks to compute units, having higher network bandwidth and faster storage access capability.

4.2 PowerRun

Normalized data set (Table 6):

Table 6. Normalized power run performance per run.

Normalized resource level	Normalized powerrun performance
1	1.000
2	2.370
2.5	2.844
3	3.223
5	4.571
6	4.389

Scalability Metric: (ScalabilityFactor = 0.6668, Confidence = 0.8987)

In this power run, the scalability factor is relatively low, and the confidence is within the allowed limit, but it is on the lower end. If we look at USL

$$C(p) = \frac{\gamma N}{1 + \alpha(p-1) + \beta p(p-1)}$$

TPC-DS queries are not pure CPU-intensive operations. Executing a distributed query plan involves running backend queries across multiple backend nodes in multiple steps. Due to dependencies between these steps, the distributed query plan runs in a specific sequence, so the backend queries cannot all run concurrently. Even if more resources are allocated to the system, the dependencies still exist. So γ is relatively low inherently. This also matches the observation that CPU and memory usage is not always high during query execution.

All backend queries will also need to access shared data. Depending on how data is distributed or partitioned and on the nature of the query itself, contention is expected while accessing shared data. So α is relatively high.

All PowerRun queries are read-only operation. But distributed queries use staged data sets generated during query execution. Query steps generate staged data sets in a certain sequence, and it will take time for all of the staged dataset to reach consistent state. So β can be high as well. That could be the explanation why ScalabilityFactor is low.

To improve PowerRun scalability (0.6668), it is necessary to improve the distributed query plan and/or the distributed plan execution mechanism to reduce waiting between dependent steps and improve execution concurrency. To improve the confidence score, more runs might be needed to reduce the noise of the test.

4.3 Throughput Run

Normalized data set (Table 7):

Table 7. Normalized through performance per run.

Normalized resource level	Normalized throughputrun performance
1	1.000
2	2.907
2.5	3.968
3	4.756
5	8.038
6	9.008

Scalability Metric: (ScalabilityFactor = 1.6106, Confidence = 0.9912)

In ThroughputRun, we see good scalability (1.6106) with high confidence. If we look at USL

$$C(p) = \frac{\gamma N}{1 + \alpha(p-1) + \beta p(p-1)}$$

In this ThroughputRun, there are 4 streams. Each individual stream still has similar challenges as in the PowerRun. But when there are more streams, the suboptimal query scalability is offset by interleaved execution from multiple streams. This also matches the observation of higher CPU and memory consumption during execution compared to the PowerRun. So γ is higher compared to the PowerRun. Both α and β should be similar to the PowerRun from each stream point of view. But because of interleaved execution between streams, at ThroughputRun stage, both α and β might be lower. The overall throughput run performance also depends on how resources are allocated when there are multiple streams executing the queries, either as fixed slices of resource or dynamically allocated resources. Scalability and total throughput are both important in this operation.

To improve throughput run scalability, one step is to improve the query plan execution for the individual streams, as in the PowerRun. Optimized resource management can also help as it is desired to dynamically allocate more resources to some streams while others are waiting for resources.

4.4 Data Maintenance Run

Normalized data set (Table 8):

Table 8. Normalized data maintenance performance per run.

Normalized resource level	Normalized data maintenance performance
1	1.000
2	1.117
2.5	1.152
3	1.233
5	1.473
6	1.510

Scalability Metric: (ScalabilityFactor = 0.1070, Confidence = 0.9861)

In Data Maintenance stage, the scalability factor is very low, and the confidence is quite high.

$$C(p) = \frac{\gamma N}{1 + \alpha(p - 1) + \beta p(p - 1)}$$

The low scalability is mainly due to the characteristics of data maintenance workload as well as the implementation of DML operations. The data volume in Data Maintenance is not very big. Even instances with a lower resource level can load the update dataset relatively fast. For loading data from views and deleting from fact table with time range, this depends on the implementation details. But overall, γ is low. These are DML operations, so different types of locking are needed for data consistency. Many cloud analytic platforms are highly optimized for loading data and read-only queries. For DML operations, both α and β are relatively high. It is observed CPU and memory consumption are low in this stage. Also, all these operations are done in sequence and each operation is relatively fast. These factors combined contribute to the low scalability of this operation.

To improve performance of data maintenance, it is required to improve the performance of view and DML operations. In TPC-DS specification, data maintenance section doesn't specify whether loading refresh data and executing refresh functions within each refreshed dataset be done in parallel or not. It is also possible to change the test drivers to increase concurrency in data maintenance run.

4.5 Overall Scalability

Database Load Test, Power Test, Throughput Test, and Data Maintenance Test demonstrate different scalability characteristics. Their Scalability Metric are (1.3923, 0.9934), (0.6668, 0.8987), (1.6106, 0.9912), (0.1070, 0.9861) and overall Scalability Metric is (0.7122, 0.9639).

When

ScalabilityFactor = 1, the system has perfect scalability.
ScalabilityFactor > 1, the system has super scalability.

ScalabilityFactor > 0 and <1, the system has suboptimal scalability.
ScalabilityFactor < 0, the system has reverse scalability.

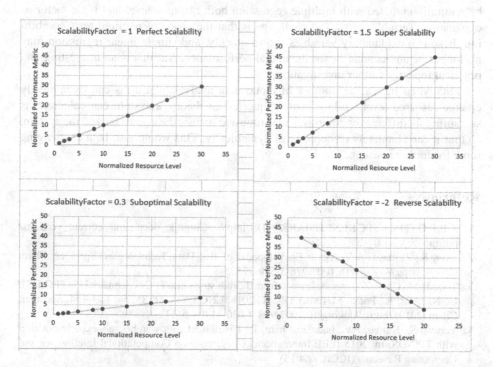

It is always a challenge for a system to achieve linear scalability. At the same time, this opens different opportunities for further improvements, and it would be interesting to see how scalability changes after improvements in different areas. To improve Scalability Metric, it is required to improve performance and scalability for each of these 4 stages in TPC-DS benchmark run.

5   Future Work

There are many ways in which this work could be extended. First, the scalability factor is calculated using a linear regression model. We can further investigate other models to see whether they can describe the scalability better. [15] We can consider including Model as part of Scalability Metric (ScalabilityFactor, Confidence, Model).

Second, we suggested that to calculate the extended TPC-DS benchmark, it is required to have data for at least six different resource levels. We might need to have more experiments across different platforms to determine the recommended size of the data set.

Next, we also only targeted the 10TB scale factor. It would be interesting to see whether scalability shows different characteristics when it reaches high scale factors like 30TB and 100TB.

In addition, in our experiments, we chose to scale only the resource level, with a fixed amount of data. Data scale factor also demonstrates interesting behavior in scalability analysis. Scaling the data size with fixed resources is another dimension of scalability analysis. Performance at different resource levels and data scale factors could also be naturally modeled with multiple regression both resource level and scale factor as explanatory variables [16]. The challenge is that the space of required tests combining these two explanatory variables grows quickly, and simple linear regression may no longer be an accurate fit for the actual performance. But this is an interesting and practical topic for further investigation.

Finally, an increasing number of cloud data analytic platforms can dynamically change resource level while executing queries. In theory, a system can calculate its scalability for different operations in real-time and surface the signals back to the system, so that it can change its resource level dynamically. This would also be a challenging topic for further research.

References

1. T. P. P. C. (TPC): TPC BENCHMARK™ DS. http://tpc.org/tpc_documents_current_versions/pdf/tpc-ds_v3.1.0.pdf
2. Sakr, S., Zomaya, A.Y. (eds.): Encyclopedia of Big Data Technologies. Springer, Cham (2019). https://doi.org/10.1007/978-3-319-77525-8
3. Trivedi, M., Chen, Z.: Lessons learned from the industry's first TPC benchmark DS (TPC-DS). In: Nambiar, R., Poess, M. (eds.) TPCTC 2018. LNCS, vol. 11135, pp. 140–154. Springer, Cham (2019). https://doi.org/10.1007/978-3-030-11404-6_11
4. Yeruva, S., Kumar, P.V., Padmanabham, P.: Distributed data warehouse - experimentation with TPC-DS. In: 2015 IEEE International Conference on Computational Intelligence and Computing Research (ICCIC) (2015)
5. Amdahl, G.M.: Validity of the single processor approach to achieving large scale computing capabilities. In: Spring Joint Computer Conference (1967)
6. Wikipedia: Amdahl's law
7. Gunther, N.J.: Guerrilla Capacity Planning. Springer-Verlag, Berlin Heidelberg (2007)
8. Gunther, N.J.: A New Interpretation of Amdahl's Law and Geometric Scalability, 17 Oct 2002. https://arxiv.org/abs/cs/0210017
9. Gunther, N.J.: How to Quantify Scalability. http://www.perfdynamics.com/Manifesto/USLscalability.html#tth_sEc1
10. Microsoft: Azure Synapse Analytics pricing. https://azure.microsoft.com/en-us/pricing/details/synapse-analytics/
11. Amazon Web Services, Inc., Amazon Redshift pricing. https://aws.amazon.com/redshift/pricing/
12. Snowflake Inc., Warehouse Size. https://docs.snowflake.com/en/user-guide/warehouses-overview.html#warehouse-size
13. Google: BigQuery pricing. https://cloud.google.com/bigquery/pricing
14. Wikipedia: Simple linear regression. https://en.wikipedia.org/wiki/Simple_linear_regression
15. Wikipedia: Linear regression. https://en.wikipedia.org/wiki/Linear_regression
16. ScienceDirect: Multiple Regression Analysis, ScienceDirect. https://www.sciencedirect.com/topics/economics-econometrics-and-finance/multiple-regression-analysis

Author Index

Printed in the United States
by Baker & Taylor Publisher Services